VERBALIZE

bring stories to life & life to stories

by Damon Suede

Published by Evil Mastermind, LLC
New York, NY
EvilMastermind.com
First Publication: 12 March 2018

Edited by Lynn West
Illustrations by Evil Mastermind, LLC
Book formatting by BB eBooks

ISBN 978-1-945043-02-4 (Ebook)
ISBN 978-1-945043-03-1 (Print)

Website: DamonSuede.com/livewire

Note: Chapters 7 and 8 include some material that first appeared in rough form as blog posts ("Add Verbs" and "Moving Target") at Romance University.

Contents

Exercises

Verbalization boosts every facet of the writing process. If you have a pressing issue in a certain craft area you want to tackle right away, use these drills and workouts to develop your skills. These exercises appear sequentially in the book and build on each other. They assume you have a basic handle on verbalization and can offer a quick fix for specific creative challenges if you're stuck.

Character

- If your **character details** feel scattered, disconnected, or forgettable, get a handle on effective alignment via the Story Line exercise on p. 42.
- If you cannot pinpoint any **character's essential action**, check out the Dark Matters exercise on p. 134.
- If you need to **create an unforgettable character** who writes their own story, amp your process with the Add Verbs exercise on p. 141.
- If your **character's impact** on their world or other characters feels disjointed, brew up some mojo with the Big Ripples exercise on p. 184.

Depth

- If you struggle to access the kind of **character complexity** that supports intense emotions, dig into the Inner Space exercise on p. 104.

- If you're interested in unpacking more of a **character's power, potential, and paradoxes**, investigate the Deep Dive exercise on p. 213.

- If you have a **scene that's not popping** for the characters participating in it, play around with the Monkey Wrench exercise on p. 231.

- If you want to drill into your **character's layers** in the most memorable, believable way, map out a strategy in the Book Self exercise on p. 251.

Genre

- If you can't meet and exceed **genre expectations** as a matter of course, take a look at the Trouble Maker exercise on p. 95.

- If you're curious about **classic genre construction** and want to push the envelope, splash around in the Fan Fave exercise on p. 118.

- If you want to **understand genre characters** in any media, spend some quality time on the Couch Potato exercise on p. 173.

- If you need a firmer handle on **genre mechanics and distinctions**, spend a little time with the Genre-flecting exercise on p. 223.

Emotion

- If you struggle to access **maximum drama and tension** in every story moment, there's real mojo in the Best Enemies exercise on p. 75.

- If your **story sometimes feels passive, aimless, or trapped** inside your character's head, check out the Trans Mission exercise on p. 154.

- If the **relationships** between characters need a boost, build that chemistry with the Counter Action exercise on p. 191.

- If you want to elicit more **emotion** in your readers, have a go at the Loaded Dice exercise on p. 238.

Arc

- If you want a better handle on your character's evolution over the course of the book via **Goal/Motivation/Conflict**, tackle the Hard Time exercise on p. 110.

- If your character's **overarching story goal** isn't clear or camera-ready, find your focus with the Big Picture exercise on p. 162.

- If you have an **info-dump addiction** or tend to deliver backstory in big slices of expo cake, charge your scenes with the Direct Object exercise on p. 244.

- If you struggle to depict **meaningful transformation** and clear emotional growth, spend some time on the Arc Aid exercise on p. 258.

Plot

- If your project lacks the kinds of **memorable moments** that dazzle genre fans, check out the Event Planning exercise on p. 80.
- If coherent, compelling **story structure** eludes you, take a whack at the Prize Fight exercise on p. 168.
- If your scenes ever get stuck in a **narrative rut** or predictable plateau, challenge your habits with the Page Directions exercise on p. 267.
- If you want to **structure your entire story** in a robust format that's useable for plotters *and* pantsers, invest time in the Grand Plan exercise on p. 277.

Words

- If you tend to **recycle character types and tropes** from book to book, shake things up with the Strong Language exercise on p. 51.
- If you struggle with **low stakes or character inaction**, you'll probably benefit from the Amp Site exercise on p. 126.
- If your story verbalization ever feels **banal, flaccid, or clichéd**, stretch beyond your comfort zone with the Booster Shot exercise on p. 179.
- If you want to amp **suspense, emotion, or surprise**, bust the rut via the Turn Signal exercise on p. 206.

Introduction

There is no *one* way to write a book.

In the pages that follow, I present an approach to genre writing that has paid my bills and won me acclaim for the better part of twenty-five years.

Why do some imaginary people move us, inspire us, and change the world? Why do audiences spend time with your book instead of any other kind of entertainment? Why do you write this story and not those others? How much mental real estate does your work deserve?

I always tell my students: **The secret of life is paying attention.** I repeat that sentence like a creative mantra. It applies to love, work, play, health, education, sports, religion, art, politics, business, and every other part of living worth mention. You name it: the root of success, the right answer, the smart move, the best solution always comes down to *attention*.

If you want to know what matters to people, notice where they invest their energy, focus their resources, and spend their time. If something matters enough, you pay attention to it; if you don't, it doesn't matter to you.

As authors, attention pushes us toward meaningful specificity. Out of all the words available, we look beyond just *some* words to the *right* words. Writers pay attention so that characters can pay attention, so that readers will pay attention. We *verbalize*.

Your mileage may vary, but the principles do not.

Readers engage with characters because as social primates we're wired to identify patterns and extract meaning from our environment to figure out what matters. The core of any story is the *emotional ride* it offers an audience.

This book explains my technique for story development through characterization that

- applies to plotters or pantsers in any genre at any level.
- provides tools and tricks with dependable, delightful results.
- requires no special knowledge, style, technology, or work habits.
- draws on brain biology, performance, and classic literary principles.
- taps your unique voice and verbal gifts to tell the best story possible.

Most writing guides look at structure and character backward: they start with garnish and peter out before they get to the entrée. How many craft books simply repeat lessons they gleaned elsewhere, undigested and unexamined? In the pages that follow, I'm offering something *else*.

Language is literally the key...putting the right words in the right order for the right audience.

No matter your voice or vibe, *verbalizing* your story will help you get the right words on the page. This book offers a new pick for an old lock, a simple, practical technique developed over years entertaining audiences for a paycheck. Verbalization uses language to tell your story so you waste less effort and find the right words faster.

To date, my approach to character and story planning has proved useful for a wide swath of writers—newbies and experts, plotters and pantsers, authors and industry professionals—in every popular genre and media. Regardless of your experience or intent, the techniques in this book can transform the way you craft your pages.

In concrete terms, this book offers theory, examples, and practical exercises. Since our topic is fiction, the majority of my examples will come from popular genre novels. We're going to tackle story and character with a method that is specific, flexible, and fun to implement. *F'realz.*

Verbalizing your work will help you

- brainstorm and gauge potential story ideas before you invest time and energy.
- populate your projects with the kinds of characters fans crave.
- drive action, anchor intimacy, spark dialogue, inspire humor, and amplify the emotional impact of any scene.
- structure narrative, steer your rough draft to completion, and guide the revision and editorial process.
- pinpoint problems, pitfalls, and dead ends before they derail a project.

- clarify your story's hook, pitch, submission, and promo package.

Not to sound like a deranged infomercial, but I believe verbalization offers a storytelling Swiss Army knife that slices, dices, spices, splices, and entices the kind of fans who line up the night before and champion your work to millions of new readers.

After all, a plot is only as thrilling as the people who populate it. A story is inevitably the record of someone changed by their journey toward happiness.

What is a person? Who matters? Why are we alive? What is happiness and who deserves it? What is good or evil, right or wrong, kindness or cruelty, nature or nurture?

Storytelling is difficult to teach because it's bound up in our beliefs about humanity, agency, responsibility, and duty. It pivots on issues of fate and free will, honor and compassion, reality and illusion. Sidestepping the big moral questions in favor of Band-Aids and blandishments may feel easier-faster-simpler, but it also reduces form to formula and character to caricature.

Instead, let's focus on what matters: to build characters who move people, afford them the attention they deserve so that your readers will do the same.

Caring about your story is the way you unleash captivating characterization, brilliant plotting, hilarious comedy, devastating pathos, scintillating dialogue, breakneck reversals, incendiary love scenes, spectacular worldbuilding, fascinating specifics, staggering creativity, and overwhelming emotions that change minds and lives. In other words, the moment you stop caring, you should stop writing because your audience will stop reading.

Paying actual, authentic, absolute attention is how we fix problems, show affection, develop virtuosity, and make the world and our lives better. Where and how you pay attention tells the real tale of who and what and why you are.

Live Wire

Writing guides occupy a strange place on any shelf. On the one hand, no one can teach you to pump out a bestseller, but solid craft can accelerate and elevate that process. What works for 98% of authors may paint you into a corner. Your voice, your muse, your process may resemble what other folks are doing successfully...or *not*.

There are forms, but no formula.

Prescriptive writing manuals seem pretty goofy to me. How-to guides for writers can't "solve" writing problems or calm a writer's anxiety, but they can aim the writer's efforts with more joy and precision. I present everything that follows as practical suggestions based on my creative and professional experience digging in the word mines.

Some writing lessons can be taught, but most must be *caught*. Consequently, I'm writing this guide to share my own storytelling process in the hopes it will inform yours pragmatically. None of us tackle storytelling the same way. What follows is only my process and shouldn't be taken as writ or cant. No two writers face the same problems with the same talent or the same outcome; I don't believe in rules, but *tools*.

When exploring craft and art, the only rubric worth your consideration is the most basic: **Does it get results?**

The Live Wire Writer Guides grew out of a series of popular workshops I offer to professional authors, playwrights, comic artists, game designers, and screenwriters. I've written full-time for more than twenty-five years, taught almost as long, and write these guides as a cross-section of the lessons that have lit my path. I'm kicking off with a book on verbalization because I think it's the linchpin of all life-changing stories.

You don't need divine grace or fairy dust to tell a story properly for profit. If those things turn up, groovy, but as a working genre fictioneer you need a technique that will get the job done, rain or shine. When I get stuck, I lean on craft, and often that takes the form of books that offer answers like this one. What's been tried before? Can I find a better way? How did someone else untangle the knot I'm facing?

Writing is an art and a craft. Supernal fire may scorch the page every time you put letters and words together...but it may not. *Tough*. Every time you start a project, you pray for miracles and take what comes.

Art and craft work in concert. Ideally they turn up simultaneously, more often their attendance is lopsided, subject to your habits and inclinations. Deadlines and duty wait for no muse. Inspiration and lightning strikes are all well and good, but you can't rely on the off-chance you'll be "in the mood" when pages are due.

You cannot build a career on moods and hope. Your craft is what keeps you moving forward until art shows up.

Origin

I came to fiction from film and theatre. My experience as a performer, director, and writer in showbiz has colored all of my subsequent professional life. Additionally, for twenty years I've taught literature in a well-funded Classics department, which gives me latitude to explore obscure subjects based on my whims and obsessions.

What that means is I've spent twenty years gripped by the challenge of consistently capturing people on paper in a compelling way so folks will pay for the privilege of spending time with them. Consequently, I arrived in genre publishing with traction and a weird bag of tricks centered on how to entertain an audience.

Once, in my twenties, I watched a project turn to garbage in my hands. An Off-Broadway theatre had commissioned a play from me for actors I loved, but halfway through drafting Act I, I hit a terrible wall. Fat check. Big names. Huge deal. Nothing worked. *Horrible*...a gun at my head *I'd* loaded. I spent a summer locked in a gorgeous mountain house straining and sweating like I was giving birth to a cinder block. I was blowing a tremendous opportunity until that August when I dragged my paltry pages up to the Williamstown Theater Festival where my amazing cast reminded me: **Stories need verbalizing.** I found the right words and finished the play in a week.

In the end, what saved me and that gig was *language*.

Scripts live and die on the strength of their verbalization. Fortunes are made and lost, ditto. To make it into production, great stories must offer more than a pu-pu platter of traits or quirks or quips—they express something universal and fascinating about the human experience. To survive and succeed, scripts need to present their actors a healthy range of playable actions juicy and compelling enough to hold everyone's attention.

Ditto teaching literature. Tackling the classics with modern students requires a certain improvisatory enthusiasm and awareness of why stories outlive their authors. Ruthless practicality drove me to develop an approach to story that helped me do the job credibly.

When scripting anything, I feel duty-bound to predispose every project for success by any means at my disposal. As a former schmactor (aka *schmuck + actor*), I know precisely how insulting it felt when a lazy, sloppy writer saddled me with a limp role or a crappy scene. Come hell or polyester triple-knit, none of *my* scripts were going to torture innocent performers with my laziness or ineptitude.

This decision was more mercenary than idealistic. Actors and directors demanded playable objectives, powerful emotions, and fascinating roles, so I ponied up. If I wanted my scripts produced so I could get *paid*, providing those things became my baseline.

I share my weird résumé not out of nostalgia or egomania, but because my approach to verbalization developed as a practical solution to a pressing need: unforgettable characters who turned up on cue and dazzled. Start with specific actions, and by default a story tells itself in the most fascinating way.

I'm a professional pragmatist; if something gets results, I'll use it until I can replace it with a better option. *Rinse, repeat.* When I began writing novels, I differed from many authors because I'd worked so long in a sphere that actively fought against writers having cast approval. To sell a script to producers, directors, and actors, I needed more than snazzy backstory and appealing details. I'd spent decades building a story-telling toolkit that opened doors, made bank, and won awards.

My approach to story has its roots in British theatre and dramaturgy, which always found pragmatic and effective solutions *within the text.* That respect for the script appealed mightily to the storyteller in me, even when I was still a working schmactor. What I present in these pages doesn't duplicate these techniques, but it shares their artistic and theatrical DNA.[1]

Language-based solutions boosted and trans-formed my showbiz career, and as I began to write full-time, I instinctively adapted it to the scripting process because it saved so much time and *agita.*

When I shifted from scripted entertainment to fiction, my approach to story and character came along for the ride, evolving to meet the needs of my new format. Even though I wasn't writing for actors any-more, I still populated each story in a way that helped the reader cast it believably in their mind's eye. My format had changed, but audiences still wanted an unforgettable emotional ride.

My approach isn't magical, just a robust masala of observations and lessons I've gleaned from canny critics and grizzled colleagues. I can only take credit for *synthesizing* the ideas in this book over a few decades earning my crust in the arts. Above all, my methods are practical and pulled from my experience in the business of entertaining people.

For most of my career, I assumed everyone tackled story and character the way I did because it felt so *logical*. In 2012, I mentioned my verbalization technique offhand in a lecture I'd posted at Romance University that elicited an enthusiastic response, happy reposts, and a startling flood of correspondence.

Then at RWA's 2016 conference, I gave a workshop on characterization with my friends Farrah Rochon and Kristan Higgins, each of us describing our personal methods. Attendees seemed flabbergasted by my approach, and the recording of that class went viral. Again, I'd wrongly supposed my verbalization method was relatively common. Writer groups on a couple of continents invited me to give in-depth workshops on my method. Those attendees urged me to write a book supporting it. Those classes and my students inspired this text.

Ideally, I hope my experience in the trenches can help you navigate your own creative process. In practice, I want these Live Wire guides to serve as an energy boost, a power outlet, a safe grounding, a fresh jolt...something you can plug into when you need a new perspective or a flexible set of tools.

Use what works, ditch what doesn't.

The best lessons come from direct experience. We all stand on the shoulders of giants.[2]

Magpies

Many, *many* years ago, a script I wrote won a schmancy award presented by playwright Edward Albee. The next day we sat on a panel and he kicked off with a softball icebreaker assigned by the event's organizers: "How would you describe your job if you couldn't use any word related to writing? Not pen or script, ink or stage."

No *way* was I going to look like a plonker in front of the playwright behind *Who's Afraid of Virginia Woolf?*. I'm not often at a loss for words, but that stumped me for a long, awkward beat. A bunch of cutesy answers crowded into my mouth, which I ignored, wary of Mr. Albee's infamously sharp tongue. "Artist" seemed pretentious and "applause-whore" needlessly cynical. I flicked through all the weird chores I tackle when I'm telling a story, and then it came to me, almost by accident.

"Magpie."

He squinted and then laughed back at me, nodding. "Exactly so, exactly so." From that moment, his polite regard melted into warm camaraderie for the rest of that weekend. Apparently I'd spoken a password to some secret guild of which he was a member. For years after, every time we saw each other at retreats and openings, Mr. Albee would clasp my hand and say, "Magpie!" as if greeting a fellow wanderer. My professional code name! Well, I learned the lesson.

All artists are bold, happy scavengers, but writers possibly more so because our tools are common and the work is invisible. Authors are scrappy, curious, audacious, clever, ruthless, and a little suspect...everyone wants to do our job, but few work up the nerve. We're a bold, odd flock, and we're always hunting and pecking for any sparkly shard that catches our imagination and makes our hearts take wing.

Over the past twenty years, "Magpie" has clarified my career through darkness and doubt. When Mr. Albee nudged that word out of me, I was more right than I knew. Even with bright eyes and glossy wings, magpies starve if we don't pay attention. We build nests out of junk and gems and then fly away when we lose interest. We take what we're given and make what we must.

I hope this book will help you be an enthusiastic magpie.

Keep a sharp eye and a strong wing at the ready so you don't miss what you mustn't. Find your flock and avoid canny predators. And as your career takes flight, stick to the sky to scan the terrain, look for the bits that glitter, swoop down when you're ready. Anything that sparkles is fair game...*snooze and you lose, heed and you lead.* Salvage what you can and share the beauty other folks abandon. Don't just borrow what's good...completely *remake* your gathered trash as treasure.

That's craft. That's *art*.

I always tell my students my only intention as a teacher is to offer a practical takeaway, some concrete solution, a spark to keep your wires firing. I hope some of these techniques will help you populate your pages more effectively, powerfully, and joyfully. Let's all build characters worth loving and stories worth living.

"The only way you can write is by the light of the bridges burning behind you."

Richard Peck[3]

Part I: Wire

"The novelist says in words what cannot be said in words."

Ursula LeGuin[4]

Chapter 1: SHOWBIZ

During my tenure in scripted entertainment, I spent a couple of decades listening to actors, directors, and producers asking me why a role was necessary, how to play a beat, and what makes any audience give a damn. Professional showbiz is precarious and *expensive*.

With scripts, I had to justify every person on the page and each plot complication down to the syllable, because the costs were *brutal* and productions are forever tottering on the edge of the abyss. A new character can add six figures to a budget, and even changing a scene's time of day can demolish a shoot schedule and cause massive overruns. Savvy scribblers learn to tread warily and choose wisely.

Writers aren't casting directors. Screenwriters don't get to dictate the nonessential performer details like coloring, vibe, or physical type. An erotic thriller you draft for Idris Elba might end up a sitcom starring Betty White. Even setting, period, special effects, and tone are all up for grabs. Plays, comics, and film are inherently collaborative, complex, and perishable. A wise writer learns quickly that superficial quirks and character traits are less than worthless.

That same volatility affects anything scripted because so many egos and zeros are involved. Deals change, budgets molt, and production slates mutate without any reference to authorial intent. Scripting anything properly demands dynamic, flexible collaboration with a team: visions and voices working in tandem. In order to survive and get paid, I had to focus on the *engine* of the story, not the chrome. Consequently, every time I start any project, I'm thinking:

- Why would someone spend millions of dollars on this heap of words?
- How cheaply can it be made? Which additional costs are justified?
- How would the actor play this for an audience? Why would they?
- How would the team build/light/lens it effectively? What are the traps?
- Who's going to care and how many of them will pay actual cash for tickets?
- What's unique enough to push boundaries? What's familiar enough to win crowds?

Scripts give you no wiggle room with the audience. They cost a fortune to mount and your viewers can't flip back to clarify confusion. Any flaws you permit will get "solved" by armies of people who range from well-meaning to vicious, from brilliant to inept. Films and shows involve hundreds of egos and salaries, all of which steer the story that plays out in front of whatever audience shows up.

Books are both easier and harder. Easier entry point, harder sell. Easier learning curve, harder to master. Less money at stake, but less bandwidth and less audience for piles of product. More artistic freedom certainly, but more time required to enjoy and brutal competition for fewer eyeballs.

Nevertheless, the struggle is the same: how do you make people pay attention?

I tend to treat genre fiction as one more essential cog in the entertainment economy. Telling stories for money is an art and a craft. Consequently, when trying to figure out how to do a better job, I tend to focus on the qualities fans love and the shortcomings colleagues loathe. That way I maximize the kind of positive word of mouth that helps the stories reach the page and the books sell themselves.

Bottom line: **Writing is show business.** There's no shame in selling to an audience. Every monument in the literary canon started out as a popular success. Euripides was the Athenian Shonda Rhimes. The Globe Theatre was Elizabethan Netflix. According to their contemporaries, Jane Austen wrote silly novels for silly women and Charles Dickens cranked out serialized potboilers for the punters. Books only become canon after they're canonized.

"Better a cruel truth than a comfortable delusion."

Edward Abbey[5]

Practice

In my experience, an awful lot of writing guides work like **underpants gnomes.**

For anyone who doesn't get the *South Park* reference..., the second season episode "Gnomes" features feisty little creatures who sneak into bedrooms at night to steal underwear. When found and finally confronted, the gnomes reveal their "brilliant" plan:

- PHASE 1: COLLECT UNDERPANTS
- PHASE 2: ???
- PHASE 3: PROFIT

Of course, the irony is that they have no plan; the gnomes are ridiculous because they spend all their time on a weird and purposeless task in the hopes that someday they'll stumble onto a windfall. We laugh at the blank question marks in Phase Two because all that tenacity is wasted. Ridiculous strategy? Willful ignorance? Bizarre confidence? You pick.

Software designers, scientists, and systems analysts have their own version of this mental spackle. When studying a problem on a blueprint or formulating a solution on a blackboard, a puffy cloud will appear at a critical point with the words [MAGIC HAPPENS HERE] or [THEN A MIRACLE OCCURS][6] to explain something completely baffling and mysterious but completely necessary to a process.

The underpants gnomes have no plan because they skipped the critical step. Essentially, that miraculous ("???") cloud camouflages a blind spot on their map, revealing what they don't know. *Here be dragons.*

That's not a plan, that's a prayer...and it accomplishes nothing.

When it comes to story planning and characterization, books on writing fiction and film constantly gloss over implementation. They recycle the same basic ideas—trait lists, archetypes, psychology, collages, etc.—regurgitating existing methods and models without any coherent logic or specificity. Iffy advice persists because we tend to reteach what we've learned elsewhere, warts and all, without asking why and how it applies.

Frankly, many of the popular methods offered to writers seem to share an underpants-gnome quality I find hilarious and baffling, a fundamental gap ("???") between the advice offered and a clear plan of action that most people dutifully ignore. Interviews, beat sheets, backstory dumps, archetypal grids and forms... how does this popular advice help anyone sit down and write compelling fiction?

I've been collecting writing guides for more than thirty years, so I have a pretty solid handle on the advice floating around, and I don't just mean in the past century. Some of it is good, some of it is ridiculous, and almost none of it deals with the core challenges of creating genre entertainment. Consider any of the following popular characterization and dramatization methods:

1. First, fill out questionnaires and personal ad interviews that establish loads of character traits and trivia based on general assumptions...

(or)

1. First, determine how your story echoes a certain archetypal system or typology...

(or)

1. First, psychoanalyze your cast of imaginary friends and dream up elaborate backstories as if they're living people...

(or)

1. First, compile resonant images and references that help you visualize your character in scenes...
2. Next, you must [*something-something-something*]. Please note that *what* exactly you must do remains a mystery, which obviously makes it *art*.
3. Somehow, powerful characterization and storytelling becomes a snap. Abracadabra!

That is some *first-class* underpants-gnomes logic. How exactly do these methods put words that characterize anyone or dramatize anything on the page? That missing phase two ("???") just hangs there in limbo, unaddressed and unexamined. Essentially, these techniques operate like prayer beads or a mandala, giving you something to contemplate while you attempt to extrapolate as best you can.

In theory, as you nail down the specific characteristics of a person, you come to know their facets until their entire character gradually emerges. Bringing them to life on page will follow naturally because understanding them in their particulars will coalesce into an ability to speak *as* the character.

That's a pretty weird assumption. Think of the story of the blind men and the elephant.[7] If you lack a clear picture of the whole, jumping to conclusions and misreading the facts is inevitable. It's like trying to reach the moon by jumping off a mountain. Facets and foibles indicate a small incoherent piece of a larger puzzle with the idea that you can somehow pull it all together on your own. *Good luck, sucker!*

The entire burden of writing shifts to your ability to synthesize connections based on sketchy, possibly contradictory materials with no clear method. In this light, creating characters works more like a jumble sale than a process...fun but not functional.

- Are character interviews and trait lists helpful? They can be, if you use them at the appropriate stage of your process. (*Cue shocked muttering.*)

- Can archetypes and stock characters act as a springboard to universal appeal? Absolutely, but only if you keep them from sliding into cliché and formula. (*Hmmph! Harrumph!*)

- Can a rich backstory and subtle psychology deepen a character? Without question, if you know where, when, and how to deploy them. (*Boo! Hiss!*)

- Will a collage of photos, text, and artwork help you flesh out a character in three dimensions? Of course, but only if they serve the story and don't distract you from the main tasks. (*Howls of execration.*)

Please know I have used all of the above methods at different points. They are terrific auxiliary solutions that address specific needs, but only when the results are useful and a solid foundation is already in place.

Authors often use research and granular detail to convince readers that characters and events matter, that they deserve attention. H.P. Lovecraft once said stories should be created with "all the care and verisimilitude of an actual hoax."[8] *Amen.* Specifics must serve the story. This is where character interviews and gimmicks start to look appealing. The trouble crops up when writers use detail as deliberate flimflam to distract the reader from bogus characters and events. If you scatter meaningless details and clichés willy-nilly without skill or logic, the story actually *is* a hoax...which is why under scrutiny, sloppy hackwork comes apart like wet tissue.

Starting with secondary details relegates the actual drafting to extrapolation: because X seems true, we can assume the character used to be Y and will one day be Z. Miscues and redirects will be inevitable because you are sewing the clothes first and then looking for someone to wear them. The logical choice would be to start with the characters you need to tell the story best and then allow details to arise from them.

You would *think.*

Unfortunately, most popular characterization methods bog down in auxiliary details, a mix of abstraction and assumption you cannot actually *write.* The leap from "foster child, Methodist, Korean, INTJ, soprano, lefty" to "OMG! This character writes herself" presumably happens in that mysterious "???" phase. [*Magic happens here*]. How, exactly? You'll figure it out at some point. It's your problem. Good luck, underpants gnome.

Of course, we're assured all the other authors do it this way, so if you can't make it work, then it must be *your ineptitude*. The obvious implication: if you can't leap that murky, miraculous underpants-gnome gap, the problem is *you*.

Nonsense.

Best I can tell, a lot of authors have been making that bizarre leap ("???") quietly and intuitively for years: extrapolating what they can and fumbling toward clarity with their bag of tricks and wasting loads of time on extraneous trivia. Artists are uncommonly tenacious and inventive, but that doesn't mean the tools we've been given are necessarily the most precise or effective.

You *can* cut a steak with scissors, but there are better tools for the job.

"Any fool can make a rule, and any fool will mind it."

Henry David Thoreau[9]

Impersonals

Why do so many writing guides obsess over character trivia?

How-to books and classes constantly urge beginning authors to churn out lists of *characteristics*: traits, description, history, beliefs, and pathologies...detailsschmetails. These hypergranular questionnaires proliferate online and in how-to manuals, often designed around a trendy psychological model or archetypal system but generally framed as some kind of story kit or character-building tool.

I think of this model of characterization as **Impersonal Ads** because it treats a character as an aggregate of *characteristics*.

Back in the days of mullets and touch-tone phones, I used these techniques myself, dutifully itemizing physical details, psychological foibles, and background quirks meant to gradually form a fragmentary mosaic of a character. As a method, it's inapt and inept.

What's missing from this kind of impersonal ad approach are the forces that drive people, the focus that steers them, the flaws that shape them, and the friction they face. As authors, we need to expose their essential core, and that requires more than a rote *eye color, hair style, job* template. If you write a mannequin, don't expect a heartbeat.

Attributes, roles, and groups are, by definition, generic. There are many redheads, many Sufis, many Capricorns, many amputees. Slotting your characters into various categories doesn't do much to put words on the page, bring them to life, or make them stand out. A list of fascinating details doesn't auto-magically fascinate anyone. Throwing darts at a gigantic list of traits and habits might serve you just as well. Plenty of writing guides encourage exactly that: scattershot trivia to fill the *terra incognita* on the map.

How any of this translates into actual writing has always remained vague, but the advice persists: *then a miracle occurs.*

This questionnaire approach to characterization refuses to die because it seems simple and sensible even though it's wildly inefficient and impractical. Most of those "quirky" details will get wasted or contradicted, but we're assured that's just the *deal*...we break eggs to make omelettes, and how else are you supposed to learn about these imaginary folks whose story you're telling? In my experience, all that nitty-gritty can be meaningful, but the majority gets wasted, and at best it tells you how to write a character only *indirectly*.

What about you personally? When was the last time you got to know someone by compiling a list of traits and categories? How many times have you been hired purely on the basis of your name and raw stats? Why mess with interviews when CVs and medical charts can provide all the pertinent necessaries? Why doesn't everyone just find love in the personal ads, ordering their romantic ideal like a Happy Meal? Hell, why bother to meet with prospective hires, partners, or spouses at all?

Because **Characteristics are not character**. We all know this, but for some reason, as authors we forget.

In fact, life experience teaches us over and over that character *contradicts* characteristics more often than not, that personal ads are misleading, and that you can't sum up an entire life in a cluster of adjectives and generalities. Men aren't always manly, geniuses aren't born wearing glasses, and blondes aren't always ditzy or what gentlemen prefer. In such nonsense are stupid assumptions and prejudices born.

When you boil a life down into characteristics, you can easily ignore the essentials required to tell a story and inadvertently exaggerate deceptive trivia based on your habits and ruts. And yet the bulk of character guides encourage writers to churn out lists and questionnaires without explaining how these cluttered, unfocused dossiers will populate the pages of your book. That's like hopping across a minefield on one foot or by dragging yourself up a mountain with your lips: possible, but *pointless*.

Don't believe me? Let's play a game. Imagine your next book is set in the mid-20th century and your protagonist

- grew up short, dark-haired, and sleight of build because of persistent poor health.
- identified as a vegetarian, nonsmoking animal lover and natural leader at a time of cataclysmic social upheaval.
- was raised devoutly Christian by a blue-collar family on a small farm before moving to a larger city without ever losing that distinctive Southern accent or rock-ribbed traditional values.
- survived a fractious divided home, then a divorce until being raised for a long stretch by a single mother who needed nursing through an agonizing, ultimately deadly struggle with cancer.
- attended a public school, dropped out at sixteen *before* graduating but finished education

outside the system years later, eventually studying radical thinkers fomenting a national revolution.

- initially aspired to an artistic, creative field but worked a number of odd jobs in a volatile, prejudiced metropolis that motivated a personal, lifelong turn into politics.
- embraced revolutionary activism in a huge resistance movement bent on saving the country from internal threats to its citizens.
- traveled the country to speak to impassioned crowds about government corruption and the need for social change.
- at the age of forty-two, suddenly assumed a splashy, public role as the center of a popular uprising that overturned the nation and then got lionized and vilified by media around the world.[10]
- married only once to a fellow member of the movement who passed away first, without having any children.
- died isolated and nearly destitute, yet cemented a global legacy as a universal icon and a symbol of the outer limits of the human spirit.

Boom! Characterization handled. There's plenty of meat on that bone, right? Loads of juicy backstory, built-in drama and stakes, more than enough to work with for any author in any genre. Can you imagine that story already, the cinematic fights and triumphs? Visualize a few pivotal scenes and vivid supporting roles? Given all this meaningful, dramatic specificity, you might feel like you really know this person intimately. Bringing them to three-dimensional life would be a breeze, a snap, a dash through daisies.

Here's the rug pull: the entire list above applies to (at least) *two* pivotal figures of the 20th century: Rosa Parks and Adolf Hitler. Yes, really.

Feel that fact.

Two diametrically opposed sociopolitical icons who stood at the extreme limits of human belief, and none of those meaty, granular details above paint a clear picture or help you flesh them out believably or authentically. Their backstory and incidentals don't tell us anything that matters. I can do the same with Mozart and Beyoncé... or Walt Disney and Ramses the Great. Traits are a perfectly nonsensical way to start building a character.

Obviously I'm cherry-picking, but the point stands: character is much more than characteristics and is far too critical to be relegated to scattershot *impersonal* ads. Character-as-sushi-order won't help us write much worth reading because it doesn't *verbalize* those traits.

Lists and interviews and other trait bouquets serve a legitimate function down the line, but slopping a list of particulars against the wall and seeing what sticks seems like a pretty inefficient way to bring a compelling person to life. We expect those fictional folks to evoke real emotions. So why would we write them willy-nilly?

But wait! Isn't it important to specify your characters' personality, coloring, class, heritage, sexuality, religion, education, employment, foibles, kinks, and the rest? *Obviously.* But why smash a hundred eggs to make an omelette?

Fun? Yes. Clear? Maybe. Useful? *Eventually.* But all that window dressing is the least and easiest of an author's tasks, and one I often leave until pretty late in the game. Until I know what's important, any decisions I make are bound to confuse my efforts. That kind of personal minutiae is the *snow* on the tip of the iceberg.

Of course if you love those lists and interviews, groovy. Shine on, you crazy diamond! I just want to offer you a tool that will take you farther and faster onto firmer ground.

Idiosyncrasies are great, but they only suggest the outer shell of character. At best, they can point you toward the real questions and the powerful answers that nail readers to the page. Rather than starting with the skin, we're going to peel back the muscle, the organs, the bones, the blood of your characters and get at the underlying spark that turns a body into a *being.*

Write is a verb.

Great characters pop off the page and stay with us. Traits are *salt* in the gravy. Worry about moods, quirks, and backstories after you *know* the character. They're the last and least part of the writer's job. To write unforgettable characters, your approach needs to go beyond pigmentation, employment, and family anec-dotes to something deeper.

Characters are not characteristics. Scattershot trivia is wildly inefficient, which is why characterization via personal ad templates is such a trap: it tricks you into paying attention to nonsense and distracts you from the real story. Start your work with trivia and your work will be trivial.

> "Work is love made visible. And if you cannot work with love but only with distaste, it is better that you should leave your work and sit at the gate of the temple and take alms from those who work with joy."
>
> Kahlil Gibran[11]

Significance

When we care about something, we pay attention, and by the same token, when we pay attention to something, we start to care about it.

You can only pay attention to specificity, so canny authors go out of their way to provide juicy detail that supports the story. Vagueness connotes laziness, sloppiness, or apathy in the writer, which is why pablum is general and generalized. Consequently, specificity is the core of solid craft and superior art. Precision makes us focus and remember.

By the same token, specifics are critical, but only in service to the tale you're telling. Plunking random specifics into a story without any awareness of their impact serves nothing. Paying attention to your story's details makes your readers follow suit. When you stop paying attention, likewise.

Every specific in a story requires a purpose, a *function*. Instead of pointless detail, what you should aim for is **significance**: meaningful patterns start with resonant focus. When weighing the effect of any detail, you should be able to answer the question "How does this help tell the story and improve the emotional ride?" Under that lens you'll quickly pinpoint facts that actually characterize and dramatize the tale you're telling.

Significant specifics don't just attract attention, they *reward* it so that the patterns of the story begin to connect to patterns already hardwired in your reader's mind. Rather than providing conclusions, show your audience respect and engage them directly by allowing them to reach conclusions on their own. Significance jacks into their consciousness directly for more potent and efficient narrative results.

A detail only becomes significant when it helps you tell the tale.

Show your readers significant specifics and you don't need to tell them anything, but try to *tell* them something, and their craving for pattern will send them looking for specifics that might contradict it. Better to have your audience as an enthusiastic ally than a dubious witness.

The great power of significance is that it forces all your words to do the heavy lifting—sometimes several jobs at once—so you can pack more of a punch into less space by showing and not telling. As Elizabeth Bowen put it, "Irrelevance, in any part, is a cloud and a drag on, a weakener of, the novel. It dilutes meaning. Relevance crystallizes meaning."[12]

Here's the great secret of writing popular fiction: your audience helps you tell the best story, but *only* if you give them the right materials.

What matters most is why characters pursue what they pursue and how they pursue it despite terrible odds. Instead of bogging down in minutiae, you can *anchor* every project in the raw, emotional power that engages readers and inspires creativity by focusing on the energy of the story. What matters to your audience and your process is the driving force behind the story, the spring in the clock, the emotional core, the *choices* of the characters. The *actions* they embody. The risks they take.

The rest is parsley on the plate.

As Aristotle noted, every plot asks the same question: **Will this character's action lead to happiness?**

Is trivia and backstory worthwhile? Can abstract conflicts inspire a scene? Will knowing stock characters and psychological profiles prove useful during your drafting and revision? Can archetypes and allusion boost characterization? Should you gather images and artwork to help visualize your cast? *Maybe.*

The truth is, you don't know because no two books or characters emerge the same way. Authors tend to treat this leftover trivia and wasted research as acceptable losses...not desirable *per se*, but par for the course and part of the cost of doing the job.

At first glance, the argument seems sound. By knowing the history and details of a person's life, we come to know them. By knowing them, we understand them; by understanding them, we can speak for them, with them, *as* them with a linked chain of black squiggles on a page.

Call it the creator's dilemma: until you've written the book, you don't know what you'll use and don't know what you don't need to know. You assemble a massive pile of likely ingredients and tools in the dark so you can start cooking blind. Maybe five percent ends up on the page. *Oof.* A hundred eggs to make an omelette. Would any competent chef work that way?

Sadly, most characterization starts backward, from the skin in: coloring and opinions, gender and occupation, archetypes and stock roles, backstory and psych profile. Inert nouns and modifiers, all of it. Think of those cool facts as the spice rack or the garnish. It's narrative *parsley*. When cooking a meal, no one starts by folding the napkins. First, you gather your core ingredients.

I think folks leap into character trivia because it's fun and feels meaningful without requiring actual effort. It's the *easiest* part of characterization, and we fixate on it to our detriment. You absolutely need to know those details, and they *can* enrich a solid story, but what readers want is a satisfying emotional ride. Build the ride and the rest will follow.

Deeply intuitive writers may say, "My character speaks to me" or "They take over." They chalk up the characterization process to a kind of subconscious channeling fed by all these personal ad details, like a blind date set up by their muse. The more trivia, the more powerful the link they feel. Again, it sounds nice, but how does it happen? And what happens when your imaginary friends go quiet?

Let me be clear: granular specifics matter in the drafting process, and deep knowledge of your cast is a must—*eventually*. I do exhaustive character research and interviews in the *final* stages of prepping a project.

It's the last and least part of characterization. But practical, applicable solutions for all characters start at the foundation.

Nobody building a house starts by polishing door-knobs.

"The artist seeks out the luminous detail and presents it."

Ezra Pound[13]

Chapter 2: DEVICES

Characters are the power source of all stories. We plug into them and they flow through us.

The secret magic of great characters happens *inside* their audience. Miss Marple, Lestat, Celie Harris, Edmond Dantès, Hermione Granger, Hannibal Lecter, Idgie Threadgoode, Easy Rawlins, Mrs. Whatsit, Nick Charles, Scout Finch—whatever feelings you harbor about beloved characters are based more on their provocative *gaps* than the exhaustive details the author provides. Writers provide jungle gyms for the reader's imagination.

Great characters seem so lifelike that we treat them accordingly, a habit that's emotionally logical but professionally *nonsensical*. Because characters make us remember events, feel emotions, and discover truths about our actual lives, it's tempting to overdetermine and mythologize their creation. Most discussion of fictional characters analyzes them from the audience's impressions rather than the author's task, a bit like trying to deduce a recipe by the expressions on diners' faces.

Unforgettable characters throw long shadows, but as authors our job is to focus on the original creation to learn from our artistic ancestors. As Picasso said, "No artist is a bastard. We all have forebears, and we build on the work of others."[14]

Once you choose to be a writer, *keep on choosing to be a writer at every step.*

Scribendo disces Scribere – "You learn to write by writing."

Samuel Johnson[15]

Psych

Part of the rampant impersonal ad trend dates back to the rise of mass media and the popularization of psychology.

Back in 1933, Shakespearean scholar L.C. Knights published a watershed essay entitled "How Many Children Had Lady Macbeth?" mocking critics who wasted time analyzing characters not as dramatic constructs, but as if they were actual human beings.

Knights' question was *ironic*; we don't need to know how many heirs Macbeth's Mrs. bore because those children aren't part of the play. Shakespeare mentions her offspring in passing without bothering with specifics because their names, number, and nature don't matter to the *story*. To paraphrase Knights, the complex emotional response experienced by audiences happens without (and in spite of) extraneous character details. Shakespeare ignored them because they didn't matter.[16]

Shakespeare created a character, not a woman. In a play that's just over two thousand lines long, Macbeth's Lady only has 252. Hell, she's one of the most famous characters in literature and Shakespeare doesn't even *name* her.

Knights objected to critical attempts to fabricate a three-dimensional human from dramatic scraps. Not only was the exercise silly, it led criticism into circular, cynical arguments about authors' "real" intentions and a text's "hidden" meaning based on fabricated, extrapolated evidence. The appeal was obvious: if everything could mean anything, then all opinions deserved an airing—great fodder for professors publishing for tenure but ridiculous and downright masturbatory as a way of analyzing art or improving the creative process.

For over a century, this rampant psychological approach has encouraged bizarre speculation and trivia to distract from actual analysis of literary craft and technique in favor of subjective interpretation. Sentimental "psychologizing" has nothing to do with the writing process but throws the doors open to theory and opinion unmoored from the actual text. It sidesteps research and language in favor of moods and gists. Some readers might dig that kind of musing, but for writers it can be paralyzing.

Aside from its devastating impact on American theater and film, psychologization still creates actual, practical problems for writers who have been told to make characters more "real" to improve their books. Characters reflect psychology as a matter of coherence, but they cannot *have* psychology because they do not have lives. Even an *autobiographical* character is an artificial construct with careful emphasis and elided details. Worse, you can only psychoanalyze a character after the fact, so the exercise has zip to do with actually putting people on paper. *Psych!*

The modern obsession with foibles and appearances has infected a lot of writing advice. Obsessing about imaginary psychology and trivia can cripple your process. Aeschylus and Cervantes and Austen did not create characters by picking neuroses and eye colors. Even details like temperament or birth date are useful but auxiliary. Your readers don't need to know every sliver of trivia for your characters to come to life. Piling on meaningless detail is where a lot of young writers go off the rails and into the swamp of blather and backstory.

Sometimes an unforgettable character can be sketched in a few sentences and alter millions of lives. Witness *To Kill a Mockingbird*'s **Boo Radley**, *Dracula*'s **Renfield**, or *The Princess Bride*'s **Inigo Montoya**. Those aren't three-dimensional humans, but narrative devices created by words to inspire feelings.

But characters are "so real," readers say. Nope: the story just feels real. It *needs* to feel real. The emotions are real, but their origin is fictional. In the emotional roller coaster you're building, your characters carry your readers for the duration of the journey. They are the car, not the ride. Your job is to build something sturdy enough to transport your audience.

If I say Perry Mason or Mrs. Danvers or Captain Frederick Wentworth, you may have memories or feelings about those characters. Perry Mason appears in over eighty Erle Stanley Gardner mysteries—we literally have much more of him than we do Wentworth (*Persuasion*) or Mrs. Danvers (*Rebecca*), several hundred thousand more words characterizing him. Do we know Mason *better* or believe he's somehow more *real* just because there are more words on various pages about him? Is *Twilight*'s Bella Swan more believable or alive than *Pride and Prejudice*'s Elizabeth Bennet (who inspired her) because her author filled several sequels with her?

Characters are not people; they're purpose-built narrative tools to extract satisfying emotion from your audience.

Stories are sketched in strokes, not photographic detail. No story, not even biography, requires the creation of an "entire" person, whatever that would look like. Rather, the author provides the specifics necessary to create a satisfying emotional ride for the audience. Artists should unlock audience imaginations. Most of our feelings and fantasies about fictional characters feel personal to us because they happen inside us, glorious creations hung on pegs provided by the author.

In that sense, **A character in a story is not a person, a profile, or an archetype, but an *action figure*, an entertaining device designed to perform a function within a story.** A character has parts and joints, limits and features, a set appearance and a specific range of motion that encourages play.

There is no such thing as a three-dimensional character. Only the illusion of existence, evoked by a few telling details. What you leave out can be as important as what you include. Trying to flesh out an entire life in exhaustive detail on the page is a waste of time and energy. What we want is not "real people" but action figures...resonant, fascinating, and fun to read and write and play with.

With well-conceived action figures, the writing becomes easier and more entertaining. The reading, ditto. Even the selling of the book ends up less of a chore if you start with the emotional experience readers expect.

> "Your reader reads first and foremost for *emotional* stimulation."
>
> Dwight Swain[17]

Ride

Genre writing is not for the fainthearted; make certain you are tall enough to ride that ride. Unless you're doodling and scribbling for your own amusement, art needs an audience, and that means you need to earn the attention of other folks. Art is the business of attention: earning, shaping, deserving, and directing it.

For genre authors in a crowded market, anything that distracts or derails your audience weakens your book and blunts your story's point. You forfeit attention at your peril. Every tool exists to control attention. Every flaw or weakness in your work degrades attention. The more you can manage different types of attention, the better your writing will be. Otherwise, why should anyone bother?

At first glance, stories are pointless. Life is rich, beautiful, and complex, so why do we spend so much time focused on narratives that revisit the past, extrapolate from our present, or imagine possibilities that can never actually happen? Why are we so addicted to story?

Emotion.

Words don't create characters, emotions do. If you want your books to move people, the burden falls to your characters. What makes a character more or less real is the *emotion* they elicit within us, which explains why reading is so personal and fandoms are so passionate. The emotions are real because they happen inside living, breathing readers, the characters only provoke them. Powerful emotions create powerful characters; words are just the medium of transmission.

Stories allow audiences to experience emotions beyond the scope of their everyday lives at a safe distance. Readers trust writers to take them on a fascinating journey. As Dr. Keith Oatley puts it, "The job of the writer is to present emotionally significant events at an aesthetic distance that enables us to recognize them, experience them, and assimilate them to ourselves."[18] Books let audiences experience other lives and worlds with startling immediacy so we can

- learn from others' mistakes and test reactions in context.
- navigate dangerous or unlikely scenarios at a remove.
- explore the norms, boundaries, and values of many cultures.

All your readers have to give you is *attention* for you to turn words into worlds. The appeal of great genre fiction is that it offers audiences a perfect blend of certainty and surprise.

Like a roller coaster, the audience *chooses* to take the ride. Your story waits for readers to buckle themselves in so that you can take them on a well-crafted emotional journey that will surprise, gratify, and delight them before returning them safely to their regularly scheduled lives. At the end of a roller coaster, the punters unbuckle, climb out, and head back to their real lives, but the emotions linger. You want them raving about the ride afterward.

In genre fiction, the author's constant opponent is boredom. Plateaus and repetition give everyone permission to tune out or forget. Once a character has overcome difficulty, lesser difficulties and even identical difficulties will leave your readers cold. The outcome is inevitable. Without stakes there is no story. **In genre entertainment, the name of the game is escalation.**

Don't let them hop off the ride. At every moment, you want your audience thinking about all the ways that make putting down the book, even glancing away, less likely. Through steady escalation, you teach your audience that they dare not waver for a moment. Whatever is happening on the page at this moment must be more fascinating than what was happening a moment ago. **Tension creates attention.**

Readers will accept anything you don't give them a reason to doubt. Any time readers cannot understand a character's actions or can predict a scene's outcome, you give them a chance to slip away. And there's the rub: clichés, logic leaps, shoddy research, and all other failures of craft loosen your hold on the audience, give readers a chance to wake from the dream you're spinning. No tension, no attention.

When you are looking for ways to make a scene more dramatic, don't be afraid to push events to extremes. Asking "what if?" or "what happens next?" only keeps the scene moving at its current intensity. Instead, try to imagine what the worst possible development might be. Push the possibilities in a believable way, and you give your characters a chance to exceed expectations. **Think laterally, not literally.**

Studying melodrama, farce, and pulp fiction can liberate a writer from the everyday constraints of taste, caution, and timidity. As legendary writing teacher Dwight Swain teaches us, disasters demand decisions, and decisions unleash ever more intense disasters.[19] What reversal, discovery, or transformation would require a change of tactics from all the people involved? How can you escalate a choice, a moment, a situation to the outer limits of dramatic possibility? Your job is to entertain people and make them feel things outside their experience.

When people ride a roller coaster, what they remember is the rush and climb, the adrenaline and relief. The punters pay money for the experience and what lasts is the emotional effect. With painstaking attention, engineers have milked those feelings in a calculated flow, but the public doesn't take pictures of the rails or the rivets. Joyful mobs don't line up to study the blueprints and the rigging.

All the structural decisions of a satisfying roller coaster take place prior to the ride and offstage behind the proverbial curtain. You don't learn to build a roller coaster simply by riding a bunch of roller coasters. You study the fundamentals and learn the limits so you can push them.

A novel is no different.

You have to lay the rails, and the character is the car readers climb aboard at the beginning for the best point of view to bring them back safe and sound at the end. Not every ride is the same, and different genres shape the reader's emotional experience differently. Certain basic structural features recur, so each new attraction must balance expectations and innovation.

Readers will pursue and avoid certain emotional rides based on their history, preferences, and word of mouth. Some readers are omnivores, happy to veer between mild and wild diversions, while others stick to a narrow slice of the spectrum. Popular fiction delivers an intense emotional ride, but all the danger is imaginary, the variations carefully and skillfully wrought, and the conclusion safe and satisfying.

The audience will get on board with anything as long as you can make them care. The moment they stop caring, they will stop reading. Your job is to make them care enough to keep turning the pages, and for them to care, you must care even more.

Don't write what you know, write what you feel.

Your job is to create coherent characters who must deal with unlikely pressure believably. Allow your characters to have remarkable reactions to everyday situations and vice versa. The uncertainty of their circumstances is such "stuff as dreams are made on."[20] Rather than waiting for lightning to strike, get down to the business of telling the tale the best way you know how.

Pay attention to your writing so that you keep exceeding your own expectations. As long as you keep paying zealous, ruthless, joyful attention, readers will return the favor.

"Your good fortune is not to need good fortune."

Seneca the Younger[21]

Process

Oceans are imaginary.

Yes, large bodies of salt water cover most of our planet's surface, but the division and dissection of the Earth's salt water is arbitrary. "Ocean" is an abstract word we use to describe a matrix of phenomena that share certain powers, features, and boundaries. Dip your toe in the Atlantic and you're touching waves created by the weather patterns in the Pacific. Glacial thaw in the Arctic Circle affects oil rigs off Scotland and the migration patterns of whales in the Indian Ocean. Tidal flows can kill off species and boost an entire ecosystem in the opposite hemisphere.

No one can study and understand oceans at a glance. Their complexity overwhelms us, so we break them into manageable parts for analysis, research, and industry. As we come to understand them, the overlaps and symbiotic relations between those parts reveal themselves. We study the water to see the sea.

As a subject of study, fiction is oceanic and equally indivisible. Studying any portion of the writing process trespasses upon every other writing topic. Trying to separate character from plot, pace, POV, dialogue, voice, intimacy, worldbuilding, comedy, symbol, theme, and anything else is almost impossible. Like any living thing, storytelling involves a complex matrix of interdependent organic systems.

I don't see plot, character, setting, emotion, voice, and theme as separate things but rather as overlapping lenses that allow us to focus on different tasks of storytelling. For the purposes of this book, our focus will be characters and story planning, which necessarily touch on every other element of writing.

Craft provides a set of tools authors use to grapple with a single strata of the vast matrix of writing. By studying our colleagues' techniques, we cobble together a flexible arsenal with infinite applications. Analyzing and experimenting help you build the kind of story you want to tell. Solid craft skills will expose dangers and steer you toward safer waters. And because no two authors or books are the same, craft produces infinite variety.

Craft apprises, advises, devises, scrutinizes, and analyzes. It breaks writing's cohesive living system into manageable bite-sized portions so we can tackle the job at hand without losing our minds or our nerve. Craft anchors all your wildest inventions and steers the process so you can do the job credibly even when you aren't inspired.

Craft *is* critical. The muse is unpredictable and inspiration doesn't operate on a schedule. When you have a deadline and pages due, craft delivers competent work on time with skill. Those tools and tricks come from training and experience, and they will save your butt, repeatedly. Knowing the various options, possibilities, and pitfalls will help you build a glorious whole out of the inert components. But for any project to come to life, it requires wholeness, harmony, and radiance, and that's where we turn to **art**.

Exceptional stories spring from a spark of magic. Sometimes a story or a character is so compelling, it supersedes crappy prose and dodgy grammar by touching on...*more*. Unforgettable books require more than competent prose studded with stylistic garnish.

Art earns the attention of its audience because it distills the attention of its creator into something simultaneously rigorous and vigorous. Art attempts to articulate the inarticulable, to show the invisible, to reveal the spark in the darkness. It turns up at odd moments and often without warning. It's the monkey in the wrench, the fortune in the cookie, the shine in the diamond.

When I say no two people write a book the same way, I mean exactly that. A hundred authors would produce a hundred idiosyncratic Cinderellas. Our processes may have overlaps and similarities, but a great character or a bestselling book cannot be assembled from a recipe or a kit. The gap between solid craft and moving transcendence is art.

Both are essential to your process: the *craft* of spinning a yarn and the *art* of saying impossible things. Art will always be erratic, fickle, and untamed, just as craft remains steady, conscious, and imperfect. You cannot guarantee beauty will turn up every time you put words on a page, but you can pursue beauty with diligence and vigilance...even when the whole enterprise starts to feel as impossible, deranged, and naïve as a blindfolded unicorn hunt on skates.

The secret is paying attention.

Knowing theoretically how to write great jokes will never make you funny without serious focus. Reading about pathos and allusion will not make everything you write meaningful or tragic without emotional legibility. Churning out "well-structured" dreck according to some vague, arbitrary formula will never win reader's hearts. On a starship, Red Shirts will never end up in the captain's chair, because they aren't paying attention. Anyone can learn to cut stone, and some craftspeople learn to place stones, but only a very few artists learn how to build palaces.

Just pay attention. Try to ditch the habit of "believing" you're a writer or "believing" a book will change your career. Belief is a pacifier for people addicted to certainty, and certainty is the one thing in the world none of us can ever have. Kick your belief habit and learn to follow your doubts and questions to their outer limits.

Without art, craft is lifeless. Without craft, art is chaotic. We need the wire and the fire that runs through it. If you are serious about your writing and want to elevate your stories and access their wholeness, harmony, and radiance for your audience, then you go from laying bricks to building palaces.

Art brings all those craft decisions to life, relinking the various areas of your story so they don't feel mechanical or arbitrary. Art breaks the rules and tests the margins. To extend the oceanic metaphor above, art is what weaves the weather patterns, the tidal flow, the marine life, and the nautical skills together, reconnecting all the various divisions we use to understand the oceans.

At its best, genre writing makes the impossible probable and the improbable possible. Verbalizing your stories will unquestionably highlight other parts of your writing process—and that's wonderful, but it will also expose all your weaknesses and shortcuts. Learn to swim in your ocean, and eventually your ocean will swim in you.

> "Art is not truth. Art is a lie that makes us realize truth."
>
> Pablo Picasso[22]

Chapter 3: ORDER

So here's the moment where you may think, "Oceanography? Shakespeare? Action figures? Roller coasters? This guy's crazy! There's no freakin' way I can juggle all these separate pieces, let alone use them to verbalize a story on deadline."

You're right, in a way. One of the worst challenges faced by any writer is the number of flaming bricks you have to keep in the air. The complexity starts to feel overwhelming and paralyzing without some kind of craft...unless you have a handle to help you hold on. Great writing technique won't stop you worrying, but it should aim your efforts with precision and a sense of joy.

Some books flow, some books ooze. What you need is madness and a method to wrestle it into publishable shape. Solid tools should be able to manage whatever story you need to tell and generate maximum emotion in minimal time.

"To create an apple pie from scratch, you must first invent the universe."

Carl Sagan[23]

Alignment

If I asked you to carry twenty books across your house, you wouldn't carry the books one at a time. You wouldn't try to balance all twenty books at twenty different places on your body and then slide or hop or roll across the floor. I'll bet any amount of money you'd build a manageable pile to save time and trips. You'd *stack* them, because alignment conserves energy and concentrates your effort on a single point.

Even the least organized person would likely stack them by size for greater balance and stability, larger and heavier books at the bottom where you have more control over them, lighter and smaller books at the top where they make the trip with less risk.

By aligning the books before you pick them up, you can focus your energy and effort on the lowermost book and the stack above comes along for the ride. That alignment is possible because they share a shape and a scale: books are flat, stackable, and dense. Aligning them allows you to complete the task swiftly, efficiently, expertly.

Frankly, a physical book is itself a miracle of alignment. Parallel lines of text, page numbers, and typesetting make it easier for us to do the job of reading them. All those pages need to be bound so they don't get damaged or disordered. Even shelving books helps us find what we want.

Of course, not everything aligns easily. If you were carrying something precarious and fragile, like test tubes or eggs, you'd carefully place them on something stable and sturdy to protect them and minimize waste.

Why do beverages come in bottles? Why do buildings have floors and lists get alphabetized? Why do we bind pages, cook food in pots, and travel on roads?

Alignment keeps effort efficient and effective.

Alignment of your story components maximizes your power and range as an author, cutting down on wasted time and meaningless toil. All the other elements stack and balance to streamline the writing process. Characterization and dramatization (and for that matter all writing) are no different. We focus our energy where it's most needed, build from a solid base, and the story tells itself. Minor details catch a lift as needed.

Pro tip: if all of the components of your story align, any one of the components will lead you to the others. Ralph Waldo Emerson compared a person's essential character to "an acrostic or Alexandrian stanza—read it forward, backward, or across, it still spells the same thing."[24]

Alignment allows energy to flow through a story and into your audience's imagination. Knowing any one element can point you in a direction, but the more aligned the effort, the more seamless the process. The first step for a writer is to nail down the *foundation* that aligns and supports all the emotion that makes books worth reading.

"Everything is relevant. Making things relevant is the creative process."

William J. J. Gordon[25]

EXERCISE: Story Line

As we dig into the nuts and bolts of verbalizing story and character, let's work backward a moment. What are the components of an unforgettable story? Who are the imaginary people you can't get out of your head? Why?

1. Take a favorite fictional character you know well.

2. Make a list of everything you remember about the character that seems meaningful and central to their behavior and experience within the book.

3. With that list before you, draw links connecting the details that seem to align for significant effects. How do the specifics, the traits, the language align with and express everything the character does and is?

4. See if you can spot traces of the author's revisions: any vestigial anomalies, any convenient reveals, any oddball pivots. Can you discern changes the author might have made to align necessary elements?

- BONUS ROUND: Name additional ways the author could have created alignment to support the char- acterization—additional specifics or resonances. Note any lingering extraneous or contradictory de- tails that might have impeded your experience of the story. What would you change? How? With what narrative repercussions?

Parts

As we start getting technical about tools and technique, I want to make sure we're all speaking the same language.

If you're an English major or a lifelong grammar devotee, feel free to skip this brief section, but for everyone else, I want to lay out some essentials to clear our path because I think language is magic and understanding it is the key to tapping it effectively.

Please know I'm not hammering grammar to make anyone feel silly or self-conscious; I know plenty of die-hard grammarphobes who live on the bestseller lists. Storytelling doesn't coincide with syntactical know-how by default, but a solid handle on the rules of English will help your stories at their roots. Getting more comfortable with grammar will have an exponential effect on your ability to verbalize stories.

Parts of speech are categories of words grouped by their function—the way words work in the wild, as it were. For our purposes, let's look at the three most common.

- VERBS express action or a state of being for the subject of a sentence. (*to write, to edit, to revise, to submit*)
- NOUNS denote a person, place, creature, thing, event, or idea. (*writer, book, inspiration, character*)
- MODIFIERS qualify or quantify other words. (adjectives for nouns, i.e. *brilliant, talented, professional, fascinating* and adverbs for verbs and other modifiers, i.e. *very, quickly, artfully, always*).

VERBALIZE

For example, in the sentence "Revisions proceeded swiftly," *revisions* is a noun and the subject of the sentence. *Proceeded* is the verb that describes the action of the subject. *Swiftly* is a modifier (in this case an adverb) qualifying the verb "proceeded" to indicate the speed of the subject's action.

Because verbs are the strongest and most dynamic part of language, by definition adverbs are almost always the weakest word choice. A stronger version of the above sentence might be "Revisions flew." Using a more specific verb clarifies the meaning and eliminates the need for a modifier.

This is why so many authors and editors loathe adverbs—since verbs provide the energy in any sentence, adverbs only exist to *hamper and distort* that energy. Stephen King claims, "The road to hell is paved with adverbs." Actually, adverbs are so weak they can even modify other *modifiers*. Similarly, William Strunk Jr. called adjectives "the leeches that infest the pond of prose, sucking the blood of words."[26] A stronger noun can make any adjective irrelevant.

Modifiers have their uses, but they offer the weakest language for writers and often hint at deeper defects. In weak writing, adjectives and adverbs proliferate like something monkeys pick off each other and eat. When editing, that goes double. Strong, clear writing makes for an easier reading experience, which helps readers pay attention.

So far, so good. Genre writing is inherently grammatical in ways that can simplify and illuminate the process if you know the rules. Truth be told, you do most of these things instinctively. Knowing some of the rules just allows you to go beyond day-to-day facility.

One of the reason verbs are so powerful is because they are both strong and flexible: they can be *conjugated*. Conjugation is a change in the form of a verb to indicate a change in its function in a sentence. For example: a verb like "write" contains infinite possibility released when we conjugate it:

- PRESENT: You <u>write</u> a book.
- PAST: You <u>wrote</u> yesterday.
- FUTURE: You <u>will write</u> tomorrow.

Clear enough, right? And that verb's just getting warmed up. That infinite urge "to write" has about a bazillion more things it wants to scribble on the universe if someone will just conjugate it and turn it loose in different directions.

Of course, some actions are done before you get around to describing them. *Perfect* verbs have completed their actions prior to the time being described in the sentence.

- PRESENT PERFECT: You <u>have written</u> today.
- PAST PERFECT: You <u>had written</u> yesterday.
- FUTURE PERFECT: You <u>will have written</u> tomorrow.

Notice that each conjugation pinpoints a different moment in time via the verb, as well as a different context for the subject of the sentence. Actions are happening and things are changing, and all it took was a little conjugating.

In addition to *tenses* that establish time, verbs even have *moods* that establish meaning and context:

- INTERROGATIVE: <u>Will</u> you <u>write</u> later? (a question)
- CONDITIONAL: You <u>might write</u> if you made time. (an opinion)
- IMPERATIVE: <u>Write</u> the book already! (a command)

And then there are *verbals*, also known as nonfinite verbs. Most verbs make stuff happen in a certain timeframe, but verbals are nonfinite or continuous because while they convey the idea of action, their action is incomplete.

- GERUND: <u>Writing</u> is hard. (...acts as a noun)
- PARTICIPLE: You have <u>writing</u> talent. (...acts as an adjective)
- INFINITIVE: You know how <u>to write</u>, anytime and anywhere. (...acts as an abstract noun expressing all the verb's potential action.)

And that is why when most people discuss verbs in the abstract, they generally use a neutral *infinitive*: it contains an unconjugated possibility of all of the potential actions buried within that verb.

Conjugation unlocks the full power of verbs, which allows you to move time and space for everyone in your story. It releases general potential so that specific, meaningful things can happen. In a very real sense, stories are built out of a chain of conjugations that change what's happening and why. More on this later.

Again: please don't panic. Grammar is just a tool to help you write better books and communicate more clearly.

For those of you who "hate" grammar or "ignore" punctuation, I say, "Buckle, up, buttercup." Yes, some working writers manage to avoid learning the essentials and pass the grammatical buck, but that avoidance does them no favors and makes the drafting and editorial process a misery in all directions.

Even if your agent and editor assure you they don't mind changing your grammatical diaper each time, you're wasting at least part of their time on diaper duty rather than tapping their real talent and insight. Learning (and relearning) the fundamental tools of your craft dramatically changes your capacities as a writer; not learning those tools telegraphs your belief that laziness and sloppiness deserve tangible rewards.

Imagine hiring a carpenter to build your house who said they knew nothing about blueprints and hated dealing with hammers, saws, and wood. Would you go to a dentist with a phobia of teeth who drilled on instinct and cleaned your teeth with whatever objects were handy? We expect expertise from professionals. Writers who behave professionally get treated as professionals. Writers interested in continued success and professional respect keep learning and experimenting every day.

Unless you're a casual hobbyist with no interest in earning a living as an author, you need to learn the basics. If all you remember of grammar is rote memorization from junior high, you have a treat in store because *now*, grammar will improve your books, amplify your voice, and simplify your drafting process. Quite literally, grammar helps you make more money and reach more fans.

If you don't know the difference between parts of speech, learn them. Grammar may have seemed boring in school, but now it can bestow magical superpowers that pay your bills better. Plenty of fun, funny, fascinating grammar resources exist. In the bibliography, I've flagged some worth a gander.

Treat writing as a serious endeavor and it will return the favor. If you're a writer, language is your raw material and grammar your toolbox. Learn the rules so that you know when, why, and how to break them. Words are what you have to work with. Raw talent can be helpful, but ignoring the rules and tools of your career directly impedes your growth as a professional artist.

Your colleagues have better things to do than clean up messes, and your readers want to understand what you're saying.

"Ill-fitting grammar are like ill-fitting shoes. You can get used to it for a bit, but then one day your toes fall off and you can't walk to the bathroom."

Jasper Fforde[27]

Control

No one wonders if a person *exists* on first meeting, but characters must earn belief.

Characters *do* things. In popular fiction they do fascinating things that move an audience. They get, find, make, take, and change things to solve that case, claim that prize, or earn that Happily Ever After. Their stories, relationships, and complications arise from those specific actions. As the characters grow and change believably, we come to love them and empathize with them. By the same token, inert, generic characters leave us cold and bored.

If I tell you a hero is *curious, swarthy,* or *skillful,* I'm hoping you'll take the provided descriptor at (literal) face value and dig no deeper. If I assign that protagonist a noun like *pirate* or *singer* or *werewolf,* I'm relying on your knowledge and imagination to do the heavy lifting by appealing to generic expectations about those roles. But as soon as I tell you that person *ravishes, inspires,* or *burgles* something, you have a clear picture

Now you know why I thought the parts of speech needed an airing.

Once a hero acts like a hero on those pages, they *show* heroism without any superfluous *telling.* All the nouns and modifiers only ornament the obvious, offering little more than *salt* in the gravy. A canny wordsmith can ditch most of the modifiers and nouns and get down to the business of spinning the yarn without tripping over the tassels.

Action is all. Characters are not people or things, they are *forces*...arcs of transformation caused by high-stakes choices. As a storyteller, modifiers encumber and nouns can become obstacles, but by definition *verbs* have the power to do anything.

Inexperienced writers will often push back: "modifiers are sexy" or "nouns are concrete." Sure...and a book of nothing but nouns, adjectives, and adverbs would be DOA because all that "sexy concrete" would sit there like a giant cinder block. **Without verbs, nothing happens.** As a skillful professional, align your efforts. Invest your time and energy where they'll have the greatest impact.

- **Modifiers tell.** Adjectives and adverbs only provide prechewed interpretation to explain other words, relying on preexisting opinion to decorate the story.
- **Nouns suggest.** They populate a story's landscape with subjects and objects by relying on general, generic assumptions.
- **Verbs show.** They express the energy of characters and direct their story because they relate actual forces shaping the narrative.

Now, I'm not saying you can write a book of nothing but verbs. All the parts of speech serve necessary storytelling functions. But action is *fundamental*. Every successful genre story begins with the kind of dynamic transformation that provokes emotions in its readers, full stop.

Language creates belief. Belief creates behavior. Behavior creates culture.

The person who makes choices drives the scene and steers the story. Their actions control the flow of the story, and, on some level, the conflict between any characters is a life or death struggle over whose story gets told and how it turns out. Verbs clash and characters steer their story thereby.

Bottom line: tinsel and tassels are nice, but what readers remember (and rave about) is the emotion of powerful actions and unavoidable clashes. Modifiers encumber writing, so their decorative specificity comes at a cost. Nouns are static and create the illusion of stasis. Dynamic verbs make for dynamic writing because they contain and express all the energy in a scene/story.

Nouns and modifiers may seem more tangible at first glance because they are literally visible, but we can only *experience* them via the dynamic interaction of verbs. Without energy, matter (and all its descriptors) is literally inert. We build the pipes to carry the flow. So when we enjoy a story, it's the journey we remember...

Not the activities, but the *actions*. Not modifiers, not nouns, but *verbs*.

"We're born to love grammar. We're taught to hate it."

Max Morenberg[28]

EXERCISE: Strong Language

How would you describe one of your characters using different parts of speech? Don't be afraid to incorporate language that also evokes the world and vibe of their story, context, and genre.

1. Choose a character from one of your projects, either planned or published, and list 5 modifiers intrinsic to them.

2. Upgrade those modifiers to 5 nouns that convey the descriptive content of those modifiers as concrete people or items.

3. Upgrade those nouns to 5 verbs that activate the solid clarity of those nouns as dynamic expressions of the character's behavior during the course of the story. What does this language capture? What does it miss?

4. Add another 5-10 supplemental verbs that seem especially appropriate and evocative for the character and their scenes.

Push your vocabulary as far as possible, absorbing new terms and tone-appropriate slang to capture the character clearly. Try to capture the fascinating energy that originally drew you to the character.

Part II: Fire

"Essential oils–are wrung–
The Attar from the Rose
Be not expressed by Suns–alone–
It is the gift of screws–"

Emily Dickinson[29]

Chapter 4: VISION

We hear music, we view sculpture, and we read literature. Art (and by extension all entertainment) is the business of attention, and we can only pay attention to *something*. To earn and move an audience, any book needs to reward the attention invested by its audience. Fiction requires literal decoding from brains up to the task, raring to go.

A painting is visible, a symphony audible, but how do you make a story resonate? When talking about songs, it's easy to grasp what listeners expect: *sound, rhythm, melody, hook*. But what readers want from fiction isn't an education or eye exercise—they read for an **emotional experience**. As a genre author, you must take their feelings for a ride, satisfying their preconceptions while delighting them via your expertise and creativity within the form.

By evoking emotions, you engage with an audience's interior experience. Impersonal ads and lazy retreads won't cut it, but give your readers something to care about and they'll follow you into Troy, Mordor, the Château d'If, and worse...because they *care*.

> "Art is the imposing of a pattern on experience, and our aesthetic enjoyment is recognition of the pattern."
>
> Alfred North Whitehead[30]

Pattern

Humans evolved as problem solvers. Plenty of stronger, swifter, sturdier animals exist, but based on sheer cognitive *oomph*, humans ascended to the top of the food chain in spite of our evolutionary shortcomings. Brawn may be useful, but our brain is the lever that has moved the world for several million years.

The skill that defines our species is **pattern recognition**. We love meaningful order and search for it constantly, instinctively. We can't stop ourselves. If I put three pennies on a table, you will see a triangle, not because I've drawn the lines, but because your brain draws them before you have time to intervene.

For humans, patterns exist everywhere and in everything, extending in a complex, interactive matrix. We identify patterns incessantly and then seek meaning in them as they oscillate between tension and release, order and chaos, creation and destruction, stimulus and response. This capacity for patterns makes language possible, as well as communities and every other rung in the ladder of human civilization.

Some patterns exist as part of the natural phenomenon we encounter, others are constructed by human consciousness, artificially, and so we call them art. All human creativity plays with patterns to create an emotional experience in its audience. We look for patterns and ascribe meaning because that is what we are wired to do. The inestimable Lisa Cron has written an entire book called *Wired for Story* that examines the direct link between brains and books, synapse and story—I cannot recommend it strenuously enough.

Short version: We love stories because of patterns. Music and painting and games, ditto. Audiences crave significance and meaningful patterns.

My goal here isn't to bludgeon you with a quickie overview of neuroplasticity, but rather to explain that as humans we are wired for story, as Cron puts it so aptly. We extrapolate meaning from the data provided: *If* something happens, *then* something results, *therefore* a change occurs. We constantly infer cause and effect and use it to determine significance because our brains seek and enjoy patterns.

If/Then/Therefore essentially sums up all of human intelligence in three words. We group things in threes because our brains work in threes: if/then/therefore, thesis/antithesis/synthesis, you/me/we, need/lack/relief, etc., which means this sequence is most likely the root of the Rule of Threes in rhetoric and narratives. *Feel that fact.*

Tension within a pattern attracts **attention** and creates **anticipation** as we try to make sense of signs and puzzles, causes and effects, actions and tactics to find **resolution**. As possibilities present themselves and fall away, that delicious anticipation rubs our brain the right way with the dual pleasure of correct prediction and unexpected resonance.

Game designer Raph Koster's *A Theory of Fun for Game Design* explains the clear links between fun and pattern recognition with far-reaching implications for all kinds of art. Koster argues that all entertainment identifies and explores patterns to attract and reward attention.[31]

- **Fun** is our word for the pleasurable feedback with which the brain rewards us whenever we pay attention to patterns in order to absorb them and learn from them.

- **Delight** recognizes and retraces a familiar pattern, producing a pleasure that is sweet but fleeting because it follows an old neural path. It rewards revisits at intervals.

- **Beauty** reveals a new pattern by exploiting the tension between expectation and reality, creating powerful and long-lasting enjoyment with depth and breadth. It also opens up new paths to revisit for later delight.

- **Boredom** is our word for the exhaustion of the possible variations in a pattern when the artist and the audience have stopped discovering delight or beauty.

Writers guarantee fun, aim for beauty, settle for delight, and avoid boredom like gum surgery. Folks don't always need new experiences, but they crave new *stimuli* that change the patterns available within the experience.

Every artist establishes a series of patterns that suggest possible resolution or hint at closure...and then *waits*. Keeping the audience in *suspense* unleashes their imagination by giving causes but withholding effects. It makes them anticipate events and guess at possible outcomes, never fully satisfying their curiosity or scratching that itch until the end. Art creates patterns, then manipulates them to reward attention, create emotion, and fascinate the audience willing to take the ride.

Our brain gets the pleasure of identifying significant patterns that create new awareness and meaning. As humans, we experience this firing and rewiring of our brains as pleasure, because our brains literally evolved to identify patterns and ascertain significance.

Stories hijack our pattern addiction and meaning quest by allowing us to share experiences with none of the risk involved. All stories use the rhythm of **tension and release** seen in human breath, our heartbeats, and every other natural cycle. Writers create patterns and shape attention to extract emotion. Playing with those patterns is both useful and fun. All those new connections in the brain feel good—and they also make that brain work better. Win-win!

If you want readers to pay attention, you must make them care.

Have you ever not finished a book because you simply couldn't bother? Not that it was awful or insulting, but it didn't feel like an actual story, as though the person who typed those words in that order had never read any book, ever. Sentences followed sentences, incidents piled up, the hook might have pulled you in, but the book just sat there dead in your hands. Maybe you gave it a whirl anyway, but after words, words, words, you simply gave up and moved on because life is too short and we're all too old.

I call this kind of writing "Names doing stuff." You open a book and watch imaginary individuals lurching through its pages, never once believing this is a person living a life, let alone *feeling* something for them. All those leaden words strung together like greasy, decomposing entrails. Writing by rote. The cast of clichés, the catalog of incidents leaves you bored and numb. Who cares? Why bother? What a scam!

Those aren't characters, but *names*. That's not a story, just *stuff*.

If you're writing popular fiction, you can't hide behind literary pretensions and lazy solutions because, in the entertainment business, you either entertain or you starve. All fiction works because it plugs directly into our human capacities, and it works best when it's allowed to do its job between our ears to make our neurons fire. How a writer directs that fire is what turns craft into art.

A great hook is what folks talk about before they read your book. A great character is what they talk about *after* they read your book. Characters make readers care.

To paraphrase a common meme: Everybody wants to be a diamond, but nobody wants to get cut. Writing, *real writing*, takes time and energy, art and craft, heart and mind, fire and wire. You know the difference because you've seen it and felt it.

Don't just type your books, write them. Give them your heart and brain and spleen and lungs. Invest in your work and it will pay spectacular dividends.

"Wisdom begins in wonder."

Socrates[32]

Leaps

Our brains are pattern factories. Not only that, each brain is itself a complex pattern created out of electro-chemical signals traveling through the three pounds of gray matter between your ears. So your brain is actually a pattern that finds and creates more patterns for other patterns to enjoy. Ideas feel good.

Old school cartoons and business infographics often represent an idea as a lightbulb. *Eureka!* We've all experienced that startling moment when realization dawns and we grasp a concept for the first time. Here's the funny thing: although it doesn't generate light, what we experience truly is a tiny spark flashing between two nerve endings. That dazzling *A-ha!* is the root of all enjoyment.

We call that gap a *synapse,* and it is literally the gap between two neurons across which a signal passes—*ZZZZT!*—like tiny lightning in the mind.[33] That sizzle you feel is real, and it happens whenever a signal leaps from one neuron to another across that synaptic divide. We experience this spark as pleasure, so we are genetically predisposed to seek out new ideas/dis-coveries/synapses, which favors new experiences and education. Our brains reward us for using them. Even better, stimulation of those cells actually increases their density—the more ideas you have, the more ideas you are capable of having.

So...education is good, thinking is fun, and our brains reward regular use. Yay, neuroscience!

One of the fascinating features of fiction is that words written by someone far away or long dead can create overwhelming emotions and compelling insight inside of me here and now. Their thoughts, transmuted into letters and words, then in turn decoded by me, somehow close the gaps between us—*ZZZZT!* Amazing. Writing closes a different kind of synaptic gap, not between cells, but between minds separated by miles and millennia.

In comic books, a set of panels drawn on a page tell a sequential story. The drawings don't move. The characters don't actually react to each other's actions. Those illustrated panels are separated by blank space, a border that comic artists call the *gutter*. That empty strip *between* drawings is where the story happens.

If I show two drawings, of eyes open and then eyes closed, you may think, "She fell asleep." If I reverse the order, you could say, "She woke up." The drawings didn't change, but the **context** did. Most action in a comic page takes place in its gutters, *between* the panels. Given a context and a set of criteria, our minds fill in the gaps. Film uses similar gaps, using individual frames to trick our minds into seeing the illusion of movement by splicing a series of stills together or cutting from scene to scene to get to the action. Our imaginations fill in the missing bits.

The term for this instinctive visual storytelling is **closure**. Our mind connects two images and closes the narrative gaps between them to create a satisfying resolution.

Closure in a novel may be less obvious, but it's still happening every moment you read. The author isn't telling you every single detail you'd experience in the scene, every thought, every breath, every gurgle. Readers connect the dots to make a line, connect the lines to make a shape...cause and effect, one enjoyable synaptic leap at a time. *ZZZZT!*

You don't *actually* know what Cleopatra, Jeeves, or Jack Reacher look like. They are cognitive mosaics built in your head out of resonant clues provided by their authors. *Their seeds, your soil.* Letters create words, words create fragmentary impressions. Based on the provided specifics, your mind produces closure and fills in the meaningful gaps.

Say I write 5+X=7. Your brain can look at the X and substitute a 2 and extrapolate the unknown component of the equation. You complete the pattern. In completing it, you connect with it, engage with it, become entangled with it. The audience fills whatever gaps you leave for them, so you'd best be careful about what you offer and what you don't. If you don't provide meaningful specifics, clear actions, and escalating stakes, then they'll fill in the gaps themselves.

Audiences always *participate*.

In fact, neurobiologists have proven that whether we experience something personally or simply read about experiencing it, the neurons in our brains fire the same way. Humans evolved to read situations and each other, and that skill transfers directly to our experience of decoding a story.[34]

Never do the audience's work *for* them. We want to decide for ourselves, experience it firsthand. People are far more likely to reach conclusions than *accept* conclusions. This explains why showing always beats telling, because making patterns too obvious and filling in the gaps for your reader steals the potential pleasure of decoding cause and effect for themselves.

In art and in life, emotional involvement is algebraic. We fill in the X based on our projection and assumptions about a situation. Authors provide compelling X's in fascinating equations. The viewer completes the "unseen danger" equation and predicts the outcome. As in life, they assess the patterns and determine what

- has happened prior.
- is currently happening.
- might happen next.

Every type of filmed entertainment operates via closure, turning frames into motion and giving us enough picture and sound to elicit senses and sensations, impressions and expressions that require analysis, interpretation, and absorption. The pattern attracts us and we find the meaning. We can't help but get involved and have feelings about imaginary circumstances, because we are code-breaking monkeys.

This is why film adaptations are often so disappointing and why "the book is always better." The book you loved actually happened in your mind and the thrill of filling in fascinating gaps feels qualitatively, quantitatively different. Authors don't "create" a character as much as readers *infer* character from on-page actions and the emotions they elicit. The best books offer cool gaps that appeal to a vast, receptive, imaginative audience.

All stories work that way. Soap opera viewers scold and praise the cast at moments of high drama. Mystery readers try to crack cases alongside the on-page sleuth. Slasher audiences will shout at victims onscreen about the maniac looming in the background.

In theatres, audience outbursts like boos, laughter, or shouted warnings are an attempt at real-world participation in the imaginary drama. When you race back to a book because you're afraid or excited about what might happen, you know the outcome is already decided—but your heart *doubts* it. The emotions are real, so our brains don't make the distinction. As social primates, we want to connect.

When two quirky attractive singles collide in a rom-com, we recognize a meet-cute in progress and immediately map out the romantic and comedic possibilities. When a dead body turns up in a mystery or an ancient evil in horror, ditto. Scenes of seduction, revenge, makeover, or triumph dramatize the characters' actions and reactions in a steady climb toward satisfying resolutions, which is why these events recur in genre fiction so often: they leave a clear, causal trail.

Anticipation and reversal of expectation keep us on our toes and in our seats. The patterns compel us and we simply can't stop ourselves getting involved tracking cause and effect to determine significance. Once we feel connected, our imaginations do the heavy lifting.

"A tip from Lubitsch: Let the audience add up two plus two. They'll love you forever."

Billy Wilder[35]

Possibility

One of the feeble truisms of authorship is that art springs from imagination. That's true enough, but not from the *author's* imagination.

Writers provide the raw materials and framework for the audience's imaginary emotional experience. Your entire job is to provide better, more meaningful patterns that will unleash your audience's imagination in an emotionally satisfying way. You provide the grit, they act as oysters, and the pearl of the story grows inside their minds.

The *audience* does most of the imaginative work of bringing fiction to life.

Admittedly, imagination is potent and flexible, but a writer's imagination is also fickle, failing us in moments of stress and doubt. Imagination can paralyze us. Perfectionism is nothing more than imagination taken off the leash, to punitive extremes. "If only I could write this scene the way I imagine it" may guarantee you cannot write a word. Imagination can hinder as much as it helps. As a working author, you need reliable tools to get the job done.

Art is the ability to remove unnecessary details, rather than dream them up. Artists choose where attention should be paid. Leave imagination to your readers. Instead, embrace **curiosity**.

Curiosity is infinitely more powerful and useful, because knowledge feeds imagination. There's always *more* to find, to know. Curiosity aims for a particular goal and serves a clear function that leads in a direction. Whatever fascinates you will heap logs on your creative bonfire. Curiosity digs up significant specifics and establishes meaningful patterns.

There's an old saying that the secret of being witty is to make *others* feel witty; the secret of being fascinating is to be fascinat-*ed*. Well, in fiction, the secret to being imaginative is to unleash the power of your audience's imaginations.

Imagination is limited by your education and capacity, by your emotional state and predilections, but curiosity is only limited by your ability to pay attention. Wise authors feed their process with a masala of challenging, complex stimuli and info. Imagination is wild and digressive. Curiosity follows patterns and leads. Imagination can falter or go cold, but curiosity is infinite. Imagination is unreliable and reactive, but insatiable curiosity is fundamental to our mental wiring.

As a professional, you must make peace with your skills and resources, your time and talent so you can kick your own ass. In testing those margins, curiosity will expose all your particular limits and genius. No two careers are the same, and they *shouldn't* be—compare and despair. Leave imagination to the audience.

Your imagination can only travel as far as you let it. Without care and feeding, your imagination will wallow in cliché like a lazy sow. Why not? We've all seen authors stuck in ruts, revisiting characters, plots, and tropes they can't seem to expand or reinvent. Clichés are comfy and easy, challenging nothing and delighting no one.

Cultivating curiosity will teach you to focus and problem solve. Inquisitive authors take spectacular risks and evolve as artists because they're constantly extending their comfort zones (and their readers' as well). When characters are curious, they see the world from unique perspectives. Curiosity forces us to pay attention to what we feel, what we sense, what we experience, and how we share.

Curiosity follows causal chains to their conclusion and it explores possibility but heeds a connected pattern. Imagination can lead you off a cliff or make you believe silliness. Relying on imagination without healthy skepticism can build castles on sand.

The reader's imagination is your single most power-ful tool: it can do more heavy lifting, paper over greater gaps and plot holes, and invoke more authentic emotion than any other trick in your arsenal. Your curiosity is the key. As you learn to look closer, dig deeper, your voice grows more powerful. All those fascinating insights, details, and solutions embed themselves in your fiction in ways that unleash *their* imaginations in the service of your story.

"Writing is nothing more than a guided dream."

Jorge Luis Borges[36]

Chapter 5: MOJO

Chiaroscuro is a Renaissance oil-painting technique that juxtaposed areas of brightness and darkness for drama and depth. You see it used with startling effect in the works of Rembrandt, Tintoretto, Rubens, and Caravaggio. Something similar turns up in Renaissance theatre, especially Shakespeare, in which buoyant comedy and grim tragedy collide with devastating impact (cf. *Hamlet*'s gravedigger, *Macbeth*'s porter, and *Twelfth Night*'s melancholy duke). High contrast makes for clear stakes and universal entertainment value. Drama, comedy, and suspense are baked into those plays because of their emotional chiaroscuro. They force audiences to pay attention because of the way our brains are wired.

Under Dr. Barry Arons, MIT's Media Lab researched the "cocktail party effect" to gather information about people's ability to listen to a single speaker during a loud gathering.[37] His study identified ways humans sort stimuli and shift attention accordingly by analyzing attention and the ways different kinds of stimuli attract focus. The single biggest factor in attracting attention was **grouping**, in every variation:

- UNGROUPED & NOTICED: Difference, Disconnection, Disruption, Uncoordinated movement, Asymmetry, Incompletion

- GROUPED & IGNORED: Similarity, Proximity, Continuity, Movement in unison, Symmetry, Closure.

Given the lessons of human evolution, this data makes perfect sense. As pattern hunters, we notice opportunities or threats because they stand out, and they stand out because they are not grouped with all the things that are not opportunities or threats. Grouping can be qualitative or quantitative, but our brains are hardwired to notice when "one of these things is not like the other." The black sheep in a field of white or the genius in a roomful of dolts. In a state of homogeny, things stand out by *differing*.

The conflict between opposing forces creates friction through a series of collisions. As they resolve their coexistence, that friction results in a new equilibrium. Opposing forces must work together or remain apart. There's the *rub*.

Bombarded by input, folks sort through details via different groupings that do or do not interest them at the moment. They filter out the noise in favor of signal, paying attention only to what they deem significant.

As an author your job is to interest people, which means this instinctive trait provides the single most powerful tool in the author's arsenal.

"Everyone thinks of changing the world, but no one thinks of changing themselves."

Leo Tolstoy[38]

Contrast

We are visual primates. We form mental pictures when reading, so a few telling details can anchor the dynamics of a scene swiftly.

In the author's arsenal, **Contrast** is the simplest, strongest, swiftest tool an author can use to generate energy and attention, whether that's contrast between actions, tactics, traits, vibe, behavior, opinions, class, history, or skills. Every dynamic and situation is heightened by contrast (and **paradox**, its conceptual offspring). Contrast is how babies first see, why opposites attract, and the reason black text on white background has been the printing standard for so long: it's clear and easy to process.

Contrast shows rather than tells, amplifying any effect because it differentiates with direct evidence. This allows readers to draw their own conclusions and closure, rather than explicitly stating differences between subjects, objects, or the actions that connect them.

While reading, the audience notes the status quo and immediately starts searching for the salt in the sugar, the ants in the pants, the grit in the pearl. A story begins the moment the ungrouped and grouped start making a mess of each other, so readers know to look for exactly that: something important to happen that can change things.

If everyone is gorgeous and rich and content at the story's open, then why bother reading? With nothing to want or get or change, who cares about what these folks think or feel? In fact, how can we think or feel anything about a bland, homogenous pudding-scape? The difference between natures, nurtures, beliefs, and circumstances throbs under a story like a heartbeat.

Readers start listening for that heartbeat before they even open the book. Based on title, artwork, blurb, they gauge the type of ride the book will give them, the potential for powerful emotion, the depth of meaning possible in this combination of characters and contexts. To be honest, that's the reason they choose one book over another: the significant contrasts and the emotional experience they promise.

Writers often refer to the need for conflict, tension, struggle, confrontation, but I prefer the word **Friction** because while it may involve outside obstacles and opponents, more than anything else it provides a source of energy and transformation. As my mother used to say, friction is what makes fights feel bad and sex feel good.

As social mammals, we're instinctively attracted to energy in action, and dramatic energy arises from friction. The tension attracts attention because opposition presupposes conflict and transformation. We watch to see how the patterns will play out. As Brian Boyd puts it, "Differences...simplify character distinctions [and] maximize emotional legibility."[39]

Friction builds up a charge between characters, potential energy that needs release. The greater the contrast between illusions and realities, thoughts and feelings, hopes and fears, the more emotional terrain the story can cover credibly.

For maximum drama and comedy in any pairing, television story departments will often divide paired characters into Straight Line and Wavy Line, a Hollywood version of Nietzsche's Apollonian and Dionysian impulses.[40]

- **Straight Lines** impose order with intention. They invest and plan within rules. Sober and stable, in situations they are the cooked meal, the boat's anchor, the civilizing drive. Like wire directing energy, they provide FORM.
- **Wavy Lines** unleash chaos on impulse. They gamble and improvise via rebellion. Intoxicated and intoxicating, in situations they are the raw ingredients, the boat's sail, the wild urge. Like fire releasing energy, they provide FORCE.

Examples of wavy/straight pairings: Bugs Bunny/Elmer Fudd, Lestat de Lioncourt/Louis de Pointe du Lac, Beloved/Sethe, Ford Prefect/Arthur Dent, Merlin/Wart, Annie Wilkes/Paul Sheldon, Jack Twist/Ennis Del Mar, Hannibal Lecter/Clarice Starling, Bertie Wooster/Reginald Jeeves.

Please note that these opposed modes aren't *necessarily* intrinsic to a character's identity. Some folks are sober at work and wacky in love. Attempts to change behavior can succeed or fail, and character transformation is dramatic. Different relationships or situations may evoke radically different interaction styles. The importance is the contrast between the people involved.

By situating relationships as opposition, in every scene you build energy just waiting to be released and amplify your characters' **emotional legibility**. Contrast maximizes the payoff for your cast and your readers. Meaningful transformation of the characters and/or the world becomes inevitable because you've seeded the conflict in the roots of the story.

In general, humans avoid conflict, and yet people crave novelty. As Cron puts it, "We don't like change, and we don't like conflict, either. So most of the time we do our best to avoid both. This isn't easy, since the only real constant is change, and change is driven by conflict."[41] The paradox of human evolution in a nutshell: risk-takers who need certainty.

Happily, stories allow us to experience the emotions of volatile and devastating situations without serious trauma. In a sense, all genre entertainment springs from this odd equilibrium, supplying emotional intensity without putting audiences in literal danger. A roller coaster can literally kill you, but no one has ever died from reading a genre novel. That's some magic trick: all of the amazing feelings with none of the physical threat or personal jeopardy.

Stories allow us to play out our eternal struggle between hope and fear in a safe, controlled space. And because stories elicit real emotions, we get several benefits of risk with none of the danger.

Contrast allows friction that releases energy into the story, but only when opposites collide.

"The gem cannot be polished without friction, nor man perfected without trials."

Confucius[42]

EXERCISE: Best Enemies

Much of entertainment is the ability to think oppositionally. Certain kinds of conflicting actions recur regularly within every genre and subgenre (e.g. *demand/defy* in Romance, *save/doom* in Thriller, *attack/defend* in Fantasy, *conceal/reveal* in Mystery, *tame/unleash* in Paranormal).

Let's identify some contrasting pairs that you think would be fun to write. What kinds of clashing actions do genre fans expect? Which would you call overused clichés and which remain timeless, classic tropes in your stretch of the bookshelf?

1. Make a list of oppositional actions that recur in your specific genre or subgenre.
2. Using a thesaurus, take a classic action duo, and come up with a list of contrasting synonyms for *each*, linking them based on the most interesting and inspiring combos.
3. Using a thesaurus, take a clichéd action duo and identify a list of unexpected, off-the-wall synonyms for *each* that might reinvent the stale duo as something fresh and unexpected.
4. Make a short list of actions you instinctively dig writing. Note any actions that leave you cold, no matter how popular they might be. Do these actions appear in other types of book? How? When?

Knowing your own tastes and tendencies in *types* of contrast will help you develop your instinctive strengths, avoid weaknesses, and also reveal possibilities for long-term career evolution.

Collision

What do readers mean when they say a book is *powerful*...moving, forceful, dazzling, brilliant, or electrifying? Where exactly is the energy in a book? How do we provide fascinating grit for all those receptive audience oysters?

If we define energy as the active forces that drive your story, then a book's mojo comes down to what happens—not within the pages, but within the reader. Shocking events and dazzling spectacle might shock or dazzle us, but then again, they might not. Unless we care about the events and spectacle, they're meaningless. Stories don't produce *physical* energy, they elicit *emotional* energy in readers. People care about characters, and characters give authors a way to tap that emotional energy.

We can't just generate energy in a vacuum. We must allow the energy of all the characters to express itself on the pages in a way that evokes real emotions in readers. Through the magic of closure, the reader connects dots and becomes entangled with imaginary lives.

Henry James summed it up nicely: "What is character but the determination of incident, what is incident but the illustration of character?"[43]

The power of a story springs directly from the collision of characters and the journey through obstacles and opponents to achieve an ultimate goal. These collisions have explosive impact, releasing energy into the story via fission or fusion...characters brought together and torn apart: "[*Subject*] wants [*object*], but [*obstacle*]."

Drama flows from these moments of conflict: between opposing desires, between reality and delusion, between the past and the present, or divided loyalties. These moments are not just anecdotes or activities, they are *events*.

In this context, **An event is any significant disruption of the status quo**...the moment a change occurs with tangible effects on everyone present: rewards and insults, discoveries and reversals, decisions and disasters, deceptions and disclosures, accidents and blessings, meetings and separations, arrivals and departures that alter the flow of the story. In stories, an event always happens for the first or the last time to amplify the stakes and the sense of occasion. Events force the characters and the readers to stop everything and pay attention.

Most pop entertainment structures itself around events, building-building-building to each and then dealing with the aftermath before building to the next: *workplace showdown, meet-cute, forbidden fruit, wacky arrest, hellish holidays, friend's wedding, serious accident, first fight, madcap makeover,* etc. Events *change* things for characters, alter their paths and perspectives.

Think of soap operas and sitcoms, popcorn movies and family sagas, comic books and reality TV; consider the kind of broad-strokes, event-driven stories they tell: births and weddings, fights and funerals, seductions and breakups, trials and punishments, diseases and miracles. Pulp entertainment pulses with stock events because they are clear and instantly dramatic. Audiences can dive into the flow at any point and swim along. **Events create instant, fascinating context.** When in doubt, look for the *WHAM*. An event pops up wherever there is collision and conflict between two different ways of seeing the world: beliefs, values, priorities. The community chugs along, beige and bland, and then—*WHAM*—aliens land or teens elope or a corpse turns up at the playground. An executive has ordered her life perfectly and then—*WHAM*—she gets transferred to Istanbul, her partners embezzle, the media runs a damning exposé. An average kid surviving school and then—*WHAM*—accepted at wizarding school or diagnosis: leukemia or a maniac moves in upstairs.

The friction between expectation and events drives all stories. Noir legend Jim Thompson once said, "There is only one plot—things are not what they seem."[44] **An event is contrast turned into context.** It exposes the crack between how things seem and a reality we can now see. For example, Jane Austen's *Pride and Prejudice* piles events upon the characters (which I cover in greater detail in the appendix).

- The Bennets *seem* content until a wildly eligible bachelor shows up at Netherfield.
- Bingley *seems* to be courting Jane with serious intent until he decamps for London.
- Darcy *seems* cold until his proposal to Lizzy shatters the polite crust between them.
- Lizzy *seems* to loathe Darcy until a visit to Pemberley reveals unexpected warmth.

- Lydia *seems* silly and harmless until she elopes with Wickham and ruins her family.

Each of these events has drastic impacts on the folks involved and reveal unknown info. And even when the characters don't cause the events, the events force them to make choices and take action in the world with serious consequences. I sometimes think of this as the tension between *if* and *is*...what *could be* vs. what *exists in reality*.

An event distills conflict into character growth much like bees turn pollen into honey.

When writing genre fiction, you must cultivate the habit of thinking *eventfully*, because these pivotal disruptions shape the flow of a narrative. If your characters are going to do significant things and inhabit a believable world, then you should have an idea of what they're doing and why.

Please know that listing events isn't plotting. You aren't structuring your story, and I'm not asking you to make up a bunch of telenovela beats out of thin air. Think of it more as a gathering of possible ingredients. What would be fun to write with these characters in this genre? Certain genres have events built into them: mysteries love a murder, adventure revels in fisticuffs, thrillers thrive on a threat. Great genre writing gives readers what they want in a way they wouldn't expect.

In fact, the genre and subgenre of a book often determines the emotional terrain it makes accessible. Audiences come to different story categories for different emotional rides. A story only succeeds to the extent that internal conflict becomes external action and external conflict creates internal action. In the words of acting teacher Sanford Meisner, "That which hinders your task is your task."

Just consider the decisive moments you know will happen in the story and build from there. You only need three or four big events to build an entire novel. We don't need to know character reactions or details yet, just the general context. Focus on the set pieces and big moments that will serve as tent poles for the story.

These events expose moments of explosive collision that release critical energy into the characters' lives. Knowing your characters will make certain events obvious and having a couple events in mind will make it easier to see what your character needs to do and who they need to be.

> "We struggle with dream figures and our blows fall on living faces."
>
> Maurice Merleau-Ponty[45]

EXERCISE: Event Planning

Dwight Swain and others have suggested that a book is little more than three or four pivotal events that lead to a satisfying resolution. Take a moment to think *eventfully* by brainstorming some of the pivotal collisions that might power your story. Look for the *WHAMs*:

- What are the dramatic, memorable events each character might face?

y

80

- How will they handle each of these events? Alone? In public? With someone loved or loathed? Knock them off balance.

- How is each the best and worst thing that could happen? Make certain the events force them to deal with incapacities and untapped strengths.

- Which events will force them to improvise on the fly, and which will allow them breathing room to react mindfully? Require high-stakes choices that change everything.

- BONUS ROUND: Imagine these events as the standout seconds in a film trailer for your story: pinpoint clear, compelling, memorable moments that will invariably hook an audience.

Look for the fun in these collisions. Create meaningful clashes and give characters opportunities to ditch their ruts. *Caveat scriptor*: Don't get sucked into the idea of structure or plotting before you have a handle on the forces at play unless it inspires or assists your process.

Spark

To close the gap between book and reader, authors must tap the story's energy, and that invariably comes from its *characters*.

Unfortunately, this is where art gets hard and the rubber meets the road: **You cannot *show* energy.** You can only show its effects.

We learn this lesson from physics: energy cannot be measured, only the impact of energy upon matter can be measured. When we say a car travels at 100 mph, we must gauge the relative speed of the vehicle in the context of its landscape. When a thermometer indicates the temperature outside is fifty degrees, we are observing the mercury's rise relative to the scale beside it.

We can *tell* an audience what makes a character tick, but we can only *show* what they do and the impact of their choices. The unique charge and force that characters bring to a situation defines who and what and how they behave in every context—the fire in the wire. Energy gives them life and makes them stick. So for best results, the characterization process starts with, and all other characterization aligns with, that core energy to form the spine of the story.

Characters turn up in a story crackling with power like clouds before a thunderstorm. Readers may sense the currents or have a hunch about the danger, but they have to wait for the rumble, the strike, the aftermath before they can find out what will happen and where. All that invisible electricity reveals itself only as it shifts from potential to kinetic energy loose in the world.

Energy moves us. Readers experience real emotion because the person may be fictional, but the energy is real. The active forces that drive your story may shift or redirect, but they don't take breaks. By definition, energy cannot stop and continue to exist. It exists by *doing*. That's another truth we learn from physics: energy can never exist in stasis.

That's why great characters straddle believable coherence and fascinating unpredictability. Audiences want to open a book and find a big glorious tempest that will satisfy them and surprise them simultaneously. Until the rain and lightning is released, nothing can happen, but in expert hands, readers have a front row seat for an electric spectacle.

Characters reveal the energy of a story by changing their surroundings. They are visible expressions of energy that allow us to observe forces at play. Want to know why characterization is so critical to fiction? What makes it so difficult and why so few writing guides dig into its challenges?

Characters are not faces, but forces.

They move us because they have *power*. They matter because they alter a world, revealing the impact of personal actions. Characters do things to the world around them...they make stuff, take stuff, fake stuff, break stuff. We evaluate their energy by assessing its consequences. We look to events to understand the people involved because the effects reveal the cause.

- Some events happen. (ACTIVITIES)
- Some events happen *to* characters. (ACCIDENTS)
- Some events are caused intentionally *by* characters. (ACTIONS)

Of these options, *actions* (intentional events) involve more people on the page and reveal exponentially more about their interactions. Activities waste time. Accidents all too easily can betray an *author's* intentions, jarring the reader. Actions portray the effects of the characters' invisible energy, making intention visible to readers, thereby providing much more narrative heft for an author.

By observing actions, we discern the underlying forces at work in a situation, which incidentally, is how we navigate our *lives*. We want to know who's doing what and why. Everything else in a narrative is auxiliary, useful perhaps, but inessential. Actions cause reactions and thereby hangs *every* tale.

The central task of characterization is harnessing energy. A character flows through a story like a charge traveling over wire; they jolt the story patterns that connect with your audience, real patterns in their real lives. All the appurtenances of character: their aspect, their affect, their actions, and their tactics all reflect that vital force to make them feel like real people to your readers. The writer must find a way to reveal that charge.

Aristotle's *Poetics* defines character (*ethos*) as "habitual action," treating character as the pattern of behavior associated with an individual. He was writing about theatre, but in a larger sense he was describing effective storytelling. That habitual action requires a context, a place to play to an audience. Authors reveal characters to the audience by creating situations that test the limits of habitual actions.

Since we can only see the effects of energy, authors must depict actions, internal and external, that have significant, meaningful impact on other actions, other characters. Every moment of the story becomes a window into the forces at play inside its people and which will change their world.

Actions speak louder than words. They express essential energy. They show rather than tell. They make scenes sizzle with static energy that needs only a touch to crackle into dramatic life. Rooting characters in action allows every detail to multitask by maximizing coherence, impact, and efficiency of emotional characterization to stir up a perfect emotional storm.

Characters must *do* so they can *be*. Once a storm blows itself out and the rain stops, the lightning vanishes from sight again. The electricity remains still *active* and present, biding its invisible time while it builds again. What happens when any energy stops? It fails and fades. Characters ditto. Most story problems start here: being and doing are mutual and simultaneous. The moment characters stop taking action and risking consequences and making high-stakes choices, they stop seeming like real people and devolve into dark squiggles on the page...names doing stuff.

Aristotle teaches us that stories don't depict human *personalities*, but human *action*, people wanting things and working past obstacles to achieve and/or acquire them. When you're aligning all the various character components, the root, the base, the core of a character will always be the most direct, visible expression of the character's energy in a story: *action*.

Characters are forces of nature because they are forces that *express their own natures*. They do stuff that matters. Their actions need to mean something and have consequences or nobody cares. If you plan to write 300 pages of names doing stuff, you might as well pack it in now and save yourself the carpal tunnel.

The root of character is *energy* and that energy reveals itself in *action*.

That means we aren't going to kick off characterization with hair color or childhood memories. The place to start is with the energy that distinguishes a character and animates them. Tap that source. Unleash the storm. Find all the invisible, emotional forces crackling inside of your characters and give them spectacular steeples to strike.

"There is another world, and it is in this one."

Paul Éluard[46]

Chapter 6: MAGIC

When I say storytelling is magical, that's only half metaphor.

The core of much folk sorcery and basic ceremony is sympathetic magic, the belief that you can use ritual or spells via items and actions associated with a target to affect that target without direct contact. Essentially, sympathetic magic influences people and events at a distance.

The most obvious example is a "voodoo doll" built to represent the target that is stuck with pins to create problems from a distance. Sympathetic magic is the reason many people avoid "unlucky" objects/places and won't "step on a crack" for fear of injuring mom's spine. It also explains the use of statues in temples so we can speak to supernatural beings and why many religions prohibit depictions of the divine out of respect. Sympathetic magic is the power of vicarious influence.

Think about that a moment. Don't we carefully craft characters to make the readers feel things at a distance? Aren't we influencing people with a few scraps and pins? In this sense, storytelling operates as a kind of *empathetic* magic.

Authors build a fictional "doll" connected to the reader through actions and qualities and then stick pins in it to make the reader feel things. If assembled correctly, every character offers us a different spectrum of emotional possibilities: new pins and new pains. Amplifying the stakes keeps readers glued to the pages because the story *matters* to them, personally; you stick pins in those characters and the audience feels them. We build up a series of associations to link their feelings to the character on the page so that we can influence them, so they can experience a series of fascinating lives and worlds vicariously. *Abracadabra.* Herein lies the colossal power of story.

Through the device of character, authors have direct and dramatic access to their readers' thoughts and emotions at a distance. Even after the author is long gone, the "spell" of a book persists and its empathetic magic makes things happen in the real world. Centuries after an author is gone, a story offers an entire cast of dolls waiting to get stuck with the right pin at the right moment to make readers feel actual, immediate emotions.

Remember: our brains do not distinguish between real-world and fictional experiences. We construct "real" people the same way we do fictional people, as a mosaic of meaningful patterns. Empathetic magic is the reason characterization moves audiences and unleashes fandoms. Through the power of suggestion, authors can (and must) create characters that change people's lives.

You cast the spell with words.

"The bridge between the words glamour and grammar is magic. According to the OED, glamour evolved through an ancient association between learning and enchantment."

Roy Peter Clark[47]

Predicament

Genre fiction can only be as dramatical as it is grammatical.

That might sound nuts, but every story in the world breaks down into subjects doing things one sentence at a time. Someone takes action that causes reactions that require new actions. *Rinse-repeat.* Whether that subject is the sole focus of the novel or part of a teeming horde, the reader only knows what you tell them one moment, one sentence at a time.

In practical terms, a sentence is built from two components:

- the SUBJECT: the person, object, idea, or entity which the sentence concerns (CHARACTER)
- the PREDICATE: an explanation of the subject's *predicament* which creates a context and adds information (CHARACTERIZATION)

No character simply exists; characters take action constantly. A character does meaningful things with consequences *so that* they can exist. In essence, every sentence is a small story. The subject introduces the main character of that sentence. The predicate goes on to characterize them more fully and dramatically to reward the attention paid.

Take the sentence "The librarian shelved the new books." The subject "The librarian" focuses our attention where it belongs so that the predicate "shelved the new books" can reveal additional information about this subject at this moment in the fictional world of the sentence.

Grammar fanatics and literary mavens have flagged this linguistic quirk as a key to clear prose. "Most sentences in English open with the subject, and they move from the known to the unknown," as grammarian Virginia Tufte put it, "Probably one of the most important grammatical observations to be made about English prose style."[48] Readers instinctively follow the known to the unknown, tracing the causal relationship from the familiar to the unfamiliar as their understanding of the characters and their world expands and leads them deeper into the story.

I tend to think of these two halves of the sentence as the **lens** and the **light**. The subject focuses attention on something significant within the story's universe, and the predicate illuminates a meaningful detail, effort, or circumstance that expands the audience's awareness of the subject, revealing something that might otherwise remain dim, hidden, or missed if someone hasn't paid attention.

Subject leads to predicate, starting from consciousness and gradually revealing the context. Each sentence operates like a narrative piñata readers whack with their imagination until the story spills out the fascinating gaps created by the author. The subject of a sentence indicates that readers need to notice a specific *something*; you've decided that a particular subject, some person/place/thing/idea deserves special focus at that moment, more than any other potential subject in the universe: pay attention to *this*. Then the predicate rewards the reader's attention with meaningful detail and a juicy predicament, spilling the bits of emotional candy and treasure readers actually want.

Another way to think about a sentence: the subject presents a package and the predicate opens the package to reveal its contents. In practical terms that means the subject is often a literal *subject*, a person or item that is the intended focus, followed by a predicate that contains the verb and any complements (aka any information regarding the subject) that illuminate the world around the subject.

Just saying the word "Gollum" doesn't summon a creature named Gollum to life. But consider: "Gollum lived on a slimy island of rock in the middle of the lake." The subject "Gollum" tells us who needs our attention. The predicate "lived on a slimy island of rock in the middle of the lake." situates this creature in the emotional and physical landscape of the story. His predicament snaps into focus around his name. Suddenly we know many things about this Gollum and his circumstances and can infer even more.

A sentence guides our attention with intention.

While the subject focuses attention on who to follow (*lens*), the predicate reveals everything we want to know (*light*), so that the subject can act upon and interact with the world of the story. At its core, a sentence tells us who to care about and why we should bother.

- "Ma Joong bit his lips till the blood trickled from his chin." (*The Chinese Nail Murders*)
- "Jessica closed her eyes, feeling tears press out beneath the lids." (*Dune*)
- "DeWitt Albright made me a little nervous." (*Devil in a Blue Dress*)
- "Caligula swore to be revenged on Neptune." (*I, Claudius*)
- "Lyra and her daemon moved through the darkening hall, taking care to keep to one side, out of sight of the kitchen." (*The Golden Compass*)
- "Vivian's lips parted slowly until her teeth caught the light and glittered like knives." (*The Big Sleep*)

Simple declarative sentences built as Subject > Verb > Object reproduce the way we perceive any experience: *Someone...Does...Something*. In story terms it creates snapshot of one moment in the narrative flow: Character > Context > Consequence. Note that this basic diction also echoes the three stages of human cognition: If/Then/Therefore. *If* we see a character, *then* their action, *therefore* we extrapolate and understand the result: narrative cause and effect at its most primal. Moving from the known to the unknown, the sentence unpacks as a dynamic moment we *experience*.

In essence, each sentence tells a brief story of its own: **Verb + Target + Progress**. Each has its own little narrative with a subject and a predicate, a person and a predicament, a character and characteristics that draw us forward, action by action. Gradually all those subjects (and objects) create the impression of a larger, living world we experience in our imaginations...an emotional ride worth taking.

By revealing fascinating subjects, actions, and objects, each mini-narrative bridges to the next and the next, sentences build into paragraphs which become chapters, and over the course of a novel those mini-stories accrete into a narrative inevitably more than the sum of its parts. Writers create patterns and shape attention to extract emotion: **Stories work dramatically *because* they work grammatically.**

Happily for authors in search of dramatic conflict, the predicament of the predicate requires moment-to-moment solutions.

Characters act because they're unhappy and want to change that. In other words, they only act to achieve or acquire happiness. If your cast begins the story completely happy, they have nothing to do. They have nothing to want or find or change, and their inertia will kill the story.

What do they want? At what do they *aim*? All your characters need to want *something* passionately or else they're furniture. And to be honest, anytime a book begins with your character talking about how bored they are, you're probably about to bore your audience. Make their lives matter.

Aristotle pointed out that every plot asks "**Will this character's action lead to happiness?** " The character's high-stakes pursuit of an objective transforms them and the world around them for good or ill. Characters want to be exactly who they are and pursue things they believe will provide happiness. Ideally, they hope their actions will cover the shortest distance between their current location and their ultimate destination. The emotions and outcome are shaped by the genre.

When discussing a story, the average person defaults to the question, "What do the characters do?" because that tells them what kind of a ride to expect. The scale of the obstacles and opponents, the depth of the predicament—establish clear stakes and the emotional extremes the story will cover. When readers pick up a picture book about toddlers searching for a stuffed animal, they don't expect raunch and mutilation or a witty discussion of late-stage capitalism.

Every character will have to face obstacles and opponents during their journey, whether it's internal, external, or a wacky combo platter. What's important is that those problems must be *significant* to the character's transformation. External troubles need to induce internal grappling with issues. Internal difficulties should impact the way the character navigates the world around them.

Problems aren't enough.

A predicament only creates stakes when it is significant to the character.

Simply piling on a bunch of accidents and attacks doesn't make a book "exciting" unless they cause *significant* internal growth and reflection. Miring a book in deep-seated trauma and painful memories won't make a book "deep" unless those issues shift the external progress in *significant* ways. The internal and external predicaments must intersect and interact meaningfully.

Genre operates like a sentence: subject and predicate need each other to create character and context. A subject needs to attract attention. A predicate needs to explain why the attention is warranted. Once your audience knows the predicament is significant, they can consider the person facing that predicament.

So...when it comes to your characters, what's the big deal?

> "Things do not happen in this world. They are brought about."
>
> Will Hays[49]

EXERCISE: Trouble Maker

One of the challenges of genre fiction is pushing the margins while still hitting your marks. Fans show up wanting a certain kind of story, but they still want you to surprise them, within limits. You have to show them something they don't know they want...*yet*.

What kinds of unique *predicaments* do you enjoy writing for your characters and how do they appeal to your audience? How do those predicaments resemble the work of other genre authors and how do they distinguish you? Get specific:

1. Name your 5 go-to tropes or troubles when you're planning a story.

2. Name 5 go-to tropes or troubles used by the stars of your genre and subgenre.
3. Identify at least 5 ways your list and the genre standards overlap and diverge. In what way do you meet reader expectations and then how do you exceed them? How is your work familiar and how is it unique?
- BONUS ROUND: Identify the one kind of trouble you write differently than anyone else in the genre. What makes it stand part? What special access or insight do you bring to that predicament?

All authors have comfort zones when it comes to character predicaments. Learn your habits and crutches, so that you're always offering a fresh emotional landscape to your readers and they'll return to take the next ride.

Problem

Nobody's perfect.

No, *seriously*...even the most gracious and blessed human who ever drew breath had doubt, pain, damage, and disappointment. We live in compromise and cope with flaws, all of us. Part of mortal existence is the awareness that things and people go wrong sometimes and the subsequent burden of that awareness.

The same is true of the imaginary friends who populate your pages. No matter how clever, gorgeous, or gifted, your characters all experience damage, need, and lack. At least, they do if you want other humans to empathize and sympathize and *pay attention* to them.

Why do we rubberneck at accidents? Why do we gossip and complain? What's so satisfying about tabloid scandal and secret flirtations and the fall of the mighty? Where's the rub between what we want and what we get, between order and chaos, change and stasis, itch and scratch, yours and mine, rich and poor, us and them?

That's the key to all storytelling: **Problems fascinate us.**

Our brains are wired to extrapolate from given details. Primate gray matter evolved to identify patterns and solve problems. We're monkeys who enjoy figuring stuff out. Trouble drags our attention toward it as our minds scramble for a solution, a fix, a balm, a bridge over the alligators. Friction between expectations and events produces energy and attention because we want to know what happens next.

When you introduce a story without a problem ("Once upon a time, they lived happily ever after.") you deny your curious audience the pleasure of figuring out what the big deal is. Without stakes, without risk, stories are boring. Your audience won't care because without friction they *cannot* care. Something needs to be going on underneath the surface.

My term for this fundamental character problem is the **Void**. Other writers may refer to it as the fatal flaw, inner obstacle, wound, scar, gap, injury, shadow, issue, or skeleton in the closet. I call it the void because each of these other monikers potentially *skews* characterization in distracting or narrow directions.

- A fatal flaw doesn't always kill you and isn't always an obvious detriment.
- A problem can be minor, ridiculous, or baffling.
- An inner obstacle may stay locked in psychology without manifesting externally or dramatically.
- A wound sounds physical and/or limited to a single incident.
- A scar that has healed may cease to trouble anyone.
- An injury might be superficial, imaginary, or temporary.
- A proverbial "skeleton in the closet" may be shared by many members of a group or family.

On the other hand, **Voids are powerful, central, and unavoidable.** Defined by absence or need, they create their own lines of force with a relentless, driving appetite that resists solution or completion. The void bends time, space, and energy like a black hole within the character. Escaping a void is impossible, but characters never stop trying.

The void is Carl Jung's Shadow. Sigmund Freud called it the Id. Pop psych refers to it as "issues" and "baggage." All of them orbit the same idea. Every believable character has a personal void that affects all of their actions and choices, which drives their steps and haunts their happiness. What does your character *a-void*?

The void motivates all character decisions and actions. Even if the audience never learns or observes that void directly, you need to plumb its depths to write any character credibly. Consider some of the examples above, and you'll notice that voids share certain simple features:

- a problematic emptiness, need, or absence that *sucks*
- deep resonance and personal significance
- an origin situated in the past
- persistent influence on character emotions and actions
- no serious relief until story's end

Remember **Voids always suck**, in every sense of the word: they're painful, hollow, and insatiable, perpetual vacuums with a bottomless capacity to darken and destroy. Like the mainspring of a clock, a void is a tight coil that never stops unwinding, which makes it the source of greatest personal danger to the character. Strong characters avoid the void and never stop battling its inexorable drag on all their efforts.

For our purposes, your character's void becomes an unsolvable problem that drives all their actions. This topic really needs more space than I can afford it in this book, but for now, ask yourself what creates problems for your character and how will they try to grapple with that essential void in pursuit of the happiness they want.

- The *murder* of Harry Potter's parents leaves him orphaned and exiled, disposing him to trust (and mistrust) the wrong people at the worst moments. (*Harry Potter and the Philosopher's/Sorcerer's Stone*)

- The *abuse* from Lizbeth Salander's father drives her into arson, an asylum, and painful isolation as a hacker while empowering enemies who threaten her life, her allies, and her country. (*The Girl with the Dragon Tattoo*)

- The *enslavement* of Kunta Kinte tears him from his home and thrusts him into a hostile, brutal country that crushes his youthful idealism and severs his descendants' links to their complex heritage. (*Roots*)

- Jon Snow's mysterious *illegitimacy* instills a crippling chivalry in him, living alongside a loving family he cannot save, then exiles him to defend the literal edge of his world where he faces betrayal and destruction. (*A Game of Thrones*)

- The *fatal illness* of Anne Elliot's mother crushes her confidence, blocks her marriage, and leaves her wrangling self-absorbed loafers determined to ruin themselves and her chance of finding her own overdue happy ending. (*Persuasion*)

- William of Baskerville's *false recantation* allows the Inquisition to burn an innocent man, profanes his faith, empowers his enemies, leaves him rootless, and promotes superstition that empowers a serial murderer and a gross miscarriage of justice. (*The Name of the Rose*)

- After the untimely *death* of Ellie Arroway's supportive father, she abandons her family and faith to embrace the freaky extremes of astrophysics, then risks a respected research career on a mission that violates all her scientific principles. (*Contact*)

For each of these characters, *their void* directs all their actions while simultaneously draining, dampening, and derailing their energy, making the goal they pursue both impossible and essential. Think of Gollum's stolen golden "birthday present" (*The Lord of the Rings*), Officer Bud White's abusive upbringing (*L.A. Confidential*), or Clarice Starling's screaming lambs (*The Silence of the Lambs*); those horrible memories define those characters and direct their actions irrevocably. The void produces excruciating tension forcing the character into dramatic action.

Knowing the persistent problem that motivates your character will help aim that at a challenging, significant, relatable goal. It helps specify their intention by anchoring their action in past pain. Through the magic of empathy, we stick pins in our action figures and cause reader feelings at a distance. Knowing the void can activate every scene and spare your audience reams of backstory.

As it happens, your readers instinctively look for a character's void, because we do the same thing every time we meet people: gauge their issues, suss their psychology, look for their tells, try to figure out what makes them tick...the unstable core in their nuclear reactor. They may not even be able to put a finger on the instinct, but the void is the reason Mary Sues and deus ex machinas ruin stories. In the absence of a void, their fakeness becomes insufferable: plastic dolls pins cannot pierce. Their bland blankness offers no point of access with which to identify and empathize.

Voids are inherently personal, and so they establish basic boundaries and expectations for the reader by indicating the outer limits of emotional experience for this set of characters in this world. Even better, the void is scalable for any story, expanding and contracting to accommodate infinite narratives and any type of emotional ride. During the writing process, a void becomes a limitless power source, a kind of emotional icing gun that directs the character as she or he emerges on the page, shaping everything your character feels, thinks, says, makes, and does.

Pro tip: **Accentuate positive intentions.** Definite *actions* and objectives will always outperform *reactions* based on fear. Rather than focusing on the negatives that motivate your character, see what kinds of positive goals you can place before them to keep them moving in clear, specific directions. Especially with your protagonist, antagonist, and other central characters, favor actions that move characters toward an object of desire rather than away from an opponent or obstacle.

When a character *flees* or *denies* something, the destination or truth may remain unspecified, blurring and obscuring their action. That undirected murkiness creates a veil that separates your reader from empathizing with the character or engaging with their action. Instead, the same character could *pursue* an adversary away from a location or *prove* their innocence via evidence. Positive actions focus character energy and create a clear arc during a scene.

We want to see a character *win* a specific challenge, not *avoid* failure. Negatives derail and deaden character efforts; a character cannot play a negative in a scene. Avoidance and deflection make your characters less specific and less intentional in their actions. In other words, give your character an objective that demands fascinating *action*, rather than a turgid backstory that permits endless *reactions*. For powerful scenes and characters, keep intentions positive so they stay significant, challenging, and relatable.

To go back to grammar for a moment, the void *creates* every predicament you'll need for all those predicates that your subjects face during the story. The void acts as a kind of hardwired power grid for a character, sparking their energy and giving it a framework to flow through.

With a void defined, a character cannot freeze and a story cannot stall because they always have something to fight. If you ever get stuck, ask how the character's void forces them, specifically, to handle the opportunities and threats in this situation.

By getting specific about the emptiness that drives each of your characters, you create meaningful history, context, subtext, and impetus for their actions. It's the key in the ignition, the gas in the tank, the foot on the pedal that starts the story rolling.

"Whether we fall by ambition, blood, or lust
Like diamonds we are cut with our own dust."

John Webster[50]

EXERCISE: Inner Space

The pain, scars, lacks, and needs of a character impact every element in their creation. Take a moment to craft a meaningful void at the center of each of your main characters. What do they *a-void*? What really *sucks* for them?

If you don't know anything specifically about the root of their troubles, start with what you do know. Consider contrasts and events that seemed evident from the start. Look at their actions and overarching *goals* and trace backward along their personal trajectory to look for the point of origin. What might motivate each of them to pursue these objectives through darkness and doubt? What gnaws at them and goads them on even when they're exhausted, dismayed, or depleted?

Frame it grammatically:

- **"Because of [***past event***], I can never satisfy [***bottomless need***], which constantly messes with my actions/efforts by [***chronic, concrete problem***]."**

Or alternatively...

- **"My [***persistent problem***] keeps me trapped in a cycle of [***negative tendency***] that [***harmful verb***]s all my attempts to accomplish my goals.** "

When working out a passionate relationship, whether amorous or clamorous, look for opportunities to make those voids exacerbate each other. Their voids power the actions, so you can set up fundamental friction that sparks gonzo chemistry.

Remember: **Voids always suck.** Don't be afraid to dig deep or go dark. Better to learn the outer limits of the character. You can always dial it back.

Want

Characters do things (*actions*) because they want things (*objectives*). So what exactly do your characters need to do and why? Before we get down to brass tacks, I want to take a moment to discuss one of the most popular rubrics in genre fiction: Goal-Motivation-Conflict.

Writing instructor Dwight Swain collated many (if not most) of the core lessons about writing mass-market fiction in the twentieth century: hooks, scene and sequel, motivation-reaction, goals and conflict. Since the 1965 publication of *Techniques of the Selling Writer*, his methods have been adopted, adapted, and outright burgled by plenty of books and classes. Through a series of happy accidents, Swain and his wife became good friends with the founders of the Romance Writers of America, cementing his influence as a teacher and theoretician of genre fiction. Because of RWA's outsize influence on genre writing, several of his ideas became established norms in modern storytelling.

Full disclosure: I'm a fierce Swain fan. Several techniques I tackle in this book expand upon Swain's no-nonsense approach to visceral entertainment.

Of course, his writing guides come to us from another era, drier and less accessible than the average modern craft manual. In 1991 a romance author named Debra Dixon boiled down several of Swain's central ideas in a much-beloved book entitled *GMC: Goal, Motivation, and Conflict* for a contemporary audience using a central characterization mnemonic:

- GOAL: the crucial outcome
- MOTIVATION: the unstoppable force
- CONFLICT: the immovable obstacle

Identifying these three essentials aligns story structure around character action with coherent, believable behavior capable of carrying a narrative. GMC's strength derives from simplicity and scalability: anyone can explain what a character wants (G), why (M), and what interferes (C).

In practice, GMC maps a character's energy by explaining their behavior in context. A character takes action to pursue a *goal* because of *motivation* despite *conflict*. Even the most instinctive author can extrapolate from GMC and get a sense of the force driving a character's action and tactics. GMC exploits tension to reveal attention and intention, helping authors focus on character *agency*.

Twenty-five years later, thanks to Dixon's canny simplification of Swain's core ideas, GMC has become an accepted truism across genre publishing. GMC is so ubiquitous in our industry that there are teachers who pretend its universality is something ineffable rather than the result of Swain's experience, craft, and tenacity or Dixon's skill at condensing his ideas.

I suspect GMC works so well for authors at every level because it creates a context for characterization usable across genres, modes, and experience levels. At its root, GMC is so flexible because it expresses *time*.

- GOAL: A clear target maps a trajectory for a story and gives readers expectations about the character's *future*.
- MOTIVATION: Wounds and scars map the history which help readers understand the character's *past*.
- CONFLICT: Obstacles and opponents define capacities and strengths which make readers identify with the character's *present*.

To be clear, I think GMC provides a rock-solid starting point for structure and scene development because it unpacks plot as an intersection in *time*, situating characters in a given moment to set up the transformations to come. All stories are expressions of time: characters operate within time and reading a book forces readers to spend their time paying attention to imaginary incidents, alchemically transmuting fake-world time to elicit real-world emotions. *Magic*.

Since all characters (and all stories) operate over a period of time, GMC presents a user-friendly rubric to break down abstract concepts about behavior and background in easily dramatized chunks, pantsing for the plot-addicted and plotting for the plot averse.

Useful? Without question. Scalable? Absolutely. Straightforward? *Well...*

GMC remains a flexible, popular tool with tangible benefits. For pantsers, it establishes enough meaningful detail without hemming them in or stifling their impulses. For plotters, it situates a character in their world and anchors their emotions with resonant purpose. For folks who've never bothered with Aristotle, it reminds them to keep action front and center. GMC is simple enough to support newbies but resonant enough to shore up the efforts of old pros.

Having said that, GMC leaves so much unspoken and undefined that it doesn't actually create characters effectively. It works, but it doesn't actually work as advertised. Great for scene structure, shaky for characterization. *Cue pitchforks!* Please bear with me.

I have serious respect for Dixon's encapsulation of Swain's ideas, but please note that GMC only addresses character *indirectly*. It establishes a context by which an author can deduce character via the process of elimination: the character who pursues *this* goal because of *this* motivation despite *this* conflict should appear in my story. Notice that GMC never answers the basic questions: *Who is my character? How do I verbalize the person on the page?* GMC only creates a negative space into which the character fits, like folded and taped wrapping paper with no present inside.

In fact, **GMC characterizes by establishing everything *other than* the character.**

It nails down the critical *objects* external to a given *subject*, without ever addressing characterization directly and specifically. GMC's method is *algebraic* (e.g. 2+X= 5 therefore X=3) because it never actually reveals X. By knowing the character's GMC, you can presumably eventually extrapolate the unknown X of character indirectly by process of elimination and then write it...somehow. Grammatically, it's all predicate with no subject.

Forensic investigators call this a "void pattern," the bare outline created when blood spatter or other markings reveal an object that's been *removed* from a crime scene, a kind of definition by negation. GMC creates a void pattern where characterization should occur and then expects you to fill the space created by the context. If nothing else, that seems specious and inefficient.

Who tries to cook a meal using a list of all the ingredients you don't need and all the preparation you won't use? Decide some stuff and once you find the gaps then [*insert characterization*]? Underpants gnomes on ice! Magic happens here...*good luck!*

GMC is helpful, but it skirts characterization and (frustratingly) doesn't address the actual writing process at all. Like impersonal ads, GMC leaves an author to *extrapolate* characters and capture them on paper as best they can...somehow...at some point down the line. When GMC assists characterization, it's not by design. It's more like cutting a steak with scissors.

There is a better way.

"To live a creative life, we must lose our fear of being wrong."

Joseph Chilton Pearce[51]

EXERCISE: Hard Time

Stories have to unfold and GMC allows you to situate the characters in time. Every character occupies a series of moments on-page and off, but without context their presence is pointless. What do you think each character in your cast would *do* for the entire story to move themselves from the past, through the present, and toward their desired future?

- Identify the goal, motivation, and conflict for your main characters.
  - GOAL: the crucial outcome in the character's *future*
  - MOTIVATION: the unstoppable force in the character's *past*
  - CONFLICT: the immovable obstacle in the character's *present*
- Make a list of things this character might do throughout the book to achieve happiness inspired by and in spite of their circumstances.

Part III: Action

Action alone is in your control,
Not the results ever.
Let not the result of action be your motive,
Nor should you keep company of inaction.

Bhagavad Gita (2.47)[52]

Chapter 7: VERBS

An action is an intentional event.

Unforgettable characters don't exist as static objects on the page, but as fascinating subjects in a process of becoming. Characters *act*. They make us care by doing things that matter in ways that reveal the dynamic, volatile energy that makes them who they are.

Remember our discussion of alignment. We carry a stack of books from the bottom, but what element anchors all those scenes in a story or characteristics of characters? Do you start with their stats and statuses? Their pains and strengths and vibes? Their attractions and interactions? The roles and ranks? Their GMCs or archetypes? Their aspects and affects? All the details and trivia in the world can only suggest a character's nature or a scene's skew. You can't write those things, underpants gnome; you can only extrapolate from them.

In genre fiction, alignment starts with character actions.

At core, characters must *do* so they can *be*. Everything that person says, does, avoids, and wants exists in alignment so that they cohere, even as they seem to morph and evolve on the page. To render the effects of energy visible, authors depict the character's intentional efforts, internal and external, that have meaning-ful impact.

Writing guides refer to this type of effort variously as *action, intention, subtext, want, task, ambition, problem, need, spine*. What you call it doesn't matter so long as your characters do meaningful things in pursuit of their own happiness.

I prefer the word *action* because it reminds us to keep our characters doing stuff to accomplish their goals with consequences. There's a reason directors call "Action!" on set when shooting footage. *Actors* need to *act* to tell the story. A statue exists separate from the hands that create it. Sculptors may need metal or marble, but in fiction character *actions* are the medium of choice.[53]

Characters are sculptures that carve each other.

For entertainment to entertain anyone, you need people paying attention, and that means providing them with an emotional experience that meets and exceeds their expectations. Scenes are driven by the issues and interests native to the characters, and all other details arise organically from the core story. If you can pinpoint a character's action, you know what they are *actually* doing as they *act* upon the other charac-ters, who will *act* upon them as a consequence.

Instead of allowing you to rely on generalizations about a character's emotional or mental state, specify-ing the precise action requires scrupulous care and attention to the situation you're writing. This in turn allows all the other narrative elements to play directly into the energetic flow of the scene for maximum efficacy.

This emphasis on action rather than impersonation comes straight from the *Poetics*, cornerstone of western lit-crit (and worth a read if you haven't).[54] Character attributes, aspect, and affect only emerge via a character's intentional efforts to attain their story goal.

Action connects the character with their goals by giving their energy purpose. If you're a GMC writer, the action is *how* they pursue their goal as a tangible expression of their motivation which opposes the conflict they face; if you think of GMC as heat, fuel, and oxygen, then the action is the *fire*.

What exactly do we mean when we say action in relation to a genre story?

An action is an intentional event caused by a character in order to achieve an objective made meaningful to the reader which makes another event possible.

That's a mouthful, so let's break that definition down. An action is

- *an intentional event*. Action involves a specific choice with a tangible impact, reflecting a character's unique energy and story goal.
- *caused by a character*. Action requires the agency of a person participating in the story, so accidents and coincidences need not apply.
- *in order to achieve an objective*. Action directs the energy of a subject toward a clear story goal, which creates stakes and suspense for the audience to keep them turning the pages all the way to the end.

- *made meaningful to the reader.* Action results in significant consequences, both to characters in the story and the audience reading it, which creates empathy and emotional resonance.
- *which makes another event possible.* Action connects causally to the events preceding and following it, allowing escalation and revealing the circumstances around the character by inference.

Energy is not visible; only its effects are visible. Audiences need action as a tangible expression of character energy so they know what is happening and why it matters. To elicit emotion, you're going to need readers to engage with your story and its characters, and that means **Action is paramount**.

Action transmutes emotional energy into intentional events, distilling a character's internal reality into tangible behavior. Since readers experience characters the way they do actual human beings, action creates emotions in them via empathetic magic, and the story's action figures take the audience for an emotional ride.

Once you involve other characters and external circumstances, that action requires applied *force* to overcome the *friction* between where they start and their ultimate *focus*. Hidden energy manifests as visible action.

The action is who a character is. An action isn't just what a character *tries* to do or *dreams* of doing, but what that person actually, constantly does, cannot help but do, on every page, in every scene, at every moment. That character embodies that action throughout the entire story, whether that's one book or a dozen.

Actions speak louder than words, more clearly and powerfully.

The audience considers what characters do and what they want to achieve, and develops opinions and feelings about them, just as they would with any person they knew. The more deeply the reader engages, closure fills in the blanks until the character seems like a living three-dimensional being.

Characters make things happen so they can have happiness. Action is what they do to achieve happiness. Since actions must change something outside the character, they are directed outward; even an "internal" process like *scrutinizing* evidence or *choosing* a ring focuses on a target outside the character. They do things (actions) so they can get things (objectives).

We all just want to be happy. In the *Nicomachean Ethics*, Aristotle argues that "every action aims at some good." Characters want happiness. They may be misguided or deranged, but characters always reveal *what* they want by their actions.

Stories don't critique actions or comment on actions; they're not *about* actions. **Stories are made of action the way that pigs are made of pork.**

"Suit the action to the word, the word to the action."

William Shakespeare[55]

EXERCISE: Fan Fave

Writers start as readers, and in a real sense, every story is a reaction to all the stories that came before it. Analyzing stories and characters you love can help you develop the skills to follow suit.

Pick one of your favorite fictional people and break down what makes them who they are on the page.

1. What does this character do in every scene? Make a list of characteristic behaviors, find a common thread, and create a list of possible options.

2. Test each possible action to see if it defines the sum total of the character's behavior in the story. The easiest way to do that is to formulate it in the mode of Descartes, "**I** [*action*]**, therefore I am.**"

3. Test the action for every moment the character appears in the story. At what points does this person get close to betraying this essential action? Is the sentence true for the character at every point?

4. If not, try to improve or perfect it. Are there better options that capture a different nuance? Notice the slight variations in meaning that shift the character's nature.

5. Test other options until you find the clear winner. Make certain it works in consistent alignment in every context.

When you've nailed down an action for a beloved character, consider how *you* would have written that action. How would the story and the character differ in your hands? How would that affect the other story elements?

Life

An action is an intentional event caused by a character.

By definition, a verb expresses all the energy in a sentence, an action or a state of being. For fictional purposes, a wise author gives characters a juicy, compelling action verb with plenty of punch. Focusing on the character's actions from the start ensures the character is active, not to mention why those actions are significant.

For any character I create, I always want to pick the most potent, unexpected, specific *action* I possibly can...a dynamic verb choice that will force me (and my readers) to salivate and sweat and shiver and soar through the course of the story. **Action always occurs in the present tense...**it is what characters do right now, rather than what they did or will do. Action must unfold in real time so that readers can *experience* it.

The action acts as a kind of emotional circuit breaker for the character through which all of the behavior, traits, and energy passes. Every problem and solution starts from and aligns with the action. All of the character's potential and failure, impact and imbalance can be traced to it.

For best results, an action should operate internally and externally with a tangible *physical* effect outside of the character as well as a *mental* image and an *emotional* impact inside them as well. When identifying your character's action, look for juicy resonance on all three levels.

- PHYSICAL: Make sure the action directs its energy externally into clear, tangible goals so audiences can engage easily.
- MENTAL: Look for actions that create dynamic, dramatic images in the mind's eye. (e.g. not take, but *pilfer*; not look, but *scrutinize*; not ask, but *interrogate*)
- EMOTIONAL: Opt for actions with a wide range of variation and intensity expressing the complexity of your character's interior life.

You're going to have to write this story and bring this character to life, so keep those actions physical and fun, visceral and vital. These same qualities appeal to audiences so this approach is a twofer.

A clear action allows you to *conjugate* the character dynamically in every situation so that what they do always matters. Identify that action and every other detail of the book will align with it for maximum emotional coherence and impact. Characters embody their actions at every moment.

Think of **Odysseus** *tricking*, **Alice** *wondering*, **Scrooge** *denying*, **Gollum** *coveting*, **Hercule Poirot** *outwitting*, **Empress Livia** *poisoning*, **Edmond Dantès** *avenging*, **Lisbeth Salander** *hacking*, **Dracula** *draining*, **Zaphod Beeblebrox** *flouting*, **Cleopatra** *seducing*, **Willie Wonka** *astonishing*, **Auntie Mame** *embracing*, **Schmendrick the Magician** *bungling*, **Lorelei Lee** *luring*, or **Allan Quatermain** *exploring*...all of them relentlessly pursue the central motivated lines of action that define them and shape their stories.

Don't worry if you disagree with my take on the above characters or others later in this book. Don't expect everyone to agree on the actions you identify for your own creations. Different writers draw power from different words, themes, symbols. You're a writer, so voice should guide your choice: **Word choice is personal.**

Verbs express different kinds of energy that moves in different directions. Weigh the differences between someone who *pushes* the world away or *pulls* it toward them, someone who *joins* things together or *splits* them apart.

The purpose of an action is to help you build a satisfying emotional ride for your readers, full stop. Verb choice reflects your voice, your experience, and your perspective on a story. What matters most is that you get results. Whenever you don't, re-verb accordingly. As long as those actions help you tell the story as powerfully as possible, you're golden.

We all know that characters take action, so why would you start anywhere else when trying to *verbalize* a story?

Consider Severus Snape from the Harry Potter series. I'd argue his action is *"to vex"* because of its layered meanings as...an act of hostility, a bluff, promise, blackmail, a defense mechanism, a looming maneuver, foreboding, a leadership tactic, a warning, a theoretical threat, a legitimate menace, and a misunderstood sacrifice. Snape seems dangerous, but more than anything, he impedes and intimidates Harry throughout all seven books...like the pebble in the shoe, hair in the butter, salt in the sugar. In every sense of the word, **Snape** *vexes*

- his family, his community, his prospects, his affections, and his reputation.
- Harry's reputation at the school and any illusions about his parents.
- James Potter's superiority, Lily Potter's infatuation and marriage.
- his students, instructors, and colleagues, their lessons and work, discipline and rules.
- Gryffindor's chances and Slytherin's assumptions.
- the leadership of Dumbledore, McGonagall, and Umbridge, whenever it suits him and often when it reflects most terribly on his reputation.
- Harry's actions publicly and Harry's enemies secretly.
- Quirrell's snooping, Lockhart's fabrications, Lupin's secret, Moody's machinations, Umbridge's interrogation, and Draco Malfoy's curse.
- Dumbledore's plans (apparently) and the Death Eater's siege (actually).
- Hogwarts, the Ministry of Magic, the new Order of the Phoenix, Dumbledore's Army, the Dementors, and ultimately Voldemort.
- the history and future of the Wizarding World.
- Harry's lifelong loathing (by revealing his memories).

- himself, constantly following his heart or head precisely when he shouldn't, doing everything the hard way and the long way round.

In every scene of the books and films, Snape *vexes*. His compulsion *to vex* actually puts him at cross-purposes with everyone and everything in his world, complicating every possibility of contentment or reward. He is vexation in human form.

Calling Snape *sinister, grim, petty, malicious, lonely, bitter, repellent, snide, stern, treacherous,* or *melodramatic* only describes how others perceive him. Likewise *brave, vulnerable, devoted, resourceful, protective, remorseful, heroic, shrewd,* or *tragic*. Modifiers invariably skim the surface, elide contradiction, and reduce a life to misleading impressions.

Describing him as a *menace*, a *magician*, a *master*, a *Machiavelli*, or *martyr* only gives a cursory sense of his role in certain scenes and books and ignores others. He isn't static enough to remain a person, thing, or idea. Nouns beg the question and erode complexity.

But by focusing on verbs, his tactics and interactions—*victimizing, disciplining, shielding, harassing, misleading, scolding, puzzling, sacrificing, conspiring, cursing, snooping, sniping, snapping, snaping*—his essential energy emerges. Using verbs, I can encapsulate all of Severus Snape in a kind of narrative rhapsody on one central, essential action of *vexing*. The tactical shifts are merely notes in his core melody in the key of *vex*.

For anyone who's skeptical of my analysis, the character's actual *name* is an archaic, regional synonym for *vex*. The verb *"to snape"* literally means:

- to criticize, shame, rebuke, or reprimand
- to offend, revile, or snub severely
- to injure, bite, or nip (as with cold)
- to limit, thwart, or impede
- to blight or stunt growth
- to call off a dog
- to taper or bevel raw materials for a snug fit (in shipbuilding)
- And (in Sussex dialect) boggy ground...just for evocative flavor and to drive the point home.

The only reason I don't propose the actual, obvious verb *to snape* as this character's action is that the word fell out of common use several centuries ago, and *to vex* covers a broader and more dramatic range of tactical possibilities. He does more than snape, but he *vexes* on every page in which he appears. All of his being *aligns* with that central urge *to vex*.

Of course, I'm not doing a lit-crit reread of J.K. Rowling's epic series, but trying to imagine a way an author could arrive at a character that appealing and complex. Likewise, I'm not suggesting that Rowling would agree with my take on her legendary antihero, but rather to point out a strong character in a memorable series full of incendiary moments all defined by a single action.

Nailing down a character action for Snape gives me a hold on his essential nature and would steer my writing process. The coherence of Snape's tactics and his multifaceted appeal spring from that relentless, counterintuitive drive he has *to vex* everyone and everything that might bring him ease and happiness.

Severus Snape *vexes*, therefore he is.

Since characters *are* their action, that action doesn't change even across multiple books. The character coheres because their action does.

Alignment is everything! For us to connect with characters, to invest in the growth and emotions of a protagonist, their actions must transform them and those actions must *cohere* over the course of the book. Casting each significant character with a specific verb immediately

- releases their energy on every page and engages reader emotions.
- anchors their relationships with enemies and allies, lovers and losers, mentors and tempters.
- reflects all your choices about them, from wardrobe to history to foibles to outcome.
- invokes their authentic voice, belief system, and idiom organically.
- telegraphs their journey's scope and core story arc in each interaction.
- articulates their goal, motivation, and conflict in clear contrast to the rest of the cast.
- builds coherence across their scenes and prevents "out of character" glitches.
- provides opposing dramatic objectives for every other character in the story.

- structures your narrative organically, *in situ*, no matter your preferred writing process.

Embrace your character's action and your character will return the favor by taking action on every page. Verbalize your story from the outset and you allow the story to tell itself.

"All fine prose is based on the verbs carrying the sentences. They make sentences move."

F. Scott Fitzgerald[56]

EXERCISE: Amp Site

Modern media has a grim habit of shrinking and homogenizing everyday speech, shaving our language down to the dimmest and dumbest options in an attempt to maximize audience share...great for ratings, terrible for writers who need to find the right words.

Reading widely and wildly can reverse that process, but you can just as easily exercise your verbal faculties as you would any essential muscle. Get in the habit of upgrading language to the most dynamic and interactive verbs possible.

1. Write down 3-5 adjectives that describe your character.
2. Write down 3-5 adverbs that express the *way* your character would do something.
3. Write down 3-5 nouns that identify your character.
4. Now expose the actions buried within all those modifiers and nouns by transforming all of them

into verbs your character might embody in a scene. (If your hero is hungry, he *gobbles*. If your heroine is a bandit, she *plunders*.)

What is gained and lost by the transition into verbs? Are the resultant verbs appropriate for your character in every circumstance? Why and why not? Note how certain verbs indicate subtle information about setting, period, career, and morality. Splash around in that vocabulary and you'll stretch your authorial voice.

Source

An action is...caused by a character...made meaningful to the reader.

Where do these magical actions come from? How can you select the strongest, sexiest action available that can sustain several hundred life-changing pages?

The action of every character arises from their void...the wound, lack, or need within them that drives all their decisions. That void is the root of their desires and the source of all their energy, so of course it exerts a gravitation pull on every possible action.

All characters (and arguably all people) struggle with an empty space they cannot fill or a mortal wound that will not heal or a dark need they cannot resist. The greater that void, the higher the stakes, the stronger the conflict, the more powerful the action. That motivating lack *always* sparks the perfect action.

The action arises from their void and points them toward a happiness they believe/hope/pray might fill that inner emptiness permanently. However and whoever they are, they *pay attention* in order to secure that happiness. The void creates the emotional context for all their decisions. Exactly *what* they pay attention to lets us know what they care about and why we should care.

What is their purpose? A character doesn't just act, they take action in order to... accomplish something. Think of it as a mad lib: "*[Character]* is *[context]* who pays attention in order to *[action]* *[objective]*."

- Rooster Cogburn is a disgraced, battle-scarred marshal out at the edge of the US territories, who pays attention in order to *recover* his grit and good name. (*True Grit*)
- Whitney Stone is a headstrong hoyden who pays attention in order to *agitate* Regency society with the only husband who can handle her. (*Whitney, My Love*)
- Hercule Poirot is a fastidious Belgian detective who pays attention in order to *outwit* criminals and police using only his little grey cells. (*Death on the Nile* et al)
- Arha is the enslaved high priestess of the Nameless Ones who pays attention in order to *master* her false fears and her real enemies. (*The Tombs of Atuan*)
- Hiro Protagonist is the mafia-pizza "Deliverator" who pays attention in order to *hack* enemies and human consciousness via his sword and "mad skillz" to save the world. (*Snow Crash*)
- Idgie Threadgoode is a Depression-era Alabama troublemaker who pays attention in order to

defy bigots and build a loving community. (*Fried Green Tomatoes at the Whistle Stop Café*)

- HAL is a ship's artificial intelligence who pays attention <u>in order to</u> *regulate* his human crew and a secret mission. (*2001*)

The strongest action comes from the void because it occupies that character's thoughts at every moment, even when alone. Its inexorable vacuum sucks everything and everyone toward it, bending each situation like a black hole at the heart of the character. The void generates energy and the action expresses it in their world.

If your heroine operates from a fear of exposure and scandal, then her action might be *to disguise* or *to dictate*. If your comic sidekick's greatest fear is silence, then his actions could be *to entertain* or *to incite* in all his blathery chattering. Whatever your character needs will force them to take the necessary actions in pursuit of their intention. By testing and discarding options in search of the strongest, most dynamic action possible, you can upgrade your character to the best choice available.

The easiest way to test actions: **Can the character undertake this action without any explanation?** If yes, groovy. If no, then you're not creating an action, just baking a big, ugly exposition cake. An action that requires explanation will confuse your readers and hobble your story. Make certain that an audience understands what's happening so they *can* pay attention.

Always kick the tires: the right action is the one readers can imagine this character pursuing without any explanation or exposition necessary.

In his book *A Sense of Direction*, theatrical legend William Ball notes that though an actor chooses an action, the audience may never consciously know it, but nevertheless senses the consistency of the character's behavior. Again, this applies perfectly to writing, but unlike impersonal ad questionnaires and other murky methods, this behind-the-scenes prep work pays off handsomely every time.

Ball also offers what he calls the "all-purpose, shortcut, surefire, knockdown, bring-em-back-alive, fail-safe, self-cleaning, inexhaustible magic trick" of identifying a character's action: *get* and *make*.[57] If you're stuck, these work as a perfect starting point for verbalizing your characters.

- What is the character trying *to get* the other person to do?
- What are you trying *to make* the other person do?

If you can answer those questions, you can identify the action of any character.

Articulating the action as a verb in its infinitive form (e.g. to get, to make, to take) allows actors and directions flexibility and clarity. (e.g. Odysseus *tricks*, but his action is *to trick*.) An infinitive verb presents a neutral, flexible starting point for whatever characterization is necessary.

From those rudimentary origins, you can easily sharpen and polish an action until the character pops off the page. If you've identified the perfect verb, good job! And if things are still murky, then let's dig further. When struggling, many authors default to what characters *see* and how they *seem*: nouns and adjectives.

For characterizations bogged down in what they see, the things and beings around them, eliminate *nouns* so that

- "She wants a <u>mansion</u>." becomes "She wants *to purchase* a mansion with her windfall." or "She wants *to demolish* a hospital to clear space for a mansion."
- "He wants <u>fame</u>." becomes "He wants *to dazzle* audiences around the world for fame." or "He wants *to blackmail* a group of celebrities for fame."
- "She wants a <u>ferret</u>." becomes "She wants *to kidnap* a ferret from its owners." or "She plans *to lobby* her co-op to legalize ferrets."

By focusing the *effort* of the character rather than their expression, on what they *do* rather than a nearby thing or a person, you pinpoint their energy in a scene and across a story. They embody the action evoked by their void. Alignment to the rescue!

For characterizations seemingly stuck in appearances, moods, and how things seem, try to find the verbs hidden by the adjectives. Rather than letting a character simply *be* "sleepy," that person *demands* a nap or *escapes* to a bedroom. A "harsh" character would instead *dominate* a discussion or *ridicule* their employees. Again, by focusing on the specific action, the character becomes clear and the context comes into focus.

In turn that leads to your other characters and *their* actions which provide an ideal source of dramatic friction and will enrich all of their on-page relationships. Consider the interesting collisions possible.

If your main character needs to *orchestrate* every situation, then you'll want to populate your book with a cast of folks who *disorder, disarm, derail* that character's actions. If you have a heroine who lives to *untangle* problems or puzzles, then give her a whole cast of *meddling, fumbling, scheming* web spinners. As the author, you can solve most of your structural difficulties from the outset by specifying actions for all the characters that will produce the most dramatic friction in the least amount of space.

Don't be afraid to use placeholders and upgrade later. You may stumble across the right action after a few days playing with possibilities. There's no shame in trying them on like shoes and discarding the ones that squeak or pinch in the wrong places.

The more you verbalize this way, the more aligned your process will be, and the more efficient your efforts. Over time, you'll develop those verbal muscles so that you can rule out clinkers and stinkers early and pinpoint a winner swiftly. As a bonus, collecting vivid verbs will strengthen your writing as a whole.

Characters may not be self-aware. Some characters can see and state their actions and the actions of others clearly. These folks may even state their action in plain language on the page, but that kind of blunt candor is rare and you should use it consciously.

Above all things, **Trust your gut**. You'll know the character's action when you find it. Identifying it resembles dowsing: as you pass over several possibilities, the correct one will tug you toward it with magnetic force because it aligns with the character's aspect and affect on multiple levels.

In my experience the perfect action for the character plucks at your strings, prods your muse, and strikes a flint. It will evoke emotions and provoke your narrative impulses. That action will have a consonance and resonance that lights up possibilities you cannot wait to commit to paper.

Whatever your strengths and habits, take the time to choose those actions and every project will write itself.

"The fact is I think I am a verb instead of a personal pronoun. A verb is anything that signifies to be; to do; or to suffer. I signify all three."

Ulysses S. Grant[58]

EXERCISE: Dark Matters

Every character's action springs from a personal void. Knowing what haunts and drives a character can shape every moment they're on the page. Look to the things they lack. Voids never stop sucking, and so the power they provide is limitless.

1. Identify the character's central void and how it impedes their happiness.
2. Based on your character's void, identify the ways this character might try to address that persistent suckage with a credible solution.
   - What would fulfill them and ease their pain?
   - What kind of effect would it have on their energy at the best and worst of times?
3. Make a list of possible goals driven by the character's void.
4. Eliminate any nouns and modifiers by boiling those essential wants into a list of possible actions, listing the verbs in their infinitive forms (*to + verb*). What action will they embody to combat this void?
5. Add any other active verbs that might spring from that void as credible solution for this character. (n.b. a perfect opportunity to break out your favorite thesaurus). Narrow that list to the best candidate.
6. Complete a rough mad lib that identifies their context and desire: "[*Character*] **is** [*context*] **who pays attention in order to** [*action*] [*objective*]."

Don't be afraid to get literal and physical. If a character's void is enslavement, their action might be "*to free*" or "*to unlock*." If a character's void is abuse, their action might be "*to heal*" or "*to nurture*." People never stop trying to outrun the thing constantly dragging them towards despair, destruction, and death.

Force

An action is an intentional event...made meaningful to the reader.

For me, every project literally starts with dynamic *verbs*.

Before I commit a word to paper, I sit down and figure out the story's verbal palette, the central forces driving my cast, and ways the resultant actions might produce enough interesting friction to elicit powerful, entertaining emotions for an audience. The verbs dictate subgenre, tropes, even niche appeal thereby.

A protagonist's action roots the entire project by clarifying and energizing every moment they appear on page. The right action can

- structure the flow of scenes and escalation of events.
- charge all intercourse, social and sexual, violent and vibrant.
- indicate moments of drama and comedy.
- spawn other characters who can assist and oppose the protagonist.
- create universal, accessible conflicts with direct emotional impact.

Using verbs to construct characters rather than nouns or adjectives taps the *energy* of the story and builds *actions* directly into the bedrock of your project. That motivated flow keeps your characters' arcs believable because they are consistent without being robotic, active without being frenetic, precise without being limited.

Action makes energy visible. Energy provokes emotion. Emotions can structure the entire story. If you know what characters do and *why*, every action produces a reaction in other characters. All you have to do is feel your way through the story by verbalizing it.

Remember the discussion of conjugation back in Chapter 3? If characters are their actions, then every character can be expressed most clearly as a *verb*. For clarity, and in order to encapsulate all of the potential in a character, I use the *infinitive* form of the verb (to + verb) as a base because with that form I can unlock all of the power of the action in whatever context a character acts.

Example: A colleague came to me excited because she'd cracked a character and his action: "Lost. He's lost!"

I was confused at first. "You mean *to lose*? He *loses* in every scene of the story?"

Nope. She meant that the character was *already* lost, and consequently spent the whole story dealing with being lost. Since "lost" was a verb and fit his personality, it *had* to be the action. So I pressed, "Lost is past perfect. It's already happened. How does he keep losing things? When? How is he going to lose something in every scene? How many ways can he lose?"

She agreed and started spitballing his habitual actions, looking for the common denominator...all of them driven by *having been* lost, past perfect. What she'd done was zero in on the character's existing pain and confusion. "Lost" was the character's *void*. He didn't *lose* things...he *was lost* (a past perfect verb) in every scene. She found the solution instantly. He was always pushing to *find* solutions and people to keep from feeling lost. He was lost and so he was constantly trying *to find*.

If you can only use an action verb in past perfect, then you're probably describing a void that drives the action. An action is not what the character *is*, but what the character *does, intentionally*. Using the infinitive *as* the character pushed her one step further to see what the void made him do in every scene.

Stories conjugate characters. Just as a writer takes a verb and alters it to specify its function in a text, a story alters a character to specify their function in the narrative. Consider the infinite power of the infinitive and make certain that action will apply to all possible moments with this character. Allow the character to act, and conjugate the character to situate them precisely in time and space.

Unlike film, fiction revels in subtle, complex actions that operate internally and externally, but clarity packs a punch. The more easily the reader can verify the success or failure of an action, the more dramatic the action will be. If you have to explain an action, you can do better. **Clear actions make for powerful, moving scenes.** If your heroine "wants" something, then you must *tell* readers what, why, and how she "wants," but if her objective is to *purloin* or *annihilate* something, you can *show* the theft or the annihilation.

And like a circuit breaker, an action really does allow you to trace all of the character's connections and the story's power when you run into trouble or need to reroute something.

Always amplify where possible, and that doesn't just mean making *lurid* word choices. Go action-shopping and give yourself options. For me, this stage of story planning always ends up as a delicious thesaurus salad. I slosh all the possibilities around in a bowl until I find the one that rings true, clear, bright, and resonant for that character in this context. Any hero can *seek*, but what about a hero that *excavates, rifles, hounds*, or *craves*. If you start out saying that your villain's action is to *punish*, you might decide *mutilate* or *torture* feel flashier, but maybe the subtler *hobble* or *dissect* create scarier, less clichéd possibilities.

Strong verb, strong character. If you take nothing else from this book, remember *that*.

At my students' urging, I've completed an author-specific action/tactic thesaurus called *Activate* that includes secondary divisions by genre and vibe. Though originally intended as an appendix to this book, its length made inclusion impractical. Having said that, any thesaurus will serve your purposes, so long as it notes transitivity and flags phrasals. You just need to consider gradations, connotations, and implications in selecting your character's core verb.

Additionally, one slim guide I recommend to all authors is *Actions: The Actors' Thesaurus* by Narina Caldarone & Maggie Lloyd-Williams, which they wrote for the express purpose of providing clear, playable actions for performers looking to squeeze maximum impact from a scene. My only caveat is that this book focuses on *performable* verbs, which are not always the same as *writable* verbs. I speak from experience when I say, **What helps an actor won't always serve a writer.** For obvious reasons, Caldarone and Lloyd-Williams emphasize presentational options appropriate for the rehearsal process with a literal cast and also leave out many subjective/internal verb options ideal for fiction.

As you dig around for the right option, look for verbs that push your creative limits. Recycling comfortable actions will also guarantee you keep repeating characters, which will leave you regurgitating the same book. If your voice or subgenre is truly focused on a single type of action (i.e. *chase* for thrillers), look for subtle variation via synonyms and other angles (e.g. hunt, pursue, track). Instead of asking "why?" ask "in order to accomplish what?" Focus on what a character wants to *do*, not what they want to *be*.

Of course, plenty of folks simply do stuff *without* taking action; we call these non-actions *activities*. An action tries to cause a change. An activity simply passes time.

For a million reasons, the life of the average person involves much more activity than action. As Swain points out, "The majority of us have drift, not drive. We fall into things through happenstance and follow the line of least resistance."[59] When readers pick up a book, they're not interested in bobbing along, bored, while nothing in particular happens.

In the spectrum of impact, character behavior can take several shapes over the course of a story.

- ACTION requires that a character tries to change the status quo with consequences, pursuing a story goal made meaningful to the audience.
- ACTIVITY allows a character to pass time in stasis without cost or impact, in pursuit of a goal meaningless to the reader, even if it's significant to *them*.
- AVOIDANCE can turn some activities into a passive action and weakens character appeal.
- ADAPTATION only happens when a character runs out of excuses or escapes and must take action.
- ADVANCEMENT moves a character closer to their goal by pushing past conflicts through sequential actions.

Establishing a clear action is both simpler and subtler than you might expect. One way to see if your character is taking action is to frame it with the phrase "in order to."

- "She jumped in the pool." is an activity.
- "She jumped in the pool in order to save her son." is an action.

The same is true of anything a character can find or mind or make or take. Great sex scenes are actions that transform the characters involved. Crappy sex scenes are activities that fill up pages and change nothing. Actions are essential beats. Activities are discardable filler that serve no function. Readers skim them, as they should. When Elmore Leonard said "Try to leave out the parts people tend to skip," he was talking about *activities.*[60]

The next time you're outlining a story or you find yourself in the weeds with a truculent plot bunny, go verb hunting. Literally populate your cast of characters with a single action for each that they will embody for the length of the narrative. Identify the void that drives each of them and the singular action they hope/believe/trust will bring them happiness.

Think laterally, not literally.

Start with several intriguing placeholders and then spiral in on the right word. Amplify the options you choose by weighing dramatic contrast and narrowing that list to the one that resonates, escalates, and refracts with other actions in play. Sometimes the character will adapt to embody the action, and sometimes you'll need a better verb to encapsulate the character. Allow each action to keep its character coherent and constantly unfolding as their actions change their world and vice versa.

Let your characters *do*, so that they can *be*.

"The art of verbs isn't an art of invention. It's the art of observation—learning to see dynamism in everyday events."

Constance Hale[61]

EXERCISE: Add Verbs

Since character is habitual action, let's build a character from the verb up. Using your favorite thesaurus, zero in on the one essential, intentional action this person will embody every time they appear. Give it a whirl, either for a possible project or for an actual work in progress. Give yourself time and do some mindful digging so that you arrive not just at the easy result, but at the *best* one.

1. Identify the character's central void and how it impedes their happiness.

2. Choose active verbs that might spring from that void as a credible solution for this character's ongoing predicament (n.b. a perfect opportunity to break out your favorite thesaurus).

3. Boil those options down to about 5-10 possibilities and try them on, see which ones the character can embody for the entire length of the story/series. Next to each verb, describe how using that action would subtly shift the character's portrayal in the story.

4. Using that list of possible actions, let's get specific. Narrow your list of possible actions to the one option which best expresses their void. Is there any way to amplify its expression as the story advances? How does this action reveal the absence that occupies all their thoughts and influences all their behavior?

- BONUS ROUND: Sell the story to an A-list actor using nothing *but* the action. Pretend you're casting the miniseries based on this book: What would you tell the lead actor who asked, "What do I get to *do* over the course of the season? What's my deal? Why should I choose this project over a cookie-cutter blockbuster?" Make sure your answer would appeal to that actor and the worldwide audience the show would require to get renewed for several seasons.

Chapter 8: OBJECTIVE

An action...achieves an objective.

Characters cannot exist in a vacuum. A story needs context and conflict. All your characters pursue actions that affect each other and the world they inhabit. Audience attention gravitates inexorably toward whoever has the highest stakes and whoever needs to achieve their objective the most. Nobody wants to read a book about a clump of boring oiks who do nothing, so all those actions need to be directed outward.

At what, though? All that force needs some kind of focus. Humans do things because they want things...basic primate appetite at work.

If a character *pulverizes, what* gets pulverized? If a character *persuades, who* gets persuaded? If a character *plants, what* gets planted? All those amazing verbs need targets for their actions. Each character needs to make stuff, take stuff, fake stuff, break stuff throughout a story...but who or what?

Every character wants something they believe will give them happiness, summing them up as a single sentence: **"I want to" + action + objective**. Their action aims at something, a story goal you make meaningful for your readers, powerful and alluring enough to lead a character all the way through the events of the book.

"The greater danger for most of us lies not in setting our aim too high and falling short; but in setting our aim too low, and achieving our mark."

Michelangelo[62]

Transitivity

An action is an intentional event...to achieve an objective.

Before we dig deeper, a word about species of verbs, because my students always urge me to break this topic down in greater detail.

This next section goes out to all the grammar nerds, who should feel free to skim or skip ahead if they like. If you aren't a grammar nerd and have never thought about verbal valency, no worries. I'm breaking it down because you're a writer and words are your bread and butter. Grammar is your *knife*.

All verbs are not created equal. There are verbs and *VERBS*.

Every verb expresses the energy at work in a sentence (and a situation), but not all energy acts and interacts with its environment. When creating active characters, a savvy writer seeks out dynamic expressive actions to elicit strong emotions in the audience. Some verbs lack the basic dramatic heft to power a story, especially those which convey

- MOODS: cry, laugh, mope, whine, glow, rage, grin, fidget, sigh, glare, feel

- STATES: sparkle, nap, become, die, meander, sit, mull, meditate, persist
- REFLEXES: blush, yawn, shiver, twitch, cringe, blink, recoil, gurgle, flinch

Notice all these ineffective verbs describe entirely internal activities unrelated to anyone or anything else. They cannot be actions because they change nothing in the world around them. They can last anywhere from a moment to a week without anyone noticing or changing or reacting. A character built upon one of these verbs would exist in a passive bubble. Useless, for the purposes of verbalizing a story.

What you want is active, expressive language that captures meaningful, characteristic action. For best results, when you're identifying any character's action, the best options will always be **transitive verbs**—verbs that impact someone or something.

That makes even more sense when you consider the nature of sentences, their subjects and predicates. A transitive verb acts upon or interacts with a person, a place, a thing, or an idea. The subject exists because it *does something* in the predicate. What makes a verb transitive is the fact that it *requires* a direct object. Used in a sentence, the simple structure would be **Subject + Verb + Object**, as in

- "Mortimer poisoned the brandy." *Mortimer* is the subject, *poisoned* is the verb, and *brandy* is the object of that poisoning.
- "Vera kissed her dog." *Vera* is the subject, *kissed* is the verb, and *dog* is the object.

Transitive verbs *require* an object to receive their action, so that the subject interacts with the object. Used incorrectly, a sentence would consist only of a subject, a transitive verb, and no object. Without an object a transitive verb makes no sense. Imagine if you read

- "Mortimer poisoned." *Mortimer poisoned...* **what exactly? Poisoning requires someone or something to be poisoned. The need for an object is intrinsic to the verb's destructive action.**
- "Vera kissed." *Vera kissed...***her BFF? A ring? A llama? A single person cannot simply** *kiss* **because kissing is an act that requires a recipient or participant to receive the action of the intimate contact.**

In the quest for your story's verbs, **Always look for transitives**, aka *verbs which take a direct object* like *give, take, steal, climb, keep, seduce, attack,* and *convince.* For each of these verbs, the predicate of the sentence requires that the subject affect something: *give* **a gift**, *take* **a bite**, *steal* **a glance**, *climb* **the hill**, *seduce* **an enemy**, *attack* **a problem**, *convince* **your editor**. The presence of an object indicates transitivity. By definition, a transitive verb requires action directed at an object which in turn means your character must do something specific to cause change with conse-quences.

Transitives keep your characters subjective by giving them an objective.

There's a reason I gave this book a transitive verb as its title: authors must **verbalize** stories. "Authors" is the subject, "verbalize" is a transitive action, and "stories" is the direct object (and objective).

For authors, writing active prose is easiest with verbs that make stuff happen, not verbs that simp-ly...*exist* free of context. This goes triple when using verbs to inform an entire character via an *action*. Characters who simply *exist* do not make for page-turning exploits, rave reviews, or boffo sales.

Those "simply existing" verbs that do not impact the outside world are *intransitive*. They cannot take a direct object because they describe a vibe, situation, or involuntary motion. Some verbs are always intransitive, like *laugh*, *wink*, *come*, *go*, *sit*, *doze*, *shudder*, *fall*, *brood*, *remain*, and *expire*. In other words, you can *doze*, can be in a state of *dozing*, but you cannot *doze* <u>something</u>. So if you wrote a character who dozed all the time, you might instead say that they *escape* their problems in their dreams. "Problems" would be the object and "escape" is a perfectly useful transitive verb as the action.

Even subtly transitive verbs can work, but they re-quire authorial dexterity and brio to activate them. In Patrick Suskind's *Perfume*, the unique talent of the main character, Jean-Baptiste Grenouille, creates a strange narrative opportunity: his action is *to scent*, in the sense of "to inhale," "to track," "to discern," and "to apply" a perfume, turning what seems like a passive reflex into a compelling motive for mass murder. As an action, that's not something you can easily portray on stage or screen, but for the internal narrative of a novel, it's delicious and Suskind uses it in a bravura display unique to fiction.

Always make certain you can identify the specific object impacted by your subject and you'll know what your character wants, why, and what's in the way. If the verb is something they can do to or with another person or thing outside of themselves, it will make a terrific action. The quickest way to spot an appropriate character action is to ask yourself *"What or who receives the effect of this verb?"*

- If your character *stalks*, <u>what or whom</u> do they stalk?
- If your character *ravishes*, <u>what or whom</u> do they ravish?
- If your character *elevates*, <u>what or whom</u> do they elevate?

Remember the Law of Inertia: objects in motion tend to stay in motion and objects at rest tend to stay at rest. Active characters will remain active and passive characters ditto. Choose those verbs so those folks can steer the story all the way to its conclusion.

Intransitive verbs present a special kind of trap in character creation because they are often verbs of passive *activity* rather than action. They describe conditions or circumstances but carefully sidestep agency, intention, and focus.

Be you ware! As actions and tactics, intransitive verbs almost guarantee dead scenes because they trap the character in a bubble, isolated from the world and unable to accomplish anything. Intransitive verbs *cannot* take an object, so they need not affect the surrounding circumstances and people. A character based on an intransitive verb would simply...be. Their entire role can be summed up as a passive *condition*.

For some reason, newer writers will often default to intransitive character actions because they feel moody and philosophical (he *gripes*, she *sparkles*, they *linger*); this can quickly gum up the works, because the character exists in a solipsistic bubble. Intransitivity in the character verbs is one of the first things I look for in beginner manuscripts because it's so common and so easily remedied.

Some intransitives, called phrasal verbs, can fool you because they pair with prepositions to seem transitive (to *yearn* <u>for</u>, to *gossip* <u>about</u>, to *interfere* <u>with</u>), in a kind of transitive drag. Most phrasals have several meanings: you can *make out* with someone or *make out* a detail. Yes, they can work, but with a caveat. The danger is that sneaky preposition that bridges the gap and filters the energy between subject and object. All too easily a character can simply start to *yearn* or *gossip* or *interfere* without <u>an object</u>, leaving them marooned inside their own head and heart. Result: passive beat, dead scene, inert character, boring book.

To complicate matters further, some verbs can operate as either transitive or intransitive depending on whether a direct object receives the action. With these flexible verbs, context is everything. For example:

- He *drives away.* In that sentence "drives" operates intransitively and "away" is the preposition indicating direction.
- He *drives* <u>a bus</u> and *drives* <u>his friends</u> bonkers. In those, "bus" and "friends" are the objects of two different kinds of driving.

Other examples of flexible verbs that go both ways (depending on presence of an object) are *think, eat, demonstrate, burn, escape, play, indulge,* and *survive.* And every one of them can be replaced with far juicier, inherently transitive synonyms. Pro tip: flat or inert verb options tend to be common, overused, and undramatic.

Even some transitive verbs present a unique challenge. Grenouille's action *to scent* only works in *Perfume* because he is so terrifying and destructive. His story manages to activate a potentially dull action. Marcel Proust does something similar with *In Search of Lost Time* and his unnamed Narrator whose action is *to recall.* A subtle action requires virtuosic prose and a tolerant audience, which may be why so much literary fiction favors "passive" transitive actions and why it's a hard sell to general audiences.

Genre readers want dramatic events so that they feel something; they demand amazing exploits by fascinating people (and notice: *want* and *demand* are transitive, and *events* and *exploits* are the objects). Any character who remains a blank, passive cypher detached from their environment will kill a story by force of inertia (also note: in that sentence "remains" is intransitive). Characters built around intransitivity don't *do, dare, take,* or *make* **anything. They can't. They have no object or objective.**

Happily, you can transmute all intransitive verbs into transitives easily:

- Mattie *shines* becomes Mattie *overcomes* <u>naysayers</u>.
- Naima *relaxes* becomes Naima *shirks* <u>work</u>.
- Sam *freaks* becomes Sam *demolishes* <u>the office</u>.
- Tyrone *sulks* becomes Tyrone *ruins* <u>the ceremony</u>.

How can you spot intransitives? The simplest way is to try and identify the object taking the action of the verb. If you cannot, the verb is intransitive. Ask yourself: what are my characters doing in this scene and to *what* or to *whom* are they doing it?

Remember Suskind and Proust. You *could* create an entire character around *remember, observe, justify,* or *mull,* but your reader isn't going to be bowled over by emotion unless you have *mad* literary skills and an indulgent publisher. Passive and intransitive verbs bog down characters because they allow inertia. The more internal and abstract the action, the more dynamic and dramatic the *targets* required for those actions to entertain.

For best results, make sure that action shows the character doing, getting, or making something (i.e. transitive verbs). States of being (aka intransitive verbs) make for very digressive, internal actions not really suited to genre fiction. Whenever editors complain about flat characters or inert scenes, look beyond passive voice to the subtler culprit: passive *verbs.*

Aim for clarity and let dynamism guide you. Choose actions with range, heft, and emotional consequences, and your characters will bring your stories to life by default. Always push your verbs as far as you can. Stronger choices and vivid language will clarify and dramatize your work instantly. For example, you could articulate the same scene as either

- INTRANSITIVE: She *washed* in the lake. (i.e. a circumstance or state of being)
- TRANSITIVE: She *scoured* the gore from her arms. (i.e. a directed action with an object, "gore")

Which seems more compelling, specific, and resonant? Which sets the scene and conveys the emotional experience clearly? Use the most dynamic, dramatic language to help readers experience those emotions for themselves.

Keep your audience focused on the page. Remember, always verify you're using the action transitively by confirming who or what receives the action in the resulting sentence. **Genre fiction is dramatic because it is grammatic.**

Over time, the transitivity habit will become second nature, and you'll avoid the dreaded swamp of intransitivity at all pains so you can make your cast take action that matters. To that end, get to know your own bad habits.

- Do you default to intransitives or bland, unmemorable actions? Train yourself to upgrade feeble "existing" verbs and activate them with a clear goal that charges the situation.

- Is your pantry of verb options limited by education or laziness? Reading more widely and mindfully is easy, educational, and inspiring. Great language makes better books.

- Do you often get stuck inside a character's head or trap them with intransitives? The simplest solution is to focus on their specific objective. What are they making, taking, breaking, or forsaking? Choose verbs that can only engage the world around the character.

- Unclear about the target of your character's action? Don't know what they want in the story? Pinpoint the specific story goal they believe will bring them happiness. Specify exactly where they put their attention and why.

But wait! There's more! This storytelling technique is a *twofer*. Because transitive verbs are so visceral and compelling, they also drive all marketing and sales language. They lubricate and fuel the purring engine at the heart of your blurb, bio, and all your promo materials. By verbalizing your stories, you have a leg up on the challenges of marketing it effectively.

Grammar to the rescue! Know your actions and you can pitch your book to anyone you meet, from agents to potential fans. Learning to use them effectively will make the story stronger *and* help you sell it once it's finished.

Remember: **Action is transitive.** Active characters deserve a verb worth doing that makes their story worth telling. So, if your character is going to be *doing* this stuff transitively, what are they doing it *to*?

"You are the prism gathering all the white light of experience and in turn throwing your spectrum onto the page."

Ray Bradbury[63]

EXERCISE: Trans Mission

Even the most dynamic character has moments in which they simply *exist*, but that kind of downtime can be dead weight. One useful trick is to activate verbs by identifying their objects. The following are intransitive activities that you can transmute into dramatic actions:

- MOODS: *cry, laugh, mope, whine, glow, rage, grin, fidget, sigh, glare*
- STATES: *sparkle, nap, become, die, meander, sit, mull, meditate, persist*
- REFLEXES: *blush, yawn, shiver, twitch, cringe, blink, recoil, gurgle, flinch*

Choose 5-7 of these (or other intransitive verbs) and see what transitive language you can come up with to turn passive *activities* into fascinating, characteristic *actions* appropriate for your character. Give them a target outside themselves so they don't bog down inside themselves.

Next time you catch a character involved in some pointless, boring activity, see how you can make that moment matter by upgrading it to a meaningful action.

MacGuffins

An action is…caused by a character in order to achieve an objective.

Modern readers are not what they once were. In the 19th century, a combination of middle-class literacy and mass-market printing created armies of readers fascinated by complexity and digression. The modern novel roared to life larded with incident and digression that padded books with shameless maximalism. Audiences wanted more: more setup, more description, more backstory, more complexity, more context, more symbol, more poesy, more *words*.

In the 21st century, not so much.

While overlaps exist between film and fiction, the differences are vast and fundamental. Fiction excels at subjective, internal transformation, but film favors external action and concrete targets. Hollywood's output has eroded patience, teaching modern audiences to expect simpler, more linear entertainment that colors inside the lines. Gradually books have adapted to that altered public appetite with regard to subjects and their objects.

Film plots have to be so streamlined and audience-friendly that literal *objects* become critical to the filmmaking process: weapons to find, wealth to steal, monsters to slay, innocents to save, trophies to claim. It's always easier to take a picture of something, *anything*, and for many movies the exact nature of the thing is almost irrelevant. *Instant story, just add goal.*

Alfred Hitchcock called this kind of overarching story bait a **MacGuffin**, a term originated by screenwriter Angus MacPhail. A MacGuffin (emphasis on the *guff*) is a physical plot device serving as the linchpin of a story's stakes by providing a literal focus for all actions, a specific target of pursuit and tension, visible onscreen, concrete in conflict, without agency of its own, that gives characters something clear to struggle over.

Think of a MacGuffin as the big rope in the tug of war between the characters. MacGuffins create intense motives in all directions merely by existing. Classic examples include

- the Maltese Falcon (*The Maltese Falcon*)
- the Arkenstone (*The Hobbit*)
- the letters of transit (*Casablanca*)
- el Corazon (*Romancing the Stone*)
- the Queen's diamond studs (*The Three Musketeers*)
- the Ark of the Covenant (*Raiders of the Lost Ark*)
- the pearl (*The Pearl*)
- the Golden Compass, the Subtle Knife, the Amber Spyglass (His Dark Materials series)
- King Solomon's Mines (*King Solomon's Mines*)
- the letter (*The Letter*)
- the One Ring of Sauron (*The Lord of the Rings*)[64]
- the White Rabbit (*Alice in Wonderland*)
- the Archive (The Dresden Files)
- Rebecca (*Rebecca*)
- the forbidden manuscript (*The Name of the Rose*)

- Clyde Wynant (*The Thin Man*)
- the Death Star plans (*Star Wars*)
- Chef Anatole (*Jeeves and Wooster* stories)
- the Holy Grail (*The Once and Future King* and Arthurian legend)
- Helen of Troy (any story based on the Trojan War)
- Rosebud (*Citizen Kane*)

...as well as any number of "critical" weapons, letters, treasures, trophies, microfilms, charms, antidotes, briefcases, serums, dossiers, rings, incriminating evidence, and other pivotal objects of desire that are critical to your characters but irrelevant to the audience. Any time several people in your story are focused on a single visible item of value that drives and shapes all their actions, you're using a MacGuffin.

Notice how many of these MacGuffins provide the literal title for the story that features them. They exist to provoke curiosity and focus attention, full stop, which is how *The Pearl*, *Rebecca*, *The Letter*, and *The Maltese Falcon* got their titles. Ditto the pivotal objects in Philip Pullman's His Dark Materials trilogy as well as Harry Potter and his series of magical MacGuffins (the Philosopher's Stone, the Chamber of Secrets, the Deathly Hallows, etc.). They foreground the objective and state outright where everyone will and should pay attention.

Another feature of MacGuffins is how often they seem arbitrary, bizarre, and valueless outside the context of their narrative. As Hitchcock said, 'The main thing I've learned over the years is that the MacGuffin is nothing...nothing at all." How many of us would be willing to die for *Citizen Kane*'s Rosebud or *Strictly Ballroom*'s big trophy for the Pan-Pacific Grand Prix Amateur Five Dance Latin finals? Their worth is strictly situational, anchored in community and communal values. Only the characters need to care about them, but they need to care *completely*.

Hitchcock purists sometimes argue that sentient objects like Helen of Sparta/Troy, the White Rabbit, or Sauron's One Ring cannot be MacGuffins because they *influence* others, but I'd counter that even if not literally inanimate, a MacGuffin is a charged target with the primary function of focusing the actions of all the other characters. Its purpose is indirect and intransitive: *it only exists to be wanted*. They pursue no action. The force a MacGuffin exerts is not intentional, but almost *gravitational*.

At the same time, even if MacGuffins lack agency, I don't believe all MacGuffins are inert. Their very desirability shifts alliances, skews conflict, and alters the path through the story. They cannot take direct action, but their inherent power and contextual value alters every beat in a story with an inexorable magnetic pull. They don't *act*, they exert gravitational force that bends all actions in their vicinity.

By using a MacGuffin, filmmakers focus intention and attention on something you can capture with a camera. Because the camera needs something to shoot, abstraction doesn't work on film. What a MacGuffin really does is make a character's actions *visible*. They do something to something.

Inevitably, MacGuffins tend to be more common in film than fiction. Film excels at passive objects of desire, which makes cinematic sense: less time wasted, less exposition, more cool objects to want. The same cannot be said of a book. In a book, passive objects of desire go stale quick because fiction affords *plenty* of room for unpacking inanimate objects beyond simply *showing* them. Literary characters can easily pursue abstract, complex, and contextual objectives...which (incidentally) is a big part of why so many movie adaptations suck. Fiction focused on MacGuffins turns formulaic quick.

MacGuffins are *objects* of desire because they require a *subject* to make stuff happen; more importantly, they are *objectives* that force *subjective* actions. Think of how many heists, fights, and rescues appear onscreen and how few moments of ambivalence, subtlety, or emotional complexity. Which is easier to film? For much of Hollywood and its audiences, any story without a MacGuffin is automatically unfilmable and unwatchable. MacGuffins exist to excite and incite tangible action.[65]

Modern audiences have little patience for elaborate or subtle goals. They come by it honestly because a steady diet of MacGuffins has taught them to crave stories that show them *what* to want, clearly and directly. Midcentury modernism at its most brutal: factories produce *things*, advertising sells *things*. Herein lies one of the primary differences between film and fiction. Herein lies a great shift in popular consciousness.

This modern MacGuffin addiction has had a profound impact on storytelling. Today's readers have learned to feel more comfortable with concrete prizes and cinematic conflict, and writers have taken the hint. External action makes a film option much more likely because abstraction and ambivalence frustrate some readers and *all* showbiz executives. Ever wonder why some genres can't seem to catch a break in Hollywood? Note how adaptations happen for books with obvious MacGuffins that look good on camera. There's a giant piece of that puzzle: stories driven by unfilmable goals fight an uphill battle for adaptation.

Novelists aren't generally focused on creating a filmable object for characters to pursue. Fiction is more internal, subjective, and psychological, so authors don't need to automatically resort to the shameless cinematic device of a MacGuffin. In point of fact, most books that translate well into film do exactly that, but MacGuffins aren't *intrinsic* to fiction.

Still, the ubiquity of MacGuffins has been engraved in the popular consciousness, and authors should harness that familiarity whenever appropriate. Giving your characters a specific target links scenes and escalates tactics throughout a story. If it makes your projects more film-friendly as well, no hardship there, but a literal external MacGuffin doesn't work in all genres and stories. The urge to make a book screen-ready can ruin a story out of the gate because unlike film, fiction happens primarily *inside* your readers.

What fiction does best, film can't do at all.

So what would the fictional, figurative equivalent of a MacGuffin be? As it happens, genre fictioneers already have a perfectly useful analog, and although it's less evocative and less tangible, our term is simpler, clearer, and infinitely more practical. What Hitchcock called a MacGuffin, many novelists would simply call an **objective**.

Objectives don't *need* to be filmable, or even visible, because fiction takes place in the reader's head. A classic MacGuffin is literally, physically visible, but an objective often isn't. In fiction, objectives tend to be internal, general, passive, unformed, hidden, and/or steady. They are big enough to pull a whole story like a locomotive and universal enough to require little explanation.

We can easily grok Dracula's thirst for <u>life</u> (*Dracula*) and Jeeves's insistence on <u>order</u> (*Code of the Woosters*) without relying on a concrete totem. Easy enough to communicate a character's inner logic and passions just based on the mechanics of point of view. When reading, a character's thoughts and emotions are the shiny bits, the ploys and not the toys.

Characters pursue the objectives they want, and wanting those objectives brings them to life and brings readers into the story.

> "We call it the 'MacGuffin.' It is the mechanical element that usually crops up in any story. In crook stories it is always the necklace and in spy stories it is always the papers. We just try to be a little more original."
>
> Alfred Hitchcock[66]

EXERCISE: Big Picture

MacGuffins don't work for all stories, but even when they don't, they can help focus abstraction so that your character's needs acquire heft and clarity. Let's get hands-on with your character's ultimate story goal.

What concrete item, person, or place might be able to represent happiness for your character? Is their satisfaction achievable with concrete film-friendly targets?

1. Choose an observable symbol of your protagonist's happiness.

2. Decide exactly what it would look and sound like in a movie trailer.

3. How long would it take you to explain the value? How could you speed that process up?

4. Write a paragraph describing a thirty-second "trailer" that makes the MacGuffin's power and possibilities for this protagonist apparent.

5. Design/describe a poster that captures this MacGuffin in one image.

- BONUS ROUND: Try to create an inherently *literary* MacGuffin that would fail on film, only revealing its full impact in fiction...something abstract, subtle, and complex that could never be summed up completely in cinema (or a poster). Great fictional objectives often revel in narration and point-of-view shifts to expose tantalizing slices of their full potency. What kind of objective couldn't be "dumbed down" into any literal object that is exactly what it seems?

Achievement

An action...achieves an objective...made meaningful to the reader.

An objective must be *achievable*.

A vague or unachievable objective leaves your character with nothing to do moment to moment because they have no clear intention, can take no steps, and accomplish no changes. Their actions and tactics will lead them nowhere in particular unless they have a shot at success or failure. Your character will only pursue their objective for the entire story, against the odds, if they believe it will bring them happiness.

As story goals, **Objectives represent the desirable future**.

As authors, we just have to provide a fascinating pattern and manipulate it to evoke emotions. An objective gives your character something to want, a goal big enough to sustain an entire story. Even if you cannot find a way to make it tangible and interactive, a character objective needs to be

- CHALLENGING enough to sustain your character throughout the story's length.
- SIGNIFICANT enough to attract character attention and to inspire escalating risks.
- RELATABLE enough that anyone can grasp the character's need to pursue it.

It must be all three, because **Objectives power the larger narrative like a locomotive.** They pull a character across a risky landscape past every moment of doubt or darkness toward the possibility of happiness...a desirable future. High stakes won't matter unless someone has a chance of beating the odds, and does so at great risk and cost.

Objectives establish the emotional scope, scale, and tone readers can expect because they tap a story's power and resonance. The kinds of objectives you give your characters will attract a specific audience with specific expectations. In a sense, objectives are the root of genre, subgenre, and voice because they mean everything to your cast of characters.

Think of each objective as a mountain that needs climbing. What a character wants gives their action and tactics a trajectory. For plotters, objectives make structure a snap, and for pantsers, it gives you a clear target upon which to riff. It gives audiences a reason to give a damn.

The relative risk attached to the objective determines your story structure and stakes: if the character succeeds in achieving the objective, happiness results; if the character fails, unhappiness results. For any amount of reader engagement and tension, failure must be at least as possible as success, if not more so.

The objective renders characters subjective (aka accessible, relatable, empathetic.) It demands meaningful decisions from your character around a universal story goal. Give them an objective worth risking everything to accomplish and worth ruining their lives for should things go wrong. The threat must be there for the reward to mean anything. The objective must be almost impossible to attain and absolutely essential.

Easiest way to know you've identified the real objective: it must force the character to face their void (aka the greatest fear, deepest wound, and/or defining error) and find a way to *live* with that void at the story's end. A real objective creates crisis and helps the character *make peace* with that void.

Will this character's actions lead to happiness? The objective is the form that happiness takes, and because it is abstract, it shares many fundamental characteristics of Hitchcock's MacGuffin. Like a MacGuffin, an objective

- can only be accessed via high-stakes choices. (DIFFICULT)
- can be achieved/acquired/accomplished...or *not*. (CONCRETE)
- only exists to be wanted and has no agency. (DESIRABLE)
- cannot affect the character directly. (DISTANT)
- focuses all the character's actions. (CLEAR)
- provides a source of energy for the character. (CHARGED)
- derives its value from circumstances and demonstrates consequences. (CONTEXTUAL)
- reflects the meaning and morals of this particular person. (CHARACTERISTIC)

Thus, an effective objective is difficult yet concrete, desirable yet distant, clear yet charged, and contextual yet characteristic. It provides the spine of the character's passage through the events of the story, and at every point in the story, it points to the knowable past and possible future of the character so readers can empathize.

Objectives shore up an entire narrative arc for a character. By being distant, the objective creates a path between where the character is and where they want to be. Readers discern the pattern of the story and the characters because their actions align with clear objectives. The events inspire real emotions because you make those objectives challenging, significant, and relatable for the audience.

So much of the reading experience is internal and subjective that objectives in fiction tend to be abstract. The constellation of objectives in a book establishes the tone and stakes in play, with each character pursuing a personal story goal that contrasts with others.

- *The Silence of the Lambs*: Clarice Starling wants justice. Hannibal Lecter wants freedom. Jame Gumb wants transformation. Dr. Chilton wants fame. Jack Crawford wants resolution. Katherine Martin wants survival. Senator Martin wants control.

- *Pride and Prejudice*: Lizzy Bennet wants respectability. Mr. Darcy wants honor. Mrs. Bennet wants attention. Mr. Bennet wants peace. Mr. Wickham wants leisure. Lydia Bennet wants permission. Charles Bingley wants approval. Caroline Bingley wants admiration. Charlotte wants security. Mr. Collins wants status. Lady Catherine wants obedience.

- *The Hitchhiker's Guide to the Galaxy*: **Arthur Dent wants stability. Ford Prefect wants adventure. Trillian wants escape. Zaphod Beeblebrox wants adulation. Marvin wants sympathy. Slartibartfast wants recognition. The Heart of Gold wants cooperation. Frankie and Benjy want success.**

Three high-stakes stories in three vastly different genres, tones, and voices. The objectives establish the narrative boundaries and emotional landscape. Wanting a date and wanting to prevent a holocaust can be equally dramatic, but the highs and lows of those options will generally indicate the emotional ride your readers can expect. Essentially, a character's energy could be denoted as (*Action*: Objective): Dracula must (*Drain*: Life). The matrix of objectives in a story becomes thematic and universal without devolving into propaganda. Audiences learn to love the kinds of experiences you can provide and resent when you fail to meet (and exceed) their expectations.

Because the objective takes the entire story to achieve (or not), the character must continually adapt and re-strategize to get it. If we consider this grammatically—**Verb + Target + Progress**—then a character's ultimate path to happiness would be rendered as **Action + Objective + Adjustment = Story**.

Remember my point about GMC as an expression of time? If a character's action expresses their energy over the course of an entire story, then their objective is the abstract focus of their persistent action for its duration. Each character's action occurs in pursuit of that personal objective. Separate scenes simply show them each working to accomplish that story goal in smaller, concrete, tactical stages.

> "The Promised Land always lies at the other side of a wilderness."
>
> Havelock Ellis[67]

EXERCISE: Prize Fight

Knowing precisely what your character wants makes a huge difference to the writing and reading experience. Unlike a MacGuffin, a fictional objective will often be internal, general, passive, unformed, hidden, and/or steady because it is the desirable *future*.

Thinking in emotional, abstract, and universal terms, pinpoint the clear thematic objective that will receive your character's action throughout the course of the entire story. What matters enough for them to risk everything they have and rattle everything they know? Make certain this story goal is

- CHALLENGING...to their illusions, their safety, their relationships, their future.
- SIGNIFICANT...to their hopes, fears, schemes, dreams, experience, growth.
- RELATABLE...to all readers, but especially in this neck of the genre woods.

Test out several options. Don't be afraid to mix and match, to expand and contract the scale of the objective.

For characters who have relationships, consider objectives in relation to each other. Note how different objectives change the trajectory of the character's participation in the story and interactions with other characters. See what happens when different characters pursue similar objectives for radically different reasons because of their voids or actions.

Chapter 9: MOTION

An action...makes another event possible.

The collision of the character's actions and the reader's imagination create the illusion of a living, conscious person with feelings and thoughts beyond the words on the page. The words are necessary in the same way a stem is necessary to hold a blossom—but the blossom is what most people remember and praise.

Great fiction depicts characters not as passive, static objects but as fascinating subjects in a continual state of emergence. I tend to approach characterization as a *process*. Character moves us, not because it's a statement, but because it's a complex question that requires a story to get close to an answer.

- What does it mean to live a life?
- What constitutes happiness?
- How do people change?
- How does the past point us toward a future?
- What is the value of intentions or actions?
- Who deserves our grace and when?
- What matters most to each of us?

Character is not aspect, affect, or attitudes, but habitual action. **Action requires intention**, a character pursuing a *goal* because of *motivation* **despite** *conflict*. What does the character want? Why do they need it? How does that challenge them? Actions always spring from the void that haunts a character and steers them toward their objective as best they know how.

In the words of Sophocles, "Knowledge must come through action."[68]

Behavior and description are all well and good, but characters reveal themselves in the doing and pursuing. Obviously, any story can only provide slivers of detail; those gaps are filled in by the audience, in much the same way we extrapolate and project onto folks we encounter in our lives. We complete the pattern because that is how we "get to know" people we meet.

The reason we form emotional bonds with these imaginary beings is because we decode their details and gaps the same way we approach all the people in our lives. Our brains and our hearts don't know the difference.

"Look at that tree. It is the protagonist of all arts. It is an ideal structure of action. Upward movement and sideways resistance, balance and growth."

Richard Boleslavsky[69]

EXERCISE: Couch Potato

Want to develop your verbalization skills while you're vegging out? This is a fun activity to do whenever you're watching a show or reading a story you're already somewhat familiar with. The next time you rewatch a beloved movie/show or reread a keeper novel,

- identify a list of potential actions for the main 3-5 characters and narrow those verbs down to the best candidate.
- pay special attention to the words *characters* use to describe their own and each other's actions. (n.b. screenwriters often telegraph actions as a crutch for lazy directors and actors.)
- note when the actor seems to be reinforcing or contradicting that action through (potentially) un-scripted choices.
- track the actions for those characters for the entire movie, verifying that the action coheres, even as the tactics stretch and adapt to meet circumstances.
- BONUS ROUND: dissect a pivotal scene between two or three primary characters and determine the tactics used in the scene that reflect their main action. Who wins? Who loses? Who compromises? What's the impact in the next scene?

You'll be amazed what this teaches you about the stories you've loved all your life. Every time you revisit a story, you may discover shades and texture that change your interpretation significantly. This game is a favorite in my house and one that pays serious craft dividends over time.

Range

An action is ... meaningful to the reader which makes another event possible.

As the Law of Inertia teaches us, objects in motion tend to stay in motion and objects at rest tend to stay at rest. Characters who start out doing, daring, getting, and making keep on rinsing and repeating until they change the *world*. Physics and energy and *verbs* are on their side.

In the same way, a healthy tree can turn the sun's energy into leaves and branches, a character can turn personal struggle into visible growth. Action makes emotions external and characters accessible, turning the black squiggles on the page into intimate friends, fascinating events, and worlds worth visiting.

Actions are character energy made visible. Action is the transmutation of external conflict as internal progress.

Characters *are* their actions on the page. The clearer and stronger those actions, the clearer and stronger the characters because readers can easily form a relationship with them, experience emotions about them, and invest in their "reality." On the other hand, if you leave characters vague or inert, the reader's only options are to *invent* actions for them to explain their presence or to discard your work in favor of an author who knows how to do their job properly.

To me, the most compelling aspect of fiction is that rather than telling us what we should believe, it shows us a story and allows us to reach conclusions. In the case of *great* fiction, a story can change the course of a life or reframe history.

Have you ever read an author who seems to be writing the same book, the same cast over and over again? They're stuck in an action *rut* using the same comfy choices they know how to navigate easily. The window dressing may change, the setting and the personalities shift, but the characters and emotional ride stays identical and the reader can feel it almost immediately, even if they can't articulate the cause.

Standing water gets stagnant. How many times can you sit on the same merry-go-round before you die of boredom? Recycle actions at your peril, because eventually you'll drive off even your most devoted fans by provoking their disdain and impatience. If you orbit the same types of action repeatedly, you need to excavate that action with fascinating new tactics each time. A professional gives readers an entertaining emotional ride or everyone stops bothering.

You don't find diamonds digging in a sandbox; give me granite and a case of dynamite.

Whenever characterization gets blurry or you cannot figure out what your people are doing on the page, just ask yourself, what do they want...and what are they doing about it? **Intensity signals intention.**

Again, the best actions will always come from characters pursuing specific objectives they want rather than avoiding something they don't want. Beware of the urge to write characters who *avoid, escape, dodge, flee, shun, evade.* Yes, those verbs are technically active, but as actions they tend to skew negative and reactive. The resultant characters can easily leech the life out of a story.

Negatives undermine, positives underline. Let them aim for the future and a win rather than escaping the past or a failure. No one can escape the past or erase failures, so that's futile and uninvolving as a dramatic choice. The void may motivate them, but it's their positive actions that inspire engagement in your audience. By focusing on the future, living forward, your characters won't become mired in backstory.

Obviously, any action can work, but **The more negative the action, the more ruthlessly specific the objective required** to keep that action active. If you have a character who avoids, they need to avoid one specific, tangible thing or person, not a concept, memory, or idea.

What is the in order to for the character? Seek the purpose rather than the cause of the action. Instead of asking why a character acts, ask for what reason. Instead of allowing the past to push them from behind, allow the future to pull them toward their goal.

Pursuit is always more specific than avoidance. Because of its generality and passivity, avoidance can also make characters less empathetic, so opting for negative actions or negative objectives makes your job harder. Remember, offer positive intentions in pursuit of a specific objective. Turn your character's energy loose on the page.

Be careful with protagonists who only take action (and use tactics) upon *things* or *ideas* rather than the other characters. Books aren't theatre and everyone doesn't have to play off their fellow actors, but anyone who stays in a bubble will start to hamper story events and alienate your audience. Give your characters chances to shape each other while they're risking their illusions and changing their world.

Choose those actions carefully! You're going to have to live with them for the duration of the project. If you're smart, they'll even turn up in the cover art process, editorial meetings, and promo efforts as well. A smart action pick at the outset will also guard against

- flat, forgettable, or frustrating characters who resist dramatization.
- sagging middles, bland storylines, ho-hum endings.
- skippable or repetitive love scenes, combat, and conversations.
- skewed harangues or choir-preaching that feel like author intrusion.
- dull obligatory encounters or "meet-n-greet" filler.
- supporting roles that feel like devices, mouthpieces, or plants.
- murky hooks, generic blurbs, and forgettable promo copy.

Don't leap to the easy explanation or pop psychology. If a specific action seems perfect for no logical reason, honor your artistic instincts. Digging deeper into your character's oddball intentions might reveal fascinating potential. Embrace placeholders! You can always upgrade.

When you feel like two separate verbs are equally appropriate, look for the common denominator, just as though you were doing arithmetic. Darcy *dismisses* and *indulges* and *obeys* and *insists* at various points in the story, but none of those behaviors are his singular driving action. Reducing him to myopia doesn't begin to capture his full characterization. In Darcy's case, what one verb could contain the full range of to *dismiss*, to *indulge*, to *snub*, to *obey*, to *bestow*, to *insist*, to *propose*, to *oppose*? Why does he do these contradictory things? *To preserve.*

Darcy *preserves* everything and everyone he encounters, for good and ill. *Preserving* is how he snubs Lizzy, dodges Caroline, manipulates Bingley, placates his aunt, and rescues his sister, why he lets Wickham off the hook both times, and how he wins Lizzy in the end. *That* is his action. Those other, contradictory verbs are only secondary tactics that appear in specific contexts. So when you're action-shopping and face that kind of contradiction, look for the common denominator to complete the emotional equation. Character actions *don't* change.

Often when someone insists that their character's action changes, they haven't actually identified the action at all. The urge to swap out an action often masks the impulse to stay down in the weeds of individual scenes and tactics rather than considering the character as a coherent figure. Character is habitual action. Your job is to balance the need for consistency and transformation.

By the same token, beware of generic assumptions or the urge to *minimize* your characters by blunting their energy with weak or vague actions (which leads to flat, hackneyed portrayals). Anytime you catch yourself saying "She just wants..." or "He's only driven because..." you're weaseling out of the action, reducing your characters' deepest personal goals to something suspect or silly.

Get in the habit of accepting their actions full force, at face value, and you'll have an easier time shading and rendering those actions believably. Minimizing and assumptions undermine characterization. Embrace the forces that drive your character and they will pour onto the page.

"Storytelling reveals meaning without committing the error of defining it."

Hannah Arendt[70]

EXERCISE: Booster Shot

One of the suckiest things about mass-market entertainment is its perpetual erosion of our language in its attempt to be all things to all people. Without continual effort and exercise, our verbal muscles can atrophy.

Let's upgrade some lackluster transitive verbs to see how you can amplify their potency and precision in ways that might reveal characters. Choose one pair of actions below and see what you can do to ramp up both antonyms in different ways.

Stretch your vocabulary and sense of character by providing 3-5 "upgraded" actions to stretch their essential energy and reveal different kinds of action. Play with each verbal pairing to see how many different types of opposition are possible and what kinds of characters result.

- *push/pull, join/split, lead/follow, start/stop, call/answer, give/take, think/feel, like/dislike, open/close, grow/shrink, win/lose, ask/answer, make/break, hurry/slow, learn/forget, teach/study, help/hurt, save/spend, clean/dirty, cook/eat, lift/drop, show/see, permit/refuse, move/still, allow/refuse, right/wrong, loan/owe*

Look to push each "meh" verb duo to several clearer choices using evocative and dynamic language. Note that the strongest option may not be the most "X-treme" or lurid. Instead, focus on clarity and dynamism. Again, try to create actions that work for you as a writer; they should inspire you and challenge you, sparking potential scenes and hinting at meaningful friction.

Chain

An action is an intentional event...which makes another event possible.

I throw a ball and you grab the ball—both are required for the action of "to catch." You offer your hand and I shake it—the action "to greet" each other. For an action to occur, a subject makes an offer and the recipient of that offer reacts to it, positively or negatively. The action creates **closure** between adjacent moments, thereby creating a causal chain.

As in our comic book example, the action occurs in the imaginary gutter between the offer and the response...which in turn leads to another action. Actions build upon each other in a long chain of cause and effect linking character to character to spin a yarn.

Without consequences, characters exist in a vacuum. Every action causes contextual counter-action. Let each cause produce each effect, which in turn become the next cause. **Action is always reciprocal.**

Write the *cause*, and the effect will follow as a matter of course. As characters interact, individual actions create closure by connecting two events via each character's intentional effort, bridging time and linking objects and people together with causality and meaning. Action stitches that character's story together like a needle, beat to beat, scene to scene, with the action threaded throughout. Energy flows through the story, transforming everything in its path.

The best part: by rooting your characters in action, every moment they appear will generate emotional impact by default.

Remember, readers need to be able to track cause and effect to create closure. Without clear dots to connect, your audience starts to lose track of the story and the emotions at play.

Different authors approach action with varying degrees of magnification. Some writers prefer broad strokes and big pictures, others need every moment hammered out in advance. Keep finding ways that characters can take actions that allow other things to happen. No matter the degree of detail, fascinating action is every author's stock in trade.

Can a character's action change? *Nope.* Not if you want them to seem like a coherent person to your readers. Not if you want readers to recognize them as themselves and empathize with them like real people. Character *beliefs* often change in stories, but they must *act* like themselves for that change to be believable. A character's action lasts for the length of the story, just as the objective is their goal for the entire story. As disasters force decisions, your character will have to rejigger their behavior to stay on course, but that course will always be aligned with the character's action because what they *do* is who they *are*.

Character is habitual action. Change the action, and you're now writing a different character. Invariably, readers experience action-hopping as disjointed or inauthentic portrayals and cry foul. The urge to change that action has more to do with quick fixes and easy buttons than actual authentic characterization. The purpose of a story is to see that clash of forces play out fully and believably.

Characters do not change, they *unfold*, gradually manifesting more of their essential energy as events force them to learn and adapt, to risk and grow. Story events can change a character's beliefs, knowledge, experience, skills, perspective, choices, and behavior, and if you're writing a series, the character's next story will dangle a new *objective* on the horizon, but that character's *action* remains consistent, so the character will.

At the end of *Emma*, Miss Woodhouse still *claims*, Mr. Knightley still *scolds*; they're just claiming and scolding in ways they hadn't previously. In the Hunger Games series, Katniss Everdeen *hunts* for her family, then hunts her enemies, and ends up hunting for vengeance, justice, peace, and love...but her essential *hunt* persists as long as she does. In his hardboiled milieu, Philip Marlowe *questions* everything and everyone with dogged skepticism. Tom Ripley *manipulates* the people and wealth he admires with relentless sociopathy.

As Brian Boyd puts it, "Story offers us intense concentrations of character information."[71] Although their behavior and circumstances might change over a story, characters remain fundamentally who they are. Their voids persist at their cores, bending all interactions inexorably, and so their action continues as well.

Over time you'll develop a robust lexicon of inspiring verbs that stoke the coals and fan the flames. Start collecting juicy transitive verbs and notice when one of them sparks an entire story idea. Test them and share them with your colleagues. No one will ever write an action the way you can—that's the magic of voice.

By stretching your language, you feed the muse exactly what she craves. Developing stronger verb options will expand the books you can verbalize, the audiences you can attract. Try to become as fluent, as adept as possible in the language of actions, because it is the language of storytelling.

"Traveler, there is no path. The path is made by walking."

Antonio Machado[72]

EXERCISE: Big Ripples

Actions have impacts. No matter how subtle, timid, or surgical characters may be, their movements through a scene affect everything and everyone around them. Take a moment to examine the reverberations around a character and how they shift the story and the other characters' paths through it.

1. Choose one of your favorite scenes, either your own or in a book you admire, and identify the point of view character's action.

2. Identify the before and after context for the character, this person's circumstances immediately prior and subsequent to this scene.

3. Spot the ways the character's action in the scene connected those dots for themselves and the reader.

▪ BONUS ROUND: Do the same for additional participants in the scene, unpacking the shifts caused by some and imposed upon others. Who or what causes the shifts? How do those shifts alter the scene's flow without altering each character's essential action?

Links

An action is...caused by a character... which makes another event possible.

As I've said, contrast is the simplest, strongest, swiftest tool an author can use to generate energy and attention. Ever wonder why so many story couples and mortal enemies start out on opposite sides of whatever divide? The contrast makes their story more emotional and easy to tell. Characters are sculptures who carve each other. Remember?

Relationships are shown by the effect characters have on each other.

If two people stand next to each other for forty years without having an effect or any kind of consequential interactions, then they don't have a relationship, they have *proximity*. Whether friend or foe, people develop feelings about each other based on growth and experience, which requires significant impact in both directions. Friction between actions creates meaningful relationships, and that's what your readers expect.

Put more simply: **No Effect = No Relationship**

Much of the beauty of a successful relationship is the paradoxical coherence that unites two personalities so that one plus one equals *possibility*. Somewhere between "opposites attract" and "birds of a feather," fictional unions embrace complexity and apparent contradiction to create an unshakable payoff for the audience. The most powerful relationships arise from the oppositional energy of **antonyms**.

Whether romantic partners, grim adversaries, and anything in between, you're looking for maximum contrast. Your primary characters must generate enormous friction, so oppositional actions will always stack the deck in your favor. For best results, always give your lead characters actions that directly conflict. Make it impossible for these opposing forces to coexist, let alone cooperate and keep them directed toward each other at close range.

Since I write romance, I always frontload the collisions of my two main characters by establishing juicy conflict from the get-go via antonymic actions: *create/destroy, purify/corrupt, charge/defuse, expose/conceal, heal/harm, disrupt/control, thrust/parry, gather/scatter, praise/curse.*

Those primal, energetic struggles compel our attention because of the actions that drive them. Many of these oppositions come down to directions: their energy moves at cross-purposes. We can't help but rubberneck because the dramatic question goes beyond right or wrong to the commitments and compromises that drive all great relationships. The actions demand the story get told.

Try and find a genre classic that doesn't pivot on that kind of binary, can't-live-with-'em-or-without-'em opposition, I double-dog-dare you.

Pride and Prejudice provides a perfect example: Lizzy *provokes* and Darcy *preserves,* each of them initially convinced the other's behavior is rude and capricious. Lizzy *provokes* family, foes, friends, censure, laughter, upheaval, consternation, and a stream of marriage proposals; her pert, precise approach to life makes for delicious repartee and a well-earned happily ever after. Darcy *preserves* his honor, his friends, his name, his fortune, and his sister's reputation, not to mention the future of the Bennet family; his adamant resistance to change and upset makes him as inscrutable and infuriating as we could wish but also hints at his solid, simple goodness under all the trappings of rank and fortune.

The innate conflict between *provoke/preserve* powers all their scenes together and apart, so that we keep looking forward to the next catastrophic collision with relish.

Moreover, Lizzy's urge to *provoke* bullies and blockheads delights us but gets her into piles of trouble with everyone she encounters. Austen surrounds her with ancillary characters who bait, defy, and inspire her worst, most provocative impulses: a detached father, a silly mother, a slutty sister, an amoral cad, a haughty hero. Those comedic foils provide additional conflicting actions perfect for making her progress through the story as arduous and wrenching as possible; their horrible actions provoke her to earn her happy ending.

And again, can you tell me what color Lizzy's "fine eyes" are? *Nope.* How about her birthday or her middle name? What she eats or when she hit puberty? Trivia counts for nothing when the clash of opposing energies creates unforgettable drama and comedy. Don't forget that this extends beyond couples: *True Grit*'s Mattie Ross (*Punish*) and Rooster Cogburn (*Recover*), *Beloved*'s Sethe (*Sacrifice*) and Beloved (*Devour*), or *Bleak House*'s Lady Dedlock (*Treasure*) and Josiah Tulkinghorn (*Corrupt*).

For the purposes of illustration, here are some other coupled **antonym** examples:

- *Persuasion*: **Anne Elliott** (*Yield*) **and Captain Frederick Wentworth** (*Command*)
- *The Girl with the Dragon Tattoo*: **Lisbeth Salander** (*Hack*) **and Mikael Blomkvist** (*Bait*)

- *The Princess Bride*: **Westley** (*Rescue*) **and Buttercup** (*Spurn*)
- *Rebecca*: **the second Mrs. de Winter** (*Expose*) **and Maxim de Winter** (*Bury*)
- *Dune*: **Paul Atreides** (*Wake*) **and Chani** (*Subdue*)
- *Brokeback Mountain*: **Ennis Del Mar** (*Hold*) **and Jack Twist** (*Share*)
- *Fried Green Tomatoes at the Whistle Stop Café*: **Ruth Jamison** (*Soothe*) **and Idgie Threadgoode** (*Defy*)
- *A Streetcar Named Desire*: **Blanche Dubois** (*Conceal*) **and Stanley Kowalski** (*Penetrate*)
- *Les Liaisons dangereuses*: **Vicomte de Valmont** (*Ruin*) **and Madame de Tourvel** (*Worship*)
- *Fingersmith*: **Sue Trinder** (*Dupe*) **and Maud Lilly** (*Copy*)
- *Sense and Sensibility*: **Marianne Dashwood** (*Indulge*) **and Colonel Brandon** (*Grant*)

Adding a third party to the mix with a love triangle just ups the complexity and possibilities, because you want *three* antonyms opposing each other. *The Hunger Games* sets up Katniss Everdeen (*Hunt*), Peeta Mellark (*Feed*), and Gale Hawthorne (*Consume*) for intense conflict because hunt/feed and hunt/consume make for two very different relationships and sets of issues. *The Color Purple*'s Celie Harris (*Question*) makes her way from Mister (*Crush*) to Shug Avery (*Celebrate*). *The Age of Innocence* allows Newland Archer (*Chal-*

lenge) to love Countess Ellen Olenska (*Defy*) even as he surrenders to May Welland (*Bend*).

In most romantic triangles the verbs almost dictate the final pairing by telegraphing the most emotionally satisfying outcome for the genre concerned. And most final pairings that leave audiences irked have ignored the powerful chemistry created by antonyms. With love triangles, mismatches, and other romantic complications, thoughtful verb choice can create enough legitimate tension to charge any situation and justify subplots.

Again, you don't have to agree with the actions I've ascribed to any of these characters; those paired antonyms are what *I'd* use to tell those stories as I understand their distinct emotional rides. You might have a completely different take, and the actions you chose would reflect your authorial voice. This is the great strength of characterizing via verbs: stories are written. All writers know *plenty* of fabulous words and use them idiosyncratically.

When in doubt look to the contrast, identify the straight line/wavy line in each relationship, and make certain their actions generate interesting friction every time they collide, whether they're your main couple canoodling or a protagonist and antagonist locked in mortal combat.

Don't forget that the need for opposition extends beyond your primary duo. All of your characters complicate each other's actions meaningfully. Secondary characters will inevitably *reflect* or *reject* the actions and tactics of your primary characters.

- REFLECT: In these instances, they boost a primary character's behavior, often taking it to an extreme that underlines the risks. For these folks, think about how to push main characters' actions to their limits.
- REJECT: These characters operate as foils, forcing your main characters to question their choices and alter their courses. With them, exacerbate doubts your main characters already harbor.

At every opportunity, look for ways to complicate the progress toward each character's goals via the opposing actions of the rest of your cast. Obviously the topic of secondary characters and casting in general deserves deeper discussion, but for now make sure that all your folks change each other. Each one of them should have a meaningful impact or else they probably don't need to show up on the page at all.

As I said at the outset, characters are sculptures who carve each other; everything they do affects the efforts of everyone around them.

> "The noun of self becomes a verb. This flashpoint of creation in the present moment is where work and play merge."
>
> Stephen Nachmanovitch[73]

EXERCISE: Counter Action

Once you have a feel for individual characters, they need to start pulling their weight every time they appear. The characters around your protagonist will *reflect* or *reject* that primary action via their own actions, creating meaningful relationships on the page.

1. Start with a character you feel confident writing and identify their action.
2. Make a list of synonyms and antonyms surrounding those opposing actions, almost an "action cloud" of narrative possibilities around them.
3. Divide those verbs into two columns to REFLECT or REJECT the characters' action.
4. Identify the *other* characters who will undertake those reflecting or rejecting actions over the course of the story.
5. Allow your story to conjugate all the characters as they hamper and hasten each other's efforts, noting how those synonyms and antonyms create alliances and tension in the story.

- BONUS ROUND: Identify the antonym that is the action of another main character (love interest, antagonist, etc.) and see how the characters identified above REFLECT/REJECT this person's action. Are additional folks necessary to fulfill those functions for character?

Part IV: Tactics

"Strategy requires thought, tactics require observation."

Max Euwe, chess champion[74]

Chapter 10: FLOW

A tactic is a strategic re-action.

Character is habitual action, and that action should be expressed as a transitive verb.

Of course, a character can't simply "be" one word relentlessly in every beat of a book. Genre audiences bore easily. One-note roles have no place in solid storytelling. No one wants to read about a protagonist who "attacks" everything in sight like a frantic piranha. And frankly, characters *react* to circumstances.

Plateaus suck narratively, so each character's actions need to develop over the course of a story. What about variety, subtlety, and complexity? For characterization to ring true and wring emotion from readers, it needs melody, shape, and resonance.

This leads us directly into the issue of **tactics**. While each character's action remains consistent and coherent for the entire narrative, the *expression* of that action shifts in response to context and consequences. As problems arise and strategies change, your character's behavior must evolve and escalate. Their action and objective remain the same, but the concrete expression in a scene will reflect the new information or altered dynamics as a range of options within the primary action. **Tactics are *re*-actions specific to a scene.**

With my main cast, I identify a fundamental action for each and then add a list of potential tactics that I can use over the arc of the novel. Scene by scene, your characters adapt to circumstances and adopt strategies to help them attain their objective by the story's end. These facets of the action reveal their different layers.

If your sidekick's main action is "to polish," that intention can take many forms over the course of the story. Polishing can be

- as literal as *scrubbing* silver with a brush.
- as abstract as *enforcing* a rigid social code.
- as complex as *training* a triage unit.
- as subtle as *rubbing* buttons obsessively.
- as drastic as *remodeling* a house.
- as simple as *cleaning* every morsel off any plate.
- as figurative as *bartering* for plastic surgery he cannot afford.

In this way, the character's action *to polish* expresses itself during the story as the tactics *to scrub, to enforce, to restaff, to rub, to clean,* and *to barter.* The character's action remains consistent, but as in life, the expression of that action shifts to new synonymous tactics in response to escalating circumstances and shifting conflict.

Action makes energy visible through the story; tactics make action visible in each scene.

The accretion of those connected tactical shifts engages readers and makes characters *feel* real. Tactics reveal texture and adaptation without abandoning coherence. Instead of *telling* folks what to feel, you're *showing* them imaginary interactions that will inspire real, powerful emotion. That relationship is personal and persuasive. The audience develops their own opinions and impressions about the people on the page the way they do in day-to-day life.

Actions are character energy made visible. The corollary?

Tactics are character actions made tangible. Tactics are the transmutation of internal conflict into external progress as characters inevitably adapt to the pressures of a given context.

Rather than trying to capture energy, we portray its visible effects. The action is what they do for the length of the story, a tactic is what they do in a given scene (or beat). Starting from concrete verbs reveals the flow of the story at that point. Each new tactic further unpacks the action.

A tactic is a strategic re-action adopted by a character in order to handle an object significant to a scene that requires an external response.

Let's break that definition down. A tactic is

- *a strategic re-action*. Tactics redirect a character's effort, shifting the action's unique energy and goal during a beat or scene.
- *adopted by a character*. Tactics result from a story participant's evaluation and decisions as they respond to new experience and information.
- *in order to handle an object*. Tactics filter the energy of a subject in pursuit of a clear scene

goal, which amplifies tension and transformation to keep readers on-edge and off-balance with anticipation.

- *significant to a scene.* Tactics take the small, necessary steps leading to the character's overall goal, making the impossible merely improbable, which amplifies stakes and emotional engagement.

- *that requires an external response.* Tactics change the game for all the other characters, forcing re-actions from them in kind, revealing the dynamics and relationships around the character.

Tactics get used and discarded, adopted and adapted depending on the character's needs in a scene. Action processes external conflict as internal progress, resulting in new, improved tactics.

Tactics should be significant to a character. They shift as external events demand new strategies from a character. Essentially the character might say, "To [*action*] in this situation, I must [*tactic*] to advance toward [*objective*]."

Since actions don't change, tactics are individual *re-actions* to events based on strategy and prior experience. They literally reframe the action based on the most recent understanding of a situation.

A balanced set of tactics will illuminate your character's internal landscape and external stakes. These facets of the action provide believable, dramatic *re-actions* to the story's events as they unfold and impact the character. Whatever your protagonist's action, tactical shifts can drive quiet contemplative scenes, oddball shenanigans, and visceral confrontations, giving your audience windows into the character's deepest and most personal impulses.

Moreover, tactics arising from an action bestow instant coherence to every person on the page—they're always acting like themselves because tactics are *synonyms* of the action. Alignment! You will never write blurry or passive characters so long as you know exactly what they are doing and why it matters so much. Characters believably pursue the goals important to them but respond to events dynamically and strategically.

Please know: my aim here is not to force you to construct tottering heaps of verbs, but rather to show how grammar and a few clear word choices can drive an entire story, charge the writing process, and spark a reader's imagination. The rest is taste and temperament. How deep you drill into that web of interconnected behavior depends on your own process and ambitions.

Notice that race, age, class, gender, and all the rest of the "impersonal ad" line items don't even factor yet, because we're still unpacking the *action* that drives the character's story. Without a word about appearance, occupation, or backstory, these tactics already suggest a rich panoply of scenes and reactions and complications regardless of characteristics.

A clear set of tactics gives you perfect leverage to shift scenes that aren't gelling or to buttress saggy stretches of plotline. Even better, you will always know what to write and how to write it because the characters will act as they must in any given situation. Actions and tactics are literally *words* to prompt your writing. Characters have meaningful things to do and life gets in their way.

- May Welland might seem like a pallid ingénue because she *bends* to propriety when necessary, but she also *bends* everyone to her will. (*The Age of Innocence*)
- Claudius isn't just a stammering cripple, he *fools* his treacherous family long enough to outlive all of them and become emperor of Rome. (*I, Claudius*)
- Auntie Mame is more than a wacky relative, she *embraces* life by adopting her nephew, marrying an oil man, and exploring the world. (*Auntie Mame*)

When a character fires on all cylinders, each tactic connects to and approaches the scene's object via cause and effect. In a story that ends with hope (aka comedy in the classical sense) the tactics will steer the action directly to a successful accomplishment of an objective. In a story that ends in despair (aka tragedy in the classical sense), the tactics will push the action inexorably toward disaster, one step at a time.

"Art, at those moments when it feels most like art—when we feel most alive, most alert, most triumphant—is less like a cocktail party than a tank full of sharks. Everything's for keeps, nothing's for exercise."

John Gardner[75]

Shifts

A tactic is a strategic re-action adopted by a character.

Tactical shifts unlock a character's action, unpacking that core verb in fascinating facets appropriate to every beat, shift, and encounter. Their subtle contradictions allow for meaningful paradox and sidestep banality or cliché. Yet because they all derive from that same action, each tactic helps paint a coherent portrait of a single complex life.

Those connections and collisions tell your story. After all, verbs express *energy*, so those tactics reveal how a character will navigate a specific scene.

In other words, the character pursues their action for the entire story but uses a new tactic in each scene (or beat, depending on story complexity). Since the tactics derive from the action, the character *coheres* and still shows significant variation and gradation that aligns with their essential nature. Think of tactics as rungs on the action ladder; as they accumulate, the character climbs toward their objective one confrontation, one discovery at a time.

You can even state the primary tactics for a character as "[*Character*] **must** [*action*] [*objective*]**, even if**

201

s/he has to [*list of tactics*] to make that happen." In essence, tactics keep a character from devolving into a type, a trope, or a narrow cliché. Handled correctly, your character's tactics can

- enrich your plot with texture, depth, and subtlety.
- flesh out your cast of characters believably.
- evoke powerful, personal emotions in your audience.
- take your story in surprising, delightful directions.
- generate unexpected pathos, suspense, wonder, and laughter.

Since every scene is an attempt to change other characters, the struggle between characters plays out in the realm of tactics. Characters can, will, and should never change their *action*—that essential verb defines and describes their energy in the story—but **Tactics change constantly due to conflict**.

In a scene with other characters, a tactic attempts to bend another character's action to obtain a desirable result. Another way to frame a tactic: "I am going to [*tactic*] because [*other character/thing*] must [*action*]."

Can tactics repeat in different scenes? Absolutely, but not with the same characters in the same context. If you are going to revisit a tactic, make sure you escalate its application and change the context—regurgitation blows, but resonance packs a punch.

Tactics that shift directions keep an audience on the hook. Bore your readers and they'll head for the hills.

Stories do not move in straight lines. Circumstances shift, emotions change, and molehills become mountains, unstoppable forces meet immovable objects.

As an example, let's tackle *Les Liaisons dangereuses* with the idea that Valmont's verb is "to ruin." Over the course of the novel's 175 letters, Valmont's action (*Ruin*) frees him to *ignore* decorum, *cheat* his friends, *indulge* his worst appetites, *spoil* his mistresses, *seduce* and *torment* a saintly woman, *manipulate* his peers, *ravish* anyone willing, *wager* his happiness for kicks, *rape* and *corrupt* a rival's virgin daughter, *wreck* his only alliance and *wage* a social war, *revel* in the shame he sows, *betray* his own moral code and the only person he's ever *loved*, *deceive* and *duel* an innocent boy into murder and exile, and finally *sacrifice* himself for the happiness he *forfeited*. All of those tactics "ruin" his friends, enemies, *and* his own carefully orchestrated life as a wealthy libertine.

In every scene, Valmont's ruinous energy practically smokes off the page. He ruins everything he touches, but his arc over the course of the story lets him ruin along a rich, complicated spectrum: *ignore, indulge, spoil, manipulate, ravish, wager, seduce, torment, rape, corrupt, wreck, revel, sow, betray, love, deceive, duel, sacrifice, forfeit.*

Once you unpack all those tactical possibilities, you can see the scope of an entire character arc laid out in charged chiaroscuro. The scope and gradations of all his tactics illustrate his appetites and reveal his character. If you squint and muse, you can almost discern a faint story outline, because they expand in power and gravity toward the finish. The tactics oscillate and escalate as Valmont goes to further lengths to ruin his life in more impossible, irrevocable ways, until he's ruined his entire world and everyone in it. In the world of that novel, the Vicomte de Valmont *is* ruin.

Of course, every other character around Valmont has their own *action* that conflicts directly with his and refracts believably in a series of unfolding *tactics* to create tension, suspense, drama, and spectacle. Actions collide with actions and others react with unexpected results. Tactic answers tactic, unlocking the energy that drives the emotions of the story one scene at a time.

By shifting each character's tactics along a dynamic spectrum, you get to explore all the possibilities of that character's energy, objective, and conflict. **Changing the direction changes the tune.** The audience gets to form their own impressions and emotional relationship with the character. And through core alignment, the character gets to express the full scope of their hidden self as they struggle toward happiness against all odds.

Talk about bang for buck!

Even better, as your protagonist's action unfolds, your *other* characters will shift to react, deflect, assist, derail, and amplify their effort. Since each character has their own action to play over the course of the story, the tactics in their scenes intersect dramatically, which will help you flag the narrative possibilities and mine the story's energy for emotional impact.

Places to grow, people to be.

Let's take our *Les Liaisons dangereuses* example again. Valmont doesn't operate in a vacuum. The rest of the novel's cast must deal with this *ruining* force directed at, around, against, and through them.

- Merteuil (*Dominate*) baits, conspires, deceives, spars, torments, preys, seduces, disarms, poisons, and punishes her ally for derailing her own plans.
- Tourvel (*Worship*) honors, refuses, prays, submits, violates, confesses, and forgives her seducer's fatal flaws with fatal results for them both.
- Cécile (*Indulge*) demurs, protests, permits, resists, relents, wallows, abandons, and then educates herself with relish.
- Danceny (*Court*) praises, trusts, woos, supplants, beseeches, betrays, quibbles, rebukes, rails, and fences his rival to his death.
- Rosemonde (*Excuse*) advises, warns, spoils, defends, apologizes, scolds, and caters to her nephew's stratagems.
- Azolan (*Serve*) labors, connives, compromises, debauches, spies, finagles, and assists as his master destroys himself.
- Volanges (*Deny*) snubs, pretends, preens, wheedles, begs, bargains, surrenders, and ignores the signs of impending doom.

All of them *ruined* by, for, and with Valmont, but each of them playing their own game in the story, because *their* personal action refracts as individual tactics in scenes. The secondary characters' tactical impact on each other illuminates their relationships in all directions and reveals the perilous emotional and energetic landscape of the story.

Even perusing those verb clusters provides a map of how the scenes would unfold, how the story would escalate, how characters would act. The tactics tell the tale: facets of each character's action reveal their individual subtext and history. Verbalizing the story characterizes and dramatizes it as well.

Readers form real emotional connections because the actions play out in real-time specifics before their mind's eye, encouraging them to engage directly and authentically with a group of imaginary French aristocrats in the 1780s.

The energy on the page fires readers' imaginations, and as they create narrative closure, the story plays out in their heads and hearts.

"When you see a good move, look out for a better."

William Wayte[76]

EXERCISE: Turn Signal

Coherence and consistency shouldn't mean predictability. Straight lines and easy answers can turn a book into lukewarm oatmeal. A savvy author learns to stir the pot and spice the stew to keep readers and characters on their toes.

Identify 3-5 contradictory tactics used by a character in a specific context. Find untried and unexpected alterations to a character's approach to the story challenges they face. The tactics always align with the action, but you should look for the surprises buried within them, waiting to sprout. Look for the salt in the sugar.

When in doubt, *dissect* those verbs, digging through the synonyms of synonyms and the subtle variations and nuances that keep a character coherent without being monotonous. Unpack the shades of meaning and paradox within the actual word to find unexpected digressions and quirks that might shake things up for all the characters.

If you're revising an existing story, look at different scenes to get at the extremes of the character; if this is for an unwritten project, list 3-5 tactics that feel appropriate for the theoretical character. Find the common denominator linking them.

Steps

A tactic is...adopted by a character...significant to a scene.

How do you eat an elephant? One bite at a time.

The best way to handle a large task is to break it up into small tasks. Your characters have intense, meaningful objectives. To accomplish them, or even get close, they need to get tactical. Actions will reveal character attributes *incrementally* via tactics. Opponents and obstacles challenge the character, which require changes in tactics that illuminate the character's strengths and flaws.

If your character's action is the staircase, the tactics are the steps.

This technique will allow you to push your fiction as far as you dare. Pay attention where it counts and your characters will do the heavy lifting in your manuscript because they *can*. Tactics are literally *re*-actions, making strategic adjustments and course corrections to keep the character on the path toward their objective, shining on that distant horizon at story's end.

Aspects of the action reveal subtext and history without need for exposition or info dumping. In the simplest terms, tactics are synonyms of the character's action; in fact, I think of them as synonyms+ because they can often extend beyond direct synonyms to encompass synonyms *of* synonyms that reveal hidden depths in a character's action.

Pro tip: **For best results, tactics must be specific to the character and personally significant.** Because you're using words the audience knows, the closure is instinctive, and the coherence inevitable. Even without knowing the verbs you're using, an audience will discern the pattern at work under the story because that's how brains work. Snooze and you lose, heed and you lead.

When assembling possible tactics for your character, *synonyms* make a great starting point, especially with verbs that reveal a range of meanings and interpretations (e.g. Hiro Protagonist's action *to hack* means "decode" but also "slice," "pirate," "invade," and "endure"). Additionally, if you want to introduce subtle variation in characters, try investigating synonyms of *those* synonyms that will lead you to tactical possibilities off the familiar, over-trod path.

For example, if a character's action is *to seduce*, list the synonyms for juicy tactical candidates and then extrapolate via the synonyms that resonate. *Seduce* yields some fabulous tactical synonyms, and they in turn offer further evocative variations that help change the tune while honoring the melody. A whole array of potential *seduce* characters presents itself in the thesaurus:

- ENTICE: lure, allure, draw, entrap, coax, persuade, induce, cajole, hook, bait
- DISHONOR: shame, humiliate, defile, discredit, stain, abuse, affront, reject, sully
- VAMP: tease, dazzle, display, flatter, costume, enchant, appeal, adorn, primp
- WRONG: violate, abuse, demean, malign, cheat, injure, discredit, harm, offend,
- MISLEAD: hoodwink, misrepresent, fool, exaggerate, delude, blindfold, impose,
- DEBAUCH: pervert, pollute, corrupt, spoil, pimp, ravish, violate, subvert, vitiate
- INVEIGLE: con, sweet-talk, manipulate, maneuver, wheedle, bamboozle, exploit
- BETRAY: double-cross, abandon, renege, dupe, expose, forsake, divulge, unmask

All of these tactics connect to the *seduce* action, and by choosing the most appropriate, resonant options for your story, you could create many different types of character who *seduce* in ways particular to them. Depending on the context and object in any given scenes, you're depicting vastly different people. A "Seduce" character who *defiled, vamped, hoodwinked,* and *unmasked* in their scenes would bear little resemblance to a "Seduce" character who *entrapped, shamed, maligned,* and *abandoned.*

Proceeding via two or three degrees of synonymous separation delineates that character's action refractively, keeping the character's behavior in different beats and scenes coherent, but variegated. Look for dramatic range by way of directions, contradictions, and paradox in the synonyms, which produce fascinating tension in a character. Take pains to eliminate any sneaky intransitives, which have a habit of insinuating themselves. Language is strange and flexible.

Think laterally, not literally. Above all, follow your gut...pushing for what your character would do, want, take, and make in scenes. Little by little the central action will be surrounded by glittering, dynamic, tactical facets that reveal internal complexity and suggest narrative arcs. Keep asking yourself "Would my character react in this way in any situation? If so, why and when? How would they use this to attain their objective?"

Verbalizing is the core work of characterization and story planning, following your instincts and choosing the right words to capture your people on paper. The more you work with verbs and zero in on solid candidates, the better you know the character and the more concrete detail and language you know for your story. Beyond theory or abstraction, you can literally write **your scenes** *with these words.*

Tactical shifts delineate the beats of a scene. Changing direction keeps things moving and fascinating as characters must now push, pull, join, and split depending on the circumstances they face. And the scenes deploy the tactics in a rising, escalating arc toward the biggest and most dramatic tactical option.

Of course, this works in stories because it reflects what successful people do in life: If/Then/Therefore.

- They want something and take concrete action to get it.
- They shift tactics to deal with complications that arise.
- They keep ramping up the tactics until they succeed or they've exhausted every possibility and accept defeat.

Every character pursues their action and eventually faces conflicts that require fresh tactics. Some tactics succeed, some fail, and some flail, but all of them occur in context as they collide with the actions and objectives of other characters. **Keep the basic primate logic of If/Then/Therefore in mind at all times.**

Obviously, inactivity and intransitivity should be avoided at all costs. They suck on the page and on the stage. Inactive characters make for deeply sucky stories. Just sitting around is not going to sustain interest for the time it takes to tell a tale. The more activity you allow in favor of legitimate action, the more likely readers will simply stop bothering.

Every once in a while, I get a student who tries to convince me that literature is littered with passive lumps. Not so! Supposedly, the classic literary example of perpetual inactivity is Hamlet. For centuries, scholars have insisted that the Prince of Denmark dithers, prevaricates, broods.

Balderdash!

Anyone who claims Hamlet is inactive hasn't read the play. His action is *to test* and his tactics get wild. He *stalks* a ghost and *traps* a murderer, *strategizes* and *plots* relentlessly, *annihilates* his fiancé, and *excoriates* the court, *avenges* his father in a *duel*, and *abdicates* his rightful throne in a violent public bloodbath that *exposes* "something rotten in the state of Denmark." All of those are intense transitive verbs impacting specific dramatic objects. His relentless *tactics* make him an unforgettable protagonist.

As it happens, Hamlet never *stops* taking action and *re*-acting via tactics; his only real hesitation concerns murdering the new king, his uncle, on supernatural hearsay, which would damn his soul, natch. His action, *to test*, unpacks in a series of fascinating, escalating dramatic tactics that destroy his illusions, rip his world apart, and leave almost everyone he knows dead on the floor around him.

Even the most immobilized, introspective character can make powerful choices with electrifying consequences. And if they don't, why are they in your book? Since each tactic is a *re*-action to a specific situation, things will happen and characters will change.

Given their action, consider the complex range of reactions of which your character is capable. Create predicaments they cannot solve with their standard bag of tricks. Learn what arouses them, what terrifies them, what enrages them, what paralyzes them. Take them right to the edge of what they think they know about themselves and push them off.

"Truly the beauty of life is its uncertainty."

Yoshida Kenko[77]

EXERCISE: Deep Dive

Unforgettable characters last because their energy spills over and into our lives and words. They stretch beyond the pages of the book that contains them. When you're verbalizing a story, you can tap into startling truths about life, love, pain, and loss if you trace an action all the way to its source. The easy option, the first attempt, the lazy solution might get the job done, but don't expect socks to be knocked off by half-assery.

Rather than going with what you know, take a moment to fully process all the possibilities embedded in a single action, allowing for paradox and unexpected texture.

1. Using several dictionaries, unpack all of that action's meanings, every nuance, root, and shade. What is that verb's origin and original meaning, history, and use? What double and quadruple meanings are buried in the word?

2. Flag anything that feels resonant or significant to the character, no matter how minor. Try to unpack

every possible facet in the action to get a sense of what possibilities exist for the character.

3. Choose 5-10 tactical re-actions that are direct synonyms of that action. Select the juiciest and most compelling, dramatic options that feel relevant and resonant for this person in this story.

4. Now expand your list with synonyms of those chosen synonyms, again looking for transitive verbs that will be fun to write and fascinating as the basis of the character's behavior in a scene.

5. Note how the character becomes clearer as you dig into that action. Notice how the character morphs to accommodate interesting possibilities.

6. Assemble a list of 20-30 tactics that all fit inside the bounds of this character. Don't be afraid to allow for paradox, surprise, and contradiction; in fact, you should aim for exactly that kind of complexity.

■ BONUS ROUND: Waste not, want not! Using the verbal scraps and notes left behind in your search, verbalize another, completely *different* character with the same action. Assemble the synonyms+ that you skipped and the quirks that didn't resonate for your original character. How would this character differ from the one you originally envisioned? What would they do to this story? Could they fit in any story? What made their components unappealing to you?

Shelves

A tactic is a strategic re-action...significant to a scene.

The way you verbalize your story will determine where you fit inside the fiction landscape. Certain actions and tactics suggest genres because they resonate for those audiences. We stand on the shoulders of giants. Thousands of authors have laid the groundwork for you within that stretch of the bookshelf.

In a sense, all conventional story patterns common to a genre (aka *tropes*) are nothing more than actions and tactics common to a genre. A "secret baby" romance requires someone to *impregnate* mom and someone to *conceal* the baby. A "revenge" thriller will cast characters who *avenge*, *stalk*, and *punish* others. Audiences seek out the emotional rides they enjoy, and they expect you to build that ride expertly, aware of their expectations and capable of exceeding them. That's your *job*.

Verb shapes vibe. By experimenting with different constellations of tactics for each character and actions for your cast, you can steer your story onto the genre shelf.

- What verbs serve your story and your characters best?
- What are the actions and tactics used by main characters in the current bestsellers in the genre? How about classics in the genre?

- Are there actions and tactics that get overused in this genre? (e.g. chase/solve/protect in thrillers or seduce/tease/indulge in erotic romance)
- How would the actions and tactics for these characters change in a different genre/subgenre? How would that alter the narrative?

As always, keep these tactics transitive and specific to the characters and context.

For my part, I suspect that audience tastes actually come down specifically to the kinds of verbs and vibes readers find entertaining. When a reader is bored by one type of book or drawn to another, it's because the actions and tactics resonate and evoke appealing emotions. Genre audiences show up expecting certain obligatory scenes, beloved archetypes, and new wine in old bottles. This is where good books provide *delight* by repeating a familiar pattern, but great books produce *beauty* because they expand the pattern's possibilities. This is a vast topic for another book, but one worth considering in some detail in your own projects: how will you meet and exceed expectations.

Always factor in the type of story you're writing and the connotations of those verbs for genre and subgenre. Subtle variations in meaning really will recast an entire scene or character. There's a great difference between a thief who *steals* something versus one who *swipes*, *pilfers*, *plucks*, *snatches*, **or** *lifts* it. Those distinctions may seem minute, but they redirect that character dramatically.

Consider the differences between mystery and romantic suspense...or even cozy and hardboiled and procedural. Fandoms thrive in such subtle gradations, and your verbalization will steer the story because verbs move the story along. Turning a boat even one degree can land you somewhere miles from the original destination.

In fact, when characters share the same *action*, their individual tactics will distinguish them as individuals and suggest trope and tone differences. Tolkien's Gollum, Jame Gumb in *The Silence of the Lambs*, and Benedetto in *The Count of Monte Cristo* share an action: *to covet*. All three characters are scary, dangerous, broken monsters, but *not* in the same way. Consider how much their differing *tactics* differentiate their paths and distinct insanities through their respective stories:

- Gollum (*Covet*): envy, beg, sneak, suffer, wheedle, cheat, steal, choke, snitch, skulk, submit, dissemble, throttle, plead, lurk, tear, connive, contrive, twist, endure, starve, manipulate, mislead, serve, strangle, snatch, divide, betray, mislead, stifle, conceal, guide, insinuate, suffer, gobble, poach, curse, slink, maim, boast. (*The Lord of the Rings*)

- Jame Gumb (*Covet*): desire, pretend, lure, disguise, disarm, hide, fetishize, pose, demand, chastise, stalk, dehumanize, violate, begrudge, abduct, strip, mutilate, bully, groom, scold, starve, hunt, design, secrete, nurture, incapacitate, dissemble, stitch, disfigure, skin,

217

glamorize, terrorize, harvest, assault, flay, startle.
(*The Silence of the Lambs*)

- Benedetto (*Covet*): resent, exploit, feign, coerce,
betray, abandon, cheat, revile, blame, disguise,
condemn, borrow, deceive, dishonor, bully,
mislead, demand, attack, escape, blackmail, rob,
forsake, accuse, pilfer, begrudge, case, feign,
dupe, elude, ambush, extort, contrive, purloin,
discard, murder, swindle, expose. (*The Count of
Monte Cristo*)

Different sets of tactics make for completely different characters in a story and different kind of books on disparate genre (and subgenre) shelves. In each tactical spectrum, you can discern the distinct emotional landscapes for each character, the ways their stories will differ, the hints of a character arc and an outline.

All these villains *murder*, *steal*, and *deceive* because they *covet*, but their unique tactics emerge powered by different voids, shaped by different aims. Their individual tactics reveal their position and capacity to interact with their worlds. As groupings, they signal the highs and lows of the emotional roller coaster each author provides to their audiences.

Likewise, each of their tactical sets reflect that character's genre. Gollum's fantasy setting pushes his coveting through four books into more mythic language (*wheedle, starve, curse, throttle, insinuate*). Jame Gumb's brutal serial killer thriller demands a covet that starts dark and gets bleaker (*stalk, abduct, groom, dehumanize, mutilate*). **Benedetto's covet** stays square in the middle of Napoleonic action-adventure tropes (*betray, forsake, blackmail, ambush, purloin*). All three people covet in drastically different modes.

Never underestimate the power of character energy to shift your book's tone and texture. When compiling a list of potential tactics, start from synonyms of a character's action and spiral outward to synonyms of those synonyms with mindful curiosity. Gather possible tactical shifts and potential *re*-actions appropriate to the *void* that pains this person and the *objective* pulling them toward the story's horizon.

Plotters and pantsers, take heart. Even if you know nothing about a story but its genre/subgenre and your looming deadline, you can easily use these tactical verbs to riff out a story using your superpower: *words*. Start with an active, transitive verb that feels inspiring or entertaining and then start digging for treasure in its synonyms and the synonyms of those synonyms. Little by little a character will emerge, which in turn suggests opposing characters, which in turn sketches out dramatic events.

In the interests of clarity, here are some examples of other tactical sets from different genres, listed after the relevant character name and parenthesized action:

- Miss Jane Marple (*Probe*): detect, overhear, irk, scrutinize, interrupt, question, encroach, track, trace, eavesdrop, interfere, recall, unearth, observe, prod, annoy, contemplate, note, unlock, rumor, dissect, inquire, organize, monitor, analyze, sift, mark, deduce, discuss, ferret, prod, examine, hinder, crack, trap, solve. (*Murder at the Vicarage*, et al)

- Hannibal Lecter (*Savor*): relish, compliment, appraise, charm, praise, twist, imply, insult, taste, inspect, degrade, teach, appreciate, study, inhale, examine, sample, torture, subvert, soak, consider, devour, savage, suggest, probe, rend, convince, spar, allude, weigh, scrutinize, enjoy, hint, indulge, corrupt, devour. (*The Silence of the Lambs*, et al)

- Willie Wonka (*Astonish*): delight, concoct, confound, surprise, trick, fabricate, explode, dismay, dumbfound, hatch, stun, insult, formulate, outsmart, daze, scold, develop, startle, expand, explore, astound, shame, shock, design, abuse, stupefy, plot, disconcert, stagger, devise, bewilder, berate, discard, embrace. (*Charlie and the Chocolate Factory*)

- Katniss Everdeen (*Hunt*): trap, track, shoot, climb, aim, provide, fake, lure, dispatch, supply, chase, snare, ambush, kill, adapt, stalk, feed, scavenge, pretend, smuggle, anticipate, slaughter, forage, prowl, attack, salvage, butcher, pursue, trace, decoy, eliminate, sacrifice, feign, shadow, execute. (The Hunger Games trilogy)

- Tyrian Lannister (*Negotiate*): conceive, pose, pay, assess, contrive, fence, bait, trace, project, steer, diagram, barter, charm, mock, effect, bribe, maneuver, plan, hire, compel, investigate, arrange, chart, fashion, defend, execute, formulate, accomplish, frame, compensate, spur, devise, manage, mastermind. (*A Game of Thrones*, et al)

- Empress Livia (*Poison*): insinuate, contaminate, defame, mastermind, spoil, conspire, pollute, corrupt, shame, excoriate, murder, dazzle, hint, exploit, infect, scheme, assassinate, tarnish, deceive, frame, pressure, devise, blame, advise, taint, debase, contrive, pervert, trap, condone, blight, tantalize, defile, afflict, beg. (*I, Claudius*)

- Tita de la Garza (*Cook*): feed, blend, hide, nurse, ignite, bake, concoct, invite, cherish, season, treasure, nourish, savor, brew, deny, prepare, obey, heat, maintain, spice, devise, inflame, nurture, relish, stir, nurture, scorch, raise, mix, boil, conceal, enrage, feed, roast, infuse, stimulate, sustain, burn. (*Like Water for Chocolate*)

- Jack Torrance (*Abuse*): drink, refuse, beg, menace, beat, chase, ignore, scold, exclude, tarnish, smear, assault, chase, neglect, scorn, promise, smash, imbibe, exploit, injure, indulge, devour, bully, mislead, drown, punish, haunt, malign, pursue, damage, batter, shun, neglect, toast, insult, attack, gulp, mortify, abandon, brutalize. (*The Shining*)

- Paul Atreides (*Wake*): rouse, discover, summon, demand, invite, study, gather, provoke, scan, boost, beckon, incite, scrutinize, stir, order, warn, assemble, analyze, shake, concentrate, tap, mobilize, excite, train, rattle, convene, rise, muster, amplify, challenge, risk, lead, terrorize, overthrow, command, rally, prophesy, ascend. (*Dune*, **et al**)

- Esteban Trueba (*Force*): crack, steer, exact, rape, coerce, impose, strong-arm, grasp, drive, split, rule, expel, push, impose, erect, oblige, oppress, lead, urge, inflict, demand, insist, bully, ruin, alienate, punish, break, order, manage, violate, squeeze, compel, smash, dictate, mutilate, direct, wrench, exile, regret, rescue. (*The House of the Spirits*)

Many of the strongest tactics will be direct synonyms of the character's action, and others will be related behaviors that help the character accomplish their primary action in unique situations. Tactics keep your characters active in every beat without forcing them to hammer the same nail from different angles.

You need never run out of actions or tactics as long as you use your words effectively.

Unlike impersonal ads or theoretical overlays, this verbal prep work anchors your hands-on knowledge of the character and lays a foundation for the scenes you'll end up writing. Not only will tactical work establish genre, trope, and tone, it forces you to think actively about how your cast acts and interacts with the events they'll face. Tactics should *elevate* stock characters and obligatory scenes.

But *wait*, there's more! Now you're writing the story from the roots, aligning your effort where it will repay the investment. Verbalizing the story encourages you splash around in the rich complexity of the actual literal words you can use for portraying those people and events on the page. When the time comes to write a scene, you know where and how and *why* you need to write it. *Win-win-win*.

How do you keep creating fresh stories, fresh twists, and fresh characters? With language. You *verbalize* them.

"Practice means to perform, over and over again in the face of all obstacles, some act of vision, of faith, of desire. Practice is a means of inviting the perfection desired."

Martha Graham[78]

EXERCISE: Genre-flecting

You may write in one genre for your entire career, but odds are you'll reach a point where you want to explore the limits of your turf. Learning how other categories verbalize themselves can unlock creative and professional doors you never imagined. Of course, other types of story bring their own musts and busts, risks and rewards.

In the interest of flexibility and curiosity, let's play a game with genre and trope shifts and verbalize a character for appearances in different genres and/or subgenres.

1. Identify a single action that suggests a character you'd enjoy writing.

2. Based on that one juicy action, come up with a list of tactics appropriate to different genres or subgenres, 10-20 each. (Bonus points for disparate genres,

e.g. Amish romance+cyberpunk+cozy mystery+occult horror)

3. Genre lists in hand, verify they each cohere for the character you originally conceived, that each tactic connects to the action and is a transitive verb appropriate to this person in a scene in this type of book.

4. Compare the range of these appearances. How do those tactics mutate when confronted with different worlds and tropes? What kind of *re*-actions become essential and/or inappropriate to the character given the genre constraints? Do any tactics overlap between genres? Are any tactics native to one genre but *verboten* in another?

5. Consider the role this character plays in the genre. What would you have to do to turn a hero into a villain or a sidekick into a hero without changing their action?

6. Focus on identity. How far do the tactics have to shift to make this character into a *different* character with the same action? See how far you can stretch the character while still basing tactics on that action.

7. Assess your odds. What unique strengths and skills would you bring to this genre? What habits and flaws would make the transition difficult? Which genre tropes and traps would need your attention?

Chapter 11: OBJECTS

A tactic...handles an object.

So you've identified the action your character embodies in the narrative and the objective throughout the entire story. Next you picked out a list of transitive tactics used in individual scenes that show re-actions to individual circumstances. Those tactics are also transitive, so they must be acting upon or interacting with *something*. What exactly are those tactics affecting moment to moment during a given scene?

After you pinpoint the overarching objective your characters care about most, you can see the dim outline of their story arc. Everything they are and do focuses on that one intention regardless of risk or damage. Maybe it's a house they want to buy, a reputation that needs rescuing, an unmerited promotion, an impossible marriage, a shocking masterpiece, a lucrative crime...over the course of your story, all their effort, anxiety, and strategy will bend toward that target with gravitational force: a single objective that means more than anything else in that character's world.

The trouble with abstract objectives is that they leave room for reader confusion and doubt, and that delays and complicates the pattern recognition process. Knowing what the character wants in a story doesn't always help you navigate individual scenes.

Learn to dramatize abstractions and make them visible on the page. I'm not suggesting you need to boil subtle complexities into cartoons, but audiences want a story, not a theoretical argument. Characters cannot interact with concepts. Give your readers something they can visualize. They want to know what the hell is going on!

Scenes are always about characters negotiating spaces, things, people, and power outside of themselves. You need to know what they want in each moment as they deal with obstacles and opponents in pursuit of that big, shiny objective that drives them through the whole story.

> "Only those who risk going too far can possibly find out how far one can go."
>
> T.S. Eliot[79]

Target

A tactic is a strategic re-action... to handle an object.

Happily, writers already have a word for those scene goals too, one that is both grammatically accurate and technically useful: *object*. An object conveys both a literal target and a simple linguistic idea: the *noun* that takes the action of the subject.

An object is a precise, discrete, visible goal during a scene. A canny author uses objects to make the objective visible, to create mini-MacGuffins to keep the modern reader connected to the action.

For best results, a singular *objective* galvanizes your character across the entire story, and you must make that objective clear and tangible in every scene via an *object*. The object acts as an avatar of that thematic objective. Thus, the action is what the character does throughout a story to accomplish an objective. The object is the person or thing they do it *to* in a scene. It creates the predicament this person needs to deal with in this moment. The objective is broken down into those objects as steps along the path of pursuit.

Every subject requires an object. You want people to pay attention, so something significant must happen, which means you need a character to do something and a target they can aim at. To do anything in a scene, a character needs an object they can be the subject for. People cannot exist in a vacuum. Stories require meaningful context, and an object provides the obstacle or opponent during a scene.

The average reader may find an abstract objective difficult to visualize and dramatize in the nitty-gritty of story events, but an *object* distills the objective into something specific, tangible, and interactive during each scene.

- An OBJECTIVE is the *story goal*, the desirable outcome pursued by the character throughout the book made specific, tangible, and interactive during each internal beat. The objective is the *why* of the story and the reason the story involves the character.

- An OBJECT is the *scene goal*, the character's objective made specific, tangible, and interactive in an external beat. The object is the *why* of the scene and the reason this particular scene includes the character.

The transitive verbs of the character's action and tactics impact the objective and objects, making the character's internal state externally visible during a scene and making the external events internally meaningful. The readers need to witness the character interacting with the object in the scene during the moment, not off-page or offstage, but as events unfold.

The tactics align with the action, so the objects align with the objective.

The easiest way to dramatize that objective is to find concrete, interactive objects that connect directly to that objective so that an audience can track the cause and effect of the character's actions. A spinster's objective may be "to get married" in the abstract over the course of a story, but giving her a specific *suitor* to pursue or *cads* to rebuff creates tangible stakes and tension. Generality resists dramatization while specifics simplify the task of telling the story by *aligning* your efforts.

When you visit your in-laws, your objective can be to "keep the peace." *Keep* is your action and peace becomes a shiny objective (story goal) for your entire visit... except that peace remains vague and slippery as a target moment to moment. What exactly does peace look like, sound like, smell like? Can you show what steps peace might require? How would an outside observer identify peace? Would anyone understand that peace if they didn't know the family intimately?

By breaking an objective down into tangible objects, you map a course for your character as they work for what they want. Your action is to "keep the peace," but your objects in individual scenes might be any number of specific targets: chores, debate, your kids, relatives, television, repairs, noise, a loan, the dinner, and finally the car keys so you can make your escape. Individually you *keep* those objects under control and thereby "keep the peace." The overall objective of <u>peace</u> is built out of the mosaic of objects that comprise its keeping. Make sense?

Objects are pieces that come together to solve the puzzle of the objective. When a character encounters an *obstacle* which creates *conflict*, they calibrate their *actions* by choosing a *tactic* that targets their *object*.

In grammatical terms, the dramatic conflict is the "but" in the dramatic sentence: "In order to [*action*], [*character*] needs to [*tactic*] [*object*], but [*conflict*]."

Notice that comma in the sentence. That slight punctuated pause signals the friction facing the sentence's subject. A character pursues an object and attains it; no pause. A character pursues an object but faces conflict—you instinctively hitch your breath to indicate the complication and escalation.

The object provides your characters with their obstacle or opponent in a scene to keep the conflict clear.

If anything, transitivity is even more critical when it comes to choosing tactics because tactics appear whenever a character's action collides with a new object in a scene. As an example, consider the infamous abortive proposal scene in *Pride and Prejudice*:

- In order to *preserve* his feelings, Mr. Darcy must *court* Lizzy, but <u>she scorns him</u>.
- In order to *preserve* his composure, Mr. Darcy must *denigrate* Lizzy's embarrassing family, but <u>she rebukes his manners</u>.
- In order to *preserve* his civility, Mr. Darcy must *brave* Lizzy's mockery, but <u>she attacks his reasons</u>.
- In order to *preserve* his honor, Mr. Darcy must *flee* Lizzy's rejection, but <u>her words haunt him</u>.

Darcy's action and objective (*Preserve:* <u>Honor</u>) remain consistent, but he shifts tactics to pursue his object: Lizzy, whom he *courts, denigrates, braves,* and *flees*. None of this happens in a vacuum. What keeps him central to the story are the conflicts that compel escalating action and, therefore, updated tactics. This complexity of Austen's famous proposal scene comes from the shifting tactics, and that level of complexity doesn't (and shouldn't) apply to every scene.

Obstacles and opponents provoke empathy in readers and ingenuity in characters. Nobody likes to be told "No." Evolution hardwired humans to create "desire paths" to get where they're going when the path doesn't exist.

Literally, a **desire path** (also known as a footpath, goat track, game trail) is a crude, organic walkway created by the erosion via regular usage of the shortest or easiest distance between two points. In other words, it's a user-created solution to a design flaw or opportunity in an environment. When kids cut across the grass or animals wear a hole through a hedge, they're creating a desire path. They know where they need to go; it's only the well-intentioned dummies who laid the pavement who got it wrong.[80]

Essentially, each scene in a story is a *desire path* that cuts across the lawn to reach the character's objective, advancing one object at a time.

Objects work best when they focus the character tactics in a scene and connect clearly through a sequence of events to a character's ultimate objective. The audience should be able to connect the dots for themselves, which creates strong emotions in the reader and satisfying closure in the scene.

"Good writing is supposed to evoke sensation in the reader—not the fact that it is raining, but the feel of being rained upon."

E.L. Doctorow[81]

EXERCISE: Monkey Wrench

Objects aren't static. By tapping their energy, you can electrify even the dullest, paint-by-numbers scene. How many ways can a single object act as an opponent or obstacle in a scene? How many different scenes can you wring from a single potent object?

1. Choose an object for a specific scene that is a step on the journey to the overall story goal (objective) for that character.

2. Make a list of all the characters in the story.
3. Decide how this object would create problems and friction for each character, noting if there are multiple possibilities for any cast members.
4. Narrow the list down to the three characters who will have the most trouble and the most types of trouble with this object.
5. Write the scene three times, each time making one of those three troubled characters the subject of the scene's object.

- BONUS ROUND: Make a list of different functions the object can serve in as many scenes as possible by steering various escalating tactics in its direction.

Pay attention to the amount of mileage you can squeeze out of an object with transformation and revelation. What happens when you combine or split objects? How (and how long) can you keep escalating an object's impact over the course of a story?

Nature

A tactic is...adopted by a character in order to handle an object.

Pinpointing the object in a scene also improves the focus and energy of every interaction and eliminates narrative vagueness or indecision so that your characters do something to *something* with consequences. In each scene, the character will pursue an object they believe will eventually lead them toward their overall objective, if they're lucky and living in the right genre.

As *scene goals*, **Objects represent the immediate opportunity**.

Objects anchor individual beats for the reader by supplying tangible, meaningful opportunities for character progress and setback. In a sense, objects put a character through their paces on the page, forcing them to weather disasters and decisions in each stage before the finish line. The kinds of objects your characters pursue will define the stories you tell and the audiences they'll attract.

Since the object connects to their objective, every scene will advance their part of the story. The object creates a meaningful context for the character and helps the audience engage and empathize. For best results, the object must be:[82]

- SPECIFIC: The object must be tangible so that the character (and your audience) knows what success or failure will look like.

- EXTERNAL: The object must appear in a measurable context so that your character (and your audience) knows how much effort and risk is required to affect it.

- DYNAMIC: The object must transform so that it presents a meaningful challenge to the characters trying to have an effect on it.

Think of each object as a problem that needs solving during the scene. What a character must deal with on the fly forces them to adapt to the world around them. For plotters, objects anchor scenes in concrete specifics, and for pantsers, an object provides a perfect springboard for improvisation. For audiences, objects help them keep track of who wants what, when, and why.

The object's *distance* creates a desire path through the scene between what the character has and what the character wants. The dynamic between the subject and the object is what unleashes all that energy on the page by creating meaningful patterns and an emotional ride.

The object holds the energy of the scene like a battery. Emma Woodhouse sketches Harriet as bait for Mr. Elton; Charlie Bucket sacrifices everything to find Wonka's golden ticket; Sethe's family is devoured by Beloved, one by one; Bilbo surrenders the Ring to Gandalf unwillingly as he leaves the Shire; Valmont deflowers Cécile to punish her mother. During a scene, powerful characters situate their energy in the object.

A heroine laughing or a villain weeping doesn't necessarily make an audience laugh or weep. By expressing the emotion, they release the emotion, providing *closure* for the reader and resolving the tension. One of the quickest ways to make an audience feel something is to *trap* the character's feelings in an object. Situating a powerful emotion outside of the character in the object gives the reader room to experience the emotion *for the character*...creating closure that the story hasn't provided.

Objects create meaningful gaps for audiences to close.

I'm reminded of a canny directorial note from Declan Donnelan: instead of saying to yourself, "What is my character doing?" ask yourself, "What is the object making my character do?"[83] As long as the object is specific, external, and dynamic, the character must take clear, visible, tactical action in the scene.

The object energizes the characters and their scenes. Vague targets leave your readers unmoored, unsure what's at stake, and why it matters. The more characters focus on themselves rather than the object, they steal energy from the scene, the more the story will sink into backstory, mood, and the second-act swamp. Witness the mopey, moody, grandstanding characterizations in hack fiction and the sleaziest TV. Generality paralyzes action as the subjects reduce themselves to objects, victims to forces beyond their control.

That doesn't mean outrageous behavior guarantees great characters. One of the most insidious traps in characterization is the belief that energetic or violent characters are inherently fascinating. Genre fiction gives us hams and grandstanders out the hoo-hoo...the louder, tougher, and pushier the better, right? Not necessarily. Plenty of forgettable books star aggressive loudmouths that leave readers numb because they don't merit attention.

Grandstanding and scene-stealing are just behaviors, sometimes effective as meaningful tactics but inappropriate for many characters. Caterwauling and aggression can only make readers pay attention if the character's object is clear and the stakes manifest. Identifying the scene's object is easy once you know:

- **Objects are** *external, specific, active, tangible, dynamic, evolving.*

- Objects are not *internal, general, passive, hidden, fixed, complete.*

As readers we expect both: life-changing *objectives* in the story that torment and inspire characters in ways we can grok, and in each scene, fascinating objects that tease and twist, incite and ignite the character's hopes of happiness.

No pressure.

Hannibal Lecter's action throughout his series is *to savor.* In *The Silence of the Lambs,* his overall objective is *freedom* in every sense of the word: freedom from restraint, stupidity, laws, scrutiny, boredom, rudeness, morals, humanity. At every moment of that book, he works like hell to savor whatever freedom he has. But in individual scenes, you cannot depict "freedom" as something specific, visible, and interactive. Trying to do so would render your characters talky, passive, and static.

Instead, we see Lecter *savoring* any number of ob-jects: his books, his art, his music, his privacy, his education, his eidetic memories, Clarice's scent and cheap shoes, her childhood traumas and tough mind, the anxiety of his captors, Chilton's panic and postur-ing, Senator Martin's rage, pain, and terror, his own brilliance, human flesh, and the game he plays against everyone in his path. By giving him different objects and character re-actions to savor, different contexts and tactics, Thomas Harris paints a fascinating portrait of a monster, with one continuous unfolding of his action and objective: *to savor his freedom.*

Lecter directs his tactics in each beat and each scene toward different objects, and the energy in those scenes comes from the object impacted and the resultant event. Almost like nuclear fission, the slamming together of his energy (*Savor*: <u>Freedom</u>) and the object of his attention in each scene creates a series of small explosions that change everything.

Objects are necessary because characters achieve objectives in stages and tactics require someone or something upon which to exert their force.

This is where transitive verbs become the Swiss Army knife of characterization.

- For pantsers, tactics allow you to just write forward because you know the energy and flow of a scene even if you aren't sure exactly what will happen in any given moment until you write it.
- For plotters, tactics energize the inert rigidity of any structure, giving scenes dramatic thrust and escalation at each point.
- For so-called "plot" writers, fascinating tactics add depth and subtlety to the "thin" characterization that fooled you into thinking you don't write character.
- For so-called "character" writers, tactical coherence and escalation will bolster the "flimsy" plotting that convinced you plot was your blind spot.

Plus, all that rigorous, vigorous language amplifies the depth, dexterity, and impact of the finished product. By aligning the characters' actions and tactics, you allow the reader to experience them as real coherent people and also make the best use of writing time. Audiences follow a character's desire path through each scene with their eyes on the horizon, eager for that objective. Verbalization pays mind-boggling dividends at every stage of your process.

> "The hope in fiction, as Aristotle says, is to discover not the history of what happened, but principles of what is possible."
>
> Dr. Keith Oatley[84]

EXERCISE: Loaded Dice

An object acts as a container for character feelings, forcing them to re-act during scenes so that situations change and an audience can create closure. How can you? How does an object share its charge with everyone in the scene? What will the object make each of them do and why? Let's trap scene energy in an object for your characters.

1. What's happening and why does it matter? Choose a scene and its object and make a list of the characters participating.

2. What's at stake and why do they care? Describe the object from each character's point of view, highlighting its personal meaning and impact for each individual.

3. How would they access and interact with this object? For each character, identify the types of

energy in the object for them and the method(s) of extraction.

4. What is each character's desire path? Indicate where and how they start the scene and the terrain they have to cover to reach that object. Don't make it easy, and don't let them wimp out in their tactics.

5. For each character, explain how the object would interact with 3-5 of their tactics to produce meaningful results during each interaction. How does the object shift, irk, and provoke re-actions from everyone present?

■ BONUS ROUND: Transform the object in a way that materially alters its desirability during the scene and/or severs its ultimate connection to character objectives. How does each character react to the reversal? How do the desire paths change? Who forfeits and who won't relent? Who imagines or invents connections between the changed object and their objective?

Challenge

A tactic...handles an object significant to a scene.

Whatever success looks like in a scene, it mustn't come easy.

Audiences have zero interest in watching someone do nothing for no reason with no consequences. Identifying your character's object gives the action of the scene somewhere to go, as the story unfolds in each instant. In a scene, the object will act as the obstacle or opponent for the other characters.

Rather than cardboard cutouts, your characters have a clear task that brings them to life and makes the *stakes* visible in a given moment. Keep it

- SPECIFIC: By definition, an object must exist at a single, clear point. Your characters need to be able to *target* the object. Generalities bore and distract people; details fascinate them. Remember, art is the business of attention. If you want your audience to pay attention, your characters must pay attention, and that means specificity is your greatest ally. **Aim requires accuracy.**

- EXTERNAL: Anything at which a character aims must exist at a specific *distance* from the character. Whether the gap between subject and object is real or imaginary, it is the source of your story stakes. Placing the object *situates* your story. Even emotional objectives require an object outside the character. The tension between "I want" and "I have" or "I need" and "I get" creates reasons for characters and audiences to care. **People can only act in context.**

- DYNAMIC: Any story-worthy object presents a challenge, otherwise the stakes are nonexistent. Because the object exists in a state of flux and motion, the character must pay attention even in difficulty and doubt. Static or inert objects make for static, inert stories. **The more dynamic the object, the more energy your character**

can draw from it and the more dramatic the resultant story.

In *The Color Purple*, **Shug Avery** (*Celebrate*: <u>Blessings</u>) faces Celie Harris as her object at different points and re-actions. Celie initially resents Shug's *welcoming* a <u>safe home</u> out of the limelight. Shug *cheers* all her <u>lovers</u>, *broadcasts* her <u>own money and clothing</u>, *toasts* <u>strong women</u>, *extols* the quiet hand of the <u>Almighty</u> in the world, and ultimately *urges* Celie's <u>brave escape</u> to a new life. At each point, Celie's action (*Question*) derails the outcome of Shug's action (*Celebrate*) in a different way because individual objects force their tactics to keep changing.

Often a single object will suffice for several different scenes. To avoid repetition and redundancy, make sure escalation and variation transform the object in each new scene appearance so that it keeps raising the stakes and forcing your character to adapt anew. Objects don't just sit there, they morph and poison, shift and tease, tempting bystanders and provoking re-actions.

Whenever audiences complain about "objectified" characters, what they're criticizing is *inertia*. If your entire cast uses another character as an <u>object</u> without that character ever taking action as a subject themselves, they stop being a person and become a device. Pro tip: An easy way to guard against sexism, racism, homophobia, and most other forms of prejudice in your fiction is to subjectify traditionally objectified characters. Let people act as the *subjects* of their own scenes and give them their own objects to act upon.

What an object reveals is the *limits* of a character's power, how far a subject is willing to go to accomplish their objective. By specifying stakes, an object situates characters within a world and a worldview. Nailing down a specific object can change an entire scene and a sequence of objects can tell an entire story. When Edmond Dantès (*Avenge*: Persecution) must *avenge* the persecution he suffered, he faces several possible objects, each with slightly different stakes and intention charging it, using a different tactic for each. To achieve his objective, he

- escapes his Chateau d'If cell as a faux corpse. (object: cell)
- reclaims the Sprada treasure to fund his revenge. (object: treasure)
- drives Fernand to suicide by shaming his family. (object: Fernand)
- ruins Villefort by exposing his treacheries. (object: Villefort)
- produces Caderousse's letter to get Benedetto arrested (object: letter)
- bankrupts Danglars, to prison and penury. (object: Danglars)
- frees Haydée from enslavement and weds her. (object: Haydée)

Each of these objects subtly shifts the focus on Dantès' behavior, the targets for different tactics without altering his essential need to (*Avenge*: Persecution). The more abstract and internal the character's tactic in a scene, the more specific, challenging, and external the object needs to be to serve as an appropriate scene goal.

Because the character must grapple with the object in a scene, the character must process developments and re-actions to improve their next strategy for the next object. If we consider this grammatically (**Verb + Target + Progress**), then in each dramatic beat, a character's steps toward happiness would be rendered as: **Tactic + Object + Response = Scene**. What does the character attempt? How does the object respond to that tactic?

Frankenstein is haunted by his <u>creature</u>. Zaphod Beeblebrox steals the <u>Heart of Gold</u> to find a lost planet. Sam Spade's entire world is rattled by that <u>Maltese Falcon</u>. Kizzy Waller's family is doomed by <u>forged papers</u>. Catherine Moreland is galvanized by <u>Northanger Abbey</u> and all it insinuates. Every corpse in every mystery unleashes havoc upon the surrounding community. Matches need making. Crimes need solving. Monsters need fighting. Bombs need defusing. Banks need robbing. Villains need thwarting. Journeys end in lovers meeting.

To put it another way: **The hunger is in the meat.**

The audience needs something they can hang on to in the flood of incidents, a story preserver that buoys them through a scene. Arthur's objective may be to unite England, but what does that *look* like? Not for nothing the folklore gives us Merlin, Excalibur, Guinevere, Camelot, a Round Table, Mordred, a Grail, and more medieval tackle as individual objects so that we grok what he's after in the long run. Herein lies one of the great truths of myth and folklore and one of the challenges of epic storytelling: massive thematic objectives require *extraordinary* objects to hold attention. The more abstract the objective, the more tangible the objects need to be so that readers can follow the flow of the narrative.

As long as the object stays in motion, the character must adapt and adopt new strategies. Remember: the audience isn't fascinated by the character changing the object, they are fascinated by the ways the object changes the *character*. They want the character to abandon their illusions and see the object as it truly is. The minute you stop providing objects to handle, the audience gets bored and you won't accomplish anything but character assassination.

"Talent hits a target no one else can hit; Genius hits a target no one else can see."

Arthur Schopenhauer[85]

EXERCISE: Direct Object

The power of transitivity can make abstractions concrete, internal states interactive, and memories tangible. Depending on your genre and subgenre, your characters' internal states can manifest as external targets that are precise, visible, and interactive to keep info active.

By creating a specific object, you're providing characters with a target for their tactics in a given scene. This prevents the dreaded exposition dump by making information active during their beats. How would you reveal...?: (Pick one of each for the character in question.)

- THOUGHTS: childhood memory, error, discovery, wit, opinion, investigation, solution
- MOMENTS: breakup, exposure, promotion, deadline, loan, abortion, fight, triumph, funeral
- CONDITIONS: addiction, wealth, illiteracy, talent, illness, scandal, insanity, probation, genius
- EMOTIONS: loneliness, joy, anxiety, calm, irritation, panic, unrequited desire, surprise
- RELATIONSHIPS: toxic family, first love, conspiracy, divorce, BFFs, affair, colleagues, distrust

The trick here is to *show*, not tell the reader what matters. Consider how one object can be understood in several ways by different people. Look for opportunities to transform, disguise, or unpack the object further without exposition. How many things can it make them do? How many forms can it take? How will it morph and adapt to their efforts?

- BONUS ROUND: Take a single object and make it charged and meaningful for 5 different contexts or characters in a way that tells an entire story starring them. Allow the objects to force the story into the open, demanding tactics from them and making their ultimate actions and objectives clear.

Chapter 12: BEATS

A tactic is...an external response.

Every time your character's tactics shift, a new beat begins. A character makes an offer that is either accepted or rejected—requiring a new offer.

Scenes are always about characters negotiating external spaces, objects, forces, and most importantly, *other* characters doing the exact same thing. Each scene will show a specific tactic impacting a specific object with consequences.

During a beat, a character attempts to change someone or something strategically. They make an *offer*: a proposal, a command, a request, an attack, a solution—and that offer is either *accepted* or *rejected*—which necessitates a new offer, which immediately begins a new beat.

An offer is the tactic presented for consideration by the other participants dealing with the object in the situation.

A simple scene may only show a single beat, but a complex scene like Darcy's infamous midpoint proposal might portray many beats as the characters try to deal with a particular object via a series of tactics. A beat change means a *tactic* change, but the object often remains the same because the character's objective remains the same. Think of them as rungs on the ladder: objects for objectives, tactics for actions, and scenes for story.

- Each object is a link in the chain leading that character to their objective.
- Each tactic is a step on a desire path through the story revealing their line of action.
- Each scene builds upon significant events to craft an overarching story.

If you want a character's journey toward their objective to entertain and move an audience, then readers need to be able to trace the line of cause and effect through tactic to tactic, from scene to scene.

Giving the audience fascinating dots to connect essentially tricks your readers into developing personal, emotional involvement with the events of the story as they unfold because they can empathize with the struggles and disappointments, just as they anticipate the growth and success ahead.

In the real world, most people don't live thrilling lives of adventure and indulgence. Genre fiction lays out an emotional smorgasbord heaped with meaning and pleasure and invites audiences to grab a plate.

When I'm verbalizing a story, I ask myself: How would this person in this situation pursue happiness? What would happiness look like and how would they reach it? Who would help or harm them? How far would they go? How much would happiness change their world?

Get into the habit of looking for the secret joy in every beat so that your characters can *play* in their scenes. Let them have their kind of fun on the page. When working with actors, I used to call this the "free prize" in a character, something unlikely you get to do in the role: you get to star in a superhero montage, you get to seduce your nemesis, you get to play a gargoyle freed from stone, you get to hunt alligators with your bare hands.

These "free prizes" act as a secret treat to keep you and your readers hooked in those moments when stress or boredom might become distracting. Look for the ways that your characters have permission to do things your readers wish they could and never will. Remember: the objects make your cast act and they also keep readers from putting the story down.

Now, lest all this talk of beats and scenes make anyone anxious: a word about story structure.

An outline only offers a snapshot of a story as you understand it right now. Outlining your story before you work up a proposal or plotting a project before you write it has more to do with efficiency and time management than anything else. You cannot *improvise* a roller coaster. Fail to plan, plan to fail.

The truth is, all genre fiction gets plotted. Anyone who writes genre fiction plots their books because genre presumes certain tropes and structural expectations your audience brings to the bookshelf. Readers buy books that provide the ride they want.

At core, stories reveal meaningful transformation that elicits the desired emotion from its audience. We structure things in our heads with different degrees of precision and skill. How deep and elaborate that structuring process is varies from writer to writer, project to project, but part of knowing how to tell a story is knowing how to build a story for maximum emotional impact.

The only difference between so-called plotters and pantsers is *when* they do their plotting to elicit the appropriate emotions.

- PLOTTERS structure a story before working and draft with that plan in mind.
- PANTSERS prefer to structure after they've rough drafted and then revise accordingly.

Here's the deal: plotters pants and pantsers plot. We're not insects and we all have idiosyncratic methods that vary project to project, let alone writer to writer. The best option is whichever one helps you finish the best book for your readers. Every author will and should come at this process via their strengths and experience.

There is no one perfect path. As you work, learn to recognize resonance, the tiny joyful click of the key turning in a lock when the solution presents itself at the perfect moment. That internal click is personal, singular, and more precious than anything else in this industry. It's the sound of your voice unlocking itself.

Above all, respect your own talent and your own process. This job is no joke. Make space for the tools you need to get your work done.

"If one does not know to which port one is sailing, no wind is favorable."

Seneca the Younger[86]

EXERCISE: Book Self

If you're willing to write from deep POV, you can even set up the primary character beats by writing sentences in first person, in order of dramatic importance.

- I MUST... character *action* + <u>objective</u>
- I WANT... external goals (*tactics*) + <u>objects</u>
- I NEED... internal goals (*tactics*) + <u>objects</u>
- I WISH... I'D LIKE... activity (and therefore cuttable).

Come up with as many tactics as seem fun to write and useful to tell the tale. Slice the objective into objects and then lead the character to the objective with the objects dotting their path like breadcrumbs. Time and space should be given to those verbs that come closest to the character's action, with the least amount of time and space afforded passive activities that can only add color and texture to an environment.

Then combine them as a single message of serious intent:

"<u>I must</u> [*action*] [*objective*] **even if I'm forced to** [*tactic 1*] [*object 1*]**,** [*tactic 2*] [*object 2*]**, and** [*tactic 3*] [*object 3*]**,** *et al*...**to make it happen.**"

Trajectory

A tactic is...an external response...significant to a scene.

People call it spinning a yarn for a reason. Stories follow a cause-and-effect chain that an audience wants to follow and enjoy.

Here's the deal: Once you know your main character's action, tactics, and genre, you've already started planning the story. Collisions, interactions, and strategies have already started sprouting in your mind. Maybe it isn't conscious or tangible, but your sense of the story has begun to take shape.

What if I told you that you could structure your entire book with a thesaurus?

If characters are their actions in pursuit of their objectives, if all their scenes are their actions understood as tactics confronting objects, then the moment you have an action identified and specific tactics in place, **Character becomes plot**.

Once you've analyzed a character's action and assembled tactics, the entire story is present, albeit in jumbled pieces. All you have to do is sort those tactics into a satisfying journey through emotional peaks and valleys that reveal character depth and breadth. A character *arc* is nothing more than the ordered sequence of their tactics, object by object, as they work to reach their objective...which means you can use their tactics to structure your story.

Plot is character in context. You know the genre, the action, and the ultimate objective, so you know where they're headed and whether the main character(s) get there in one piece.

All that remains is to order those tactics in a rising trajectory toward the ending required by your genre via a blend of success and failure, internal and external progress that organizes character action for maximum emotional impact.

For real: make a list.

When verbalizing a story scene by scene, plotters will probably dive in early and pantsers wait till they've laid some tracks, but when you're ready, sort all those tactics in a rising crest from least to most dramatic verbs and alternating between internals and externals, between good and bad strategies, depending on the character and contexts. Even without knowing the entire story or the particulars, the beats and scenes will start to emerge, especially once you know the story's *climax*.

Climax is the Greek word for "ladder." Narratively a climax involves a series of sequential steps building to a high point: tactics comprise an action, objects lead to the objective, scenes build a story.

At the start of any story, you always want to position characters as far as possible from where they will wind up at the finale. Sir Laurence Olivier used to do something similar when rehearsing Shakespeare. Conscious of the musicality of the plays and his own voice, he would read through the text and then sit at a piano and plink out notes. Once he had pinpointed the highest, loudest note his character would hit while speaking those lines, he knew the outer limits of that *character's* voice. No other word or moment in the play would be as high and loud, and so every other word and moment had to be pitched lower and softer. By establishing the peak, he could map the rest of the vocal and emotional terrain toward and away from it. He could shape his entire performance. Aside from portraying the character, he gave himself a clear, tangible objective *as an actor*. You can do the same as an author.

Stack your story beats toward the most emotionally satisfying resolution; once a character has overcome a problem, subsequent problems must be greater. The audience already knows they can master something equivalent, so smaller problems become pointless and digressive. No *new* closure on that prior pattern is possible. Audience boredom is the source of all "rising action" in entertainment.

New, worse, and bigger stuff has to keep happening to force the audience to create closure anew. Any story can be built one predicament (subject + predicate) at a time. All you have to do is keep creating the worst possible consequences and forcing your characters to make the hardest possible decisions about them from that list of tactics.

Pro tip: **Each subsequent tactic needs to outshine and surpass everything that has gone before.** In fiction there is only one rule: whatever happens must be more interesting than what just happened. The climax must come late so that characters can climb to their objectives, tactic by tactic, object by object.

By way of evidence I'll use my simplest and most dramatic example. In Tennessee Williams' *A Streetcar Named Desire*, **Stanley Kowalski** (*Penetrate*) **and Blanche Dubois** (*Conceal*) **cause a series of increasingly ugly confrontations. As** (*Penetrate*), **Stanley** *bullies, insults, seduces, rips, bellows, smears, fondles, smashes, jeers;* **as** (*Conceal*), **Blanche** *deflects, veils, shades, paints, fabricates, dresses, drapes, disguises,* **and** *deceives.* **Tactic slams into tactic, slowly ramping up, with victories back and forth until their final horrible rendezvous.**

What is the most horrifying, tragic *penetrate* possible? Stanley's repulsive final tactic: *to rape*. And what is the most horrifying tragic *conceal* possible? *To imprison*. Blanche's devastating mental collapse leaves her imprisoned inside her own mind in an asylum depending "on the kindness of strangers." The entire play builds inexorably toward that harrowing tactical collision.

So while you're rummaging around, take a moment to pull out the three or four most shocking tactics. Those verbs will become your character's tactics for your linchpin scenes (e.g. the act breaks and midpoint, or their equivalent). As you work, bear in mind your story's:

- FLOW: Situate new tactics along a rising arc aimed at the objective.
- DIGRESSION: Allow tactical maneuvers to backfire, surprise, and deepen character by pushing in unexpected-yet-inevitable directions.
- DEVELOPMENT: Advance each character via success and failure to the most shocking or pivotal tactic they hold in reserve.

Exercise novelty and irony by mapping those tactics so that they guide the readers toward your ending, a whole story in active verbs. Whatever your character's action and tactics, continually drop them into a situation that requires the opposite approach, that prevents the easy choice, that demands unexpected adaptation. As the old saw says, the plot makes characters heroic, and subplots make them human.

Whenever an audience complains that a story sags in the middle, the problem is always the same: an apparent resolution that comes too soon in the story. As the author, you know what's coming: the friction ahead, the looming troubles, the ticking bombs...but all the readers can see is the comfy plateau you've given them. Any saggy lull is only an ostensible resting place for the character that lets readers check out before they ought.

Adieu, attention! Sayonara, suspense! Bore your audience and you let them off the hook. To keep them reading, keep them on edge.

You must make characters do the things they cannot do so they can take the reader on a satisfying emotional ride. Disasters force decisions. Decisions create disasters.

Once you've mapped out the dynamic arc for your primary character, do something similar for your other characters. You might not write or even fully imagine all of those potential scenes, but a character's tactics must affect everyone else's tactics, so you'll need to know where various players are coming from and where they're going as well, bearing in mind:

- CONTEXT: Consider the settings and relationships in play.
- HISTORY: Let characters learn from past behavior...or not.
- IMPACT: Ensure that their tactics affect everyone else's significantly.

Require adaptation from all the characters you expect readers to care about. Every character needs an arc because every character has an action and an objective. Anyone without an arc is furniture.

The real art of writing fascinating scenes is finding the music in human impulse and interaction. Allow a mix of internal and external re-actions so your character feels three-dimensional. Remember to let some tactics backfire and disappoint and some to work against the odds. Force your characters to adapt. Inevitable triumph or failure will bore readers, so Mary Sues and Sad Sacks stink on ice.

- MARY SUES are what happens when a character never needs to adapt or adopt a new strategy. They suck because they always succeed, so who cares?
- SAD SACKS are what happens when everything tortures and dooms a character regardless of effort. They tank because of their inevitable angst, so why bother?

On that tip, let all your characters screw up sometimes, especially your heroes. Likewise, let all your characters succeed sometimes, especially your villains.

Each tactic of a character is an attempt to change the tactics of other characters. Confronted by an object, the character struggles for control of the scene. All the characters try to reframe conflict to favor their personal action. For the most powerful results, make sure to aim those tactical verbs at other characters "in order to" make them change *their* tactics.

Actions collide with actions, tactics parry tactics, and characters carve each other for our entertainment. As meaningful changes change your cast and their world, your story will unfold in the most dramatic way possible.

"If there is no possibility for change in a character, we have no interest in him."

Flannery O'Connor[87]

EXERCISE Arc Aid

A character has a beginning, middle, and end just like the story. Identify the three major climaxes for your protagonist. This needn't box you in; if you're a plotter, these can help structure your story organically, and if you think of yourself as a pantser, just approach these as a series of *potential* story beats.

For the sake of balance and variety, try to cover a wide range of possibilities at differing levels of escalation and intensity.

1. Select a character for whom you've identified a powerful action and a list of tactics.

2. Sort your character's list of tactical verbs by intensity, impact, and interest level. Arrange them sequentially in order of *force* from least to most potent. When would each tactic be the most dramatic choice to make?

3. Consider your story goals, other members of your cast, the genre-appropriate ending toward which you may be working.

4. Match your tactical verbs to that list of moments, organizing them in a sloping arc of intensity that ends at the climactic tactic.

5. Try to alternate between internal and external tactics (need vs. want) to prevent monotony and increase character growth.

6. Identify the 3 most dramatic tactics, the most extreme tactical possibilities afforded by their action and objective. Look for the *pivot* potential.

Once you've arranged the tactics into an escalating list, confirm their relevance to the main action once more and read the list to gauge the character's arc. Place the 3 pivotal tactics where your 3 big events might fall, spaced appropriately.

Even without details or description, does this list of tactics *feel* like the flow of their story? Does it represent the way they're likely to act as events unfold?

If you're structure averse, please note this isn't a plot, just a verbalization of the character's energy shifts in the story. The more range and texture you cover, the more fascinating the resultant characters and their journeys.

Direction

A tactic is a strategic re-action...that requires an external response.

Characters have to change if you want readers to feel anything for them. Over the course of a narrative, your fictional folks will need to weather disasters and make decisions that transform their world and their role in it. We want to amplify tension and emotion so readers keep turning pages.

How, exactly? Writers do this instinctively, but for those moments when instinct falters, let's examine the process. An author who understands that writing is the application of energy to a task can easily focus energy where it can do the best job.

Contrast creates opposition and friction, and so character transformation requires a tactical cocktail that mixes it up. Yes, your characters will pursue their singular actions, but their tactics need to cover a range of possibilities in order to be fully realized.

Transformation and escalation don't happen in straight lines.

A character who sticks with a single tactical mode would get old fast, and so writers instinctively change the tune to keep readers paying attention. Now, for those of you who want to get technical, tactics can be divided in several ways. This chapter aims to break down tactics into fundamental modes. If you tend to overthink the writing process, please don't obsess.

Verbs move, so we can add texture and drama to any character arc by considering *direction*.

Back in the first section, we looked at ways that character energy is both central and invisible without action on the page. Energy moves (and moves people) in different ways, and by varying its expression on the page via character actions, you reveal a character's moves in moving ways.

Without getting too wonky or wanky, I'd like to suggest a simple, logical division of energy originally proposed by pre-Socratic philosophy.[88] Bear in mind that these are vast and drastic oversimplifications intended only to help you introduce contrast and escalation as you verbalize your stories.

If we treat any character as a distinct point of view, then energy moves along one axis in relation to a character and another in relation to the external world. Because energy moves, the *direction* of that movement will shift and evolve in response to context.

From the character's POV, their energy can either move away from or toward them, either *Push or Pull*. This division includes actions and tactics that *give/take, repel/attract, command/request,* and *threaten/persuade*. You can think of Push/Pull as the forces of will and desire, (or brawn and brains, *viz* Achilles vs. Odysseus for any Homer fans). With these verbs, ask yourself: Is this character's action moving to or from? Does Muhammad go to the mountain or the mountain come to Muhammad?

Of course, not all verbs involve the character personally. Often a character does stuff to or with the world that changes other things and people.

With verbs affecting the world outside the character, their energy unites or divides people, things, ideas, relationships, either *Join* or *Split*. These modes also include actions and tactics that *heal/harm, create/destroy, protect/attack,* and *teach/confuse*. You can think of Join/Split as the forces of love and war (or Eros and Eris for the mythologically minded). Ask yourself: Is this character's action moving things together or apart? Is their energy a spoon that gathers the food or a knife that cuts it?

Of course, what I'm describing is essential direction, and many verbs hybridize them. It may help to visualize them like so:

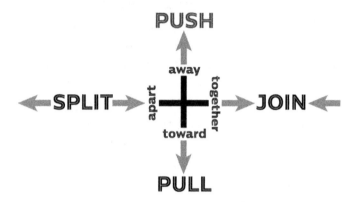

Most verbs fall somewhere between both axes. *To seduce* is primarily a pull verb, because seduction can unite *and* divide people, depending on context. A CEO might choose *to punish* a staffer to push them away, but the action of punishing *divides* the employee from the company, which makes punish a split verb.

The goal is *contrast*. By revealing the different directions, you provide a dimensional portrait of a character.

Surprise your readers with texture and depth that reveals the complex range of your character's nature. A person who *pushes-pushes-pushes* and never tries to *pull* any supporters will seem as insufferable as someone who *joins-joins-joins* in all directions, without ever *splitting* for a sanity break. Even Satan, Sauron, and Dolores Umbridge *crave* adulation while *dominating* victims....and *unite* their minions while *tearing* everyone else into wet chunks.

For best results, keep changing the tactical tune of your lead characters, and change it meaningfully. Consider the direction of their *action* and include tactics that reveal appropriate subtlety and variation via contrasting directions. Tactics allow you to change the tune and riff on different emotions. Whenever folks complain a character is "one-note" or scenes seem stuck at a plateau, a direction shift can oxygenate the story instantly. As Elizabeth Bowen puts it, "Roughly, the action of a character should be unpredictable before it has been shown, inevitable when it has been shown."[89]

Please don't obsess. Most genre fictioneers make these directional shifts instinctively. Categorizing tactical directions is tertiary to the writing process as long as you're changing the tune. Just allow enough variety that your characters aren't one-note caricatures. I include this direction concept not to drive you bonkers, but so you think about the flow of those verbs alone and as a collective. If scenes get stuck in a rut or a character gets stuck in a loop, a shift of direction might make the difference.

You probably vary tactics instinctively, so these divisions may be of most use when doing repairs or revisions on a project. Directions only help deepen depiction of a character or scene by changing the tactical tune:

- PUSH: verbs of authority and order that impose a POV upon the world by asserting internals and extending energy.

- PULL: verbs of influence and appetite that handle the outside world by attracting externals and assimilating energy.
- JOIN: verbs of inclusion and compromise, often seen as affection because of their unifying force and the emphasis on constructive, social coherence.
- SPLIT: verbs of separation and disturbance, often seen as aggression because of the potential for retaliation or ill will in a winners/losers dynamic.

Note that there's no inherent moral valence to any of these modes and that all of them can operate internally or externally. To *bestow* a fortune (push) needn't be an act of assertion any more than to *interrogate* a captive (pull) is an act of passivity. Villains can *brainwash* victims (join) and students can *flee* a class (split). What's significant is the *meaningful variation*.

All these directions have value and detriments in different contexts and come into play for different characters in different contexts. For maximum variety and texture in a character's tactics, consider using a mix that reflects the development of their tactics as they encounter the obstacles within their action's path. In *The Maltese Falcon*, Brigid O'Shaughnessy uses the full range in her tactics when it suits her:

- PULL: She *hires* detectives for a false case, then *seduces* and *ropes* Sam into a treasure hunt.
- PUSH: Whenever she's trapped, she *needles*, *demands*, and *reveals* ugly truths.

- JOIN: Bit by bit, she *coaches* Sam, *rationalizes* wrongs, and *confesses* her treachery.
- SPLIT: She *hides* that she has *deceived*, *betrayed*, and *murdered* in cold blood.

Braiding back and forth between these directions, Dashiell Hammett uses her aggressive Push tactics and vicious Split tactics as a series of dramatic reversals to escalate the action. Because Hammett tells the story entirely in external actions, without any description of character's thoughts, the dramatic pivots from Pull to Push, and (most shockingly) from Join to Split, reveal her as a two-faced femme fatale to Sam Spade and the reader simultaneously. His paranoia becomes ours. His betrayal becomes ours.

The contrast in her tactical directions creates drama; the shifts beat-to-beat reveal character nuance and history without any exposition necessary. We understand directions instinctively. We extrapolate meaning from them before we can speak.

Exercise all your story muscles and all your character modes as you verbalize. When in doubt, look to the object receiving the action of the verb.

- PUSH verbs move away from the subject toward the object into the environment beyond. (*pay, attack, hype, manhandle*)
- PULL verbs move the object from the environment toward or into the subject. (*borrow, lure, interrogate, hog*)

- JOIN verbs create common ground between people, things, groups, and concepts. (*teach, exonerate, rally, manufacture*)
- SPLIT verbs isolate or damage people, things, groups, and concepts. (*hide, demolish, insult, lacerate*)

Think of your story's emotional landscape and the audience out there waiting to traverse it. The directions of your character tactics provide the ups and downs, ins and outs of the genre roller coaster you're building for them to ride. Directions provide different types of pins to stick in your characters so you can affect your audience via empathetic magic.

By tweaking and organizing tactics, an author shapes the feelings within your audience, across miles and years. In the end, that's the definition of a genre writer, someone who can pull and push, join and split the pieces of a story to wring as much satisfying emotion from a reader as possible, every time.

Those tactical directions map the audience's journey across the narrative landscape and steer each reader's emotional voyage on the fly. Make this ride unforgettable and an eager crowd will line up for the next.

"With respect to the requirement of art, the probable impossible is always preferable to the improbable possible."

Aristotle[90]

EXERCISE: Page Directions

Readers want a *ride* and you are always battling inertia. What is an emotional roller coaster without crests and dips, loops and flips? Learning to reverse expectations and riff on a character's facets can elevate any prose.

Let's try mixing it up on the page. Take a completed page from a work in progress that feels a little flat.

1. Identify the tactic(s) being used by the character(s) participating in the scene.
2. Determine the DIRECTION of the tactic (s): Push/Pull/Join/Split.
3. Brainstorm 3 alternative tactics, one each from the other directions, so that you end up with 4 different DIRECTIONAL options for this character's tactics in this scene.
4. Verify that all 4 of those tactics still spring from their *action*.
5. Rewrite the scene 3 times, once for each of the new tactics, to see how changing the direction will alter the flow and outcome of the scene.

What does the character reveal when acting in these new directions? How does that change the tactics of other characters? Does the object remain the same each time? How do the tactical directions of other characters reflect or reject this character? How do their offers and demands shift to accommodate those new tactics?

> - BONUS ROUND: Map a character's directions throughout a story. Exactly *when* do their tactics change directions? Why and with whom? Does this person seem erratic or stuck moving in one direction for long stretches of the story? How do the directions reflect or reject the direction of that character's action?

Transformation

A tactic is...adopted by a character...that requires an external response.

I don't believe that plot and character are different things. I think they are two different ways of looking at the same task in writing: transforming a character in ways that evoke emotions within your audience. When authors say they "don't plot," what they generally mean is that they prefer to think about story as a process of internal transformation rather than a sequence of external events. They "don't plot" until later, when character can do the heavy lifting for them.

I tend to treat character not as a statement, but as a *question*.

Characters are not people or things, but arcs of transformation revealed by high-stakes choices...what George Eliot calls "a process and unfolding."[91] A character is a question it takes an entire story to answer, and the "right" answer is something each reader finds for themselves as they create closure.

My main point: actions and events occur in all genres. Many genres *are* a plot (e.g. a love story with an HEA, a crime with a solution, a disaster prevented).

Actions (characters) cause events (plots), and events (plots) inspire actions (characters). Whatever genre you write, plot and character are nothing more than the story seen through two lenses.

- PLOT is the story's collective actions as understood as an external sequence of cause and effect...which reveals the *why*.
- CHARACTER is the story's individual actions understood as an internal sequence of cause and effect...which reveals the *who*.
- STORY is the emotional ride experienced by the reader empathizing with the cause and effect of actions... which reveals the *how*.

Action cannot occur without characters to cause it. People cannot take action without creating a plot. Plot and character are flip sides of the same challenge all writers face: how to extract as much satisfying emotion from the audience as possible by telling a story.

The tricky part is that transformation can go two ways.

Some stories focus on the ways a character evolves in response to circumstances (i.e. romance, YA, horror). Other stories allow the character to remain largely unchanged, which forces the world to adapt to them (especially in thriller, action adventure, and cozy mystery). Some folks call these character-driven and plot-driven, but that seems myopic and nonsensical. Character and plot are two ways of describing the same thing, so I prefer:

- INTERNAL STORIES: Transformation of character

- **EXTERNAL STORIES:** Transformation of the world

Please note, when I say transformation of character, I'm not suggesting a new action, but a new mode of expressing that action. A character's action doesn't change. Their tactics change, but a character is *indistinguishable* from their action. Change the action, and you've changed the character.

Character is plot in context. Or to put it another way, story structure is a way of understanding the agency of characters, the effects of their actions, and the possibilities unlocked by the internal and external transformation.

When most people talk about plot, they describe it like tinker toys or an elaborate bomb, something deadly and intricate that might cost them a limb. Some writers labor under the belief that plot is a four-letter word, inherently vulgar and somehow insulting.

Of course, any genre fiction is *defined* by its plot; there is no such thing as an unplotted genre novel. To take the most obvious examples, romances end happily, horror scares people, and mysteries end with a solution; generic expectations provide the overall structural expectations of the readership. Fans turn up expecting certain obligatory scenes. **Genre is structure.**

In his book *Reading for Plot*, **Peter Brooks** boils structure down to a fantastic sentence that deserves some scrutiny. As he puts it, "Plotting...makes us read forward, seeking in the unfolding of the narrative a line of intention and a portent of design that hold the promise of progress toward meaning."[92]

At first glance, that may seem like a murky mouthful, so let's unpack that some. Plotting

- "makes us read forward." Structure creates a sense of interest and anticipation that focuses the reader's attention on what happens next, establishing sequence, context, and cause/effect by leveraging subject and predicate, person and predicament.

- "seeking in the unfolding of the narrative." Structure confirms the reader can expect a hidden reward for discerning meaning and significance in the story's events if they take the author's emotional ride.

- "a line of intention and a portent of design." Structure communicates the author's thought and feeling, art and craft, meaning and manners, with conscious care via alignment that will reward the reader's attention.

- "that hold the promise of progress toward meaning." Structure guarantees value, aspiration, and resonance within the story to make it more than the sum of its parts, so that the value and significance of the book can impact the reader's interior life and real world experiences.

Plotting simply reveals the ways character transformation creates meaning on the page and within the reader. Story structure isn't a mechanical contrivance but a framework to transfer human reason and emotion into a reader from the pages of a book. Story tells you what happened; plot tells you *why* it happened.

Plot is not a cage, but an empathy transmitter.

To that end, make your characters live *through* their story on an **arc**. Why do they start, where do they stop, and how do they manage it? Disasters and decisions cause and effect transformation.

The character's arc is not the goal, but a *trajectory* aimed toward the goal like a compass, based on the character's essential nature as reflected by their action in the story. Obviously, that overarching story goal can be broken into smaller scene goals, but without a driving action and an objective to focus characters, they can dissolve into a blurry clump of urges and wishes that head nowhere in particular. Action simultaneously aligns your creative process and the reader's emotional experience into a single clear trajectory toward an emotionally satisfying resolution.

Verbalize your own tasks as an author. Think like a character and ask yourself, "What is my intention?" Every time you get to a murky bit in your project, ask yourself what your authorial "in order to" is. The surgeon lives in a trailer park in order to create contrast. The prom queen visits the cemetery in order to unpack her intense backstory. The banker gets shot at this moment in order to highlight his recklessness.

Plot is a verb. Structure is a verb. Write is a verb.

Rather than thinking of plot as a noun, treat it as the active, intentional, transitive *verb* it is. Forget about creating a static, rigid, abstract thing called a plot, limited by your assumptions (as all nouns are limited). Instead, use dynamic language to align your story elements effectively to untangle the snags and improve its effect. *Plot* your book as an intentional, transitive action. Verbalize it.

Plotting should be like lunch: it sits in your stomach, nourishes you as necessary, and nobody else needs to look at it. Everyone will need it eventually, but they can decide for themselves how long they can wait. Only you need to know it's there.

This isn't math. You don't need to show your work.

In film, a montage provides a way to elide time swiftly, piling a bunch of consequential events in rapid succession to show something drastic shifting in the story: courtship, training, grief, rehearsal, construction. Film doesn't have time to waste and so cut-cut-cut with background music and suddenly the audience understands that everything is different.

Books abhor montages. Powerful moments in fiction need time to develop and space to play out. Anything that flicks by in rapid succession had better be unmoving and unimportant, otherwise you are cheating your reader of the full scope of the emotional ride. Think of musical numbers, action sequences, sex scenes, and any montage ever…something should always be changing. You cannot cut the high points of a roller coaster together and get the same effect. Anticipation, suspense, and release play a critical part in the experience.

If you give your readers a dial tone, don't be surprised if they hang up.

In every moment of a story, situations have to matter. On stage or in film, anything important happens either for the first time or the last time. That *significance* charges context and escalates actions. First and last moments between characters act as an emotional summation of the relationship. First and last moments in a circumstance require meaningful adaptations and decisions.

Who would want to read (or play) a character who remains static for an entire story? Even Harry Potter has to learn, train, and fail... and he's "the boy who lived" through certain death before he could walk.

Always focus on those pivotal *events* that release energy through meaningful collision. Don't write by rote. Supply your genre's obligatory scenes in fresh, unexpected iterations. Think of Olivier's high note and give your character as much room to grow and ground to cover as you can manage. Follow the desire path through their scenes, shifting directions as necessary. A character arc that runs from A to D is going to be much less interesting than one which laps the alphabet more than once. The more drastic the ups and downs, the more intense the emotions and the more unforgettable the dramatic payoff.

Weigh the first actions and first spoken words of your character on page. I once had a director who said that every character in Shakespeare could be understood by their first words, because it represented the start of their rhetorical argument. If a character is "making a case" to the audience, their opening statement is almost as critical as their closing statement.

Each character arc offers its *own* beginning. Meeting a new character later in a book *starts* a new arc. The first time we encounter your character, show us who they *are* at that moment, rather than who they might potentially become. This is actually a much greater problem than it seems. Newer authors often fall into the trap of playing the end of a book at the beginning. The heroine starts out just as brave, strong, and brilliant as she needs to be in order to face her final conflict. *Eesh.*

The beginning of any book is defined by the place on the character arc it occupies. Opening with a strong piece of physical conflict or danger has become stylish because of film and television. Trouble is, if the reader doesn't also care about the characters, that struggle serves no purpose. Stakes become essential so that you avoid activity in favor of action.

On the flipside, the ending of your story should feature the most impactful moments. Entire genres and worldviews are predicated on types of endings. For that matter, the final word of a sentence, the final sentence of a paragraph, and the final chapter of a book are the most powerful. The final note of a song is what stays with you. Ditto, the closing argument, the last word.

I refer to this as the *end position*.

We remember the end, even if the start is murky, because we took the journey too. Based on where a character began, where do they end up? Even if nothing has changed within them, the altered circumstances around a character will change how they are able to exist in the world they inhabit. Think of it as a *period* on the arc of the character. **End position is what readers take away.**

One of the most common mistakes is playing the end of the book before the characters have gotten there. As the author, you know a couple will wind up together or the murder will be solved, and so you immediately begin signaling to us how blissful it all will be in the future before anyone has met each other or investigated anything. You telegraph what the eventual outcome will be and then don't bother to actually get them to that outcome with us.

It's like anti-foreshadowing. Why should anyone read a book if THE END appears on page two? Skipping over all the important escalation that brings characters together is both lazy and dishonest, because it steals the part that the readers crave: watching characters grow and change and choose in the face of impossible odds.

Never play the Happily Ever After or unmask the villain before your characters have gotten there or your audience won't bother to watch them do it. Let the character take the journey with us and vice versa. If your characters start out satisfied, why should they bother to do anything and why do we care?

One of the things readers find most satisfying about genre fiction is that, unlike life, it guarantees satisfying closure. Romances promise that HEA. Mysteries will untangle the knot, either by solving a crime or by illuminating its dark root. Adventures end with the world saved, the baddies bagged, and the treasure claimed. In one sense, genres are completely defined by the endings they promise. Folks get to take the emotional ride to its conclusion and enjoy the inevitable ending they should have and couldn't have expected.

'To accomplish any action with the least amount of effort, that is grace."

Anton Chekhov[93]

EXERCISE: Grand Plan

Plot is character. Character is plot. Whether you're a plotter, a pantser, or a fancy dancer, knowing where you're going doesn't have to ruin the trip.

Using the character arc you built from your protagonist's tactics at the beginning of this chapter, let's map out a sequence of possible scenes that change the flow and world of the story, noting specific scene possibilities and potential resistance to that central character's line of action.

1. Make a list of other characters in the story along with their actions (as you currently understand them).

2. Make a list of your protagonist's tactics arranged in the arc you built in the last exercise with their *3 pivotal climaxes* clearly identified. If any tactics recur, verify that they escalate or evolve in some credible way.

3. Note any obligatory scenes out of that list of tactics (i.e. genre-specific or trope-specific events which must appear at certain points).

4. Populate your protagonist's arc with other characters, giving them suitably oppositional tactics in each and noting any obvious objects.
5. Place characters in the obligatory scenes as needed.
6. Decide which characters will take place in the protagonist's 3 big climaxes, paying special attention to the final, catastrophic tactic.
7. Now slot characters into the remaining gaps, allowing for variety and size of the roles.
8. Make note of any settings and circumstantial detail that seems necessary.

Give yourself a full roster of potential scenes. Fill in that list with any obligatory scenes. Make sure you aren't repeating the same tactics or avoiding any juicy possibilities out of anxiety or laziness.

- BONUS ROUND: This works best over a dedicated writing weekend between 2-4 seriously brave, trustworthy colleagues with ample brio. Find a partner willing to experiment and complete individual grand plans on your own...then TRADE plans. Take each other's completed grand plan and compose a 150-250 word blurb that tells the story of your colleague's unwritten book described by that preliminary list of verbs, events, and names. Once you're done, compare output to input to individual intention. See what you each learned about their story as well as your own.

Finale

Thank you...for taking this ride with me and for continually pushing to write better books.

By working on your craft, nurturing your art, you literally help the entire genre fiction community. The more beauty you create, the better your genre gets, the more fans will flock toward you and your colleagues. One book at a time, you write your success and rewrite the future.

What you do is more important than you may realize. You'll never know the sentence that helps someone through chemo or a divorce or depression. At a minimum, stories help people survive and grow through the concrete of their lives like sidewalk grass. At their best, books stand and shine like lighthouses on a dark, stormy shore...helping weary travelers navigate strange seas and bringing them home safe and loaded with treasure.

As we're wrapping up, I'd like to recap the entire book and distill the process of verbalization into a single run-on sentence just to remind you what we've covered.

> Writers and readers in search of **meaning** pay **attention** via **alignment** to **characters** with **significance** that suggests **patterns** created by **contrast** that causes **friction** and **escalation** during **events** in order to generate **energy** expressed through a **void** that inspires **action** in pursuit of an **objective** through **relationships** that require **tactics** to handle **objects** in an **arc** varying **directions** to maximize **transformation** to reach the kind of **emotional experience** fans crave.

Here's the deal: **Verbalization** *works.* It improves stories and eases their creation for writers of all types and stripes. All you have to do is pay attention and let words tell your story. They want to, if you'll give them a chance.

- ATTENTION: Decide why and who and what deserves attention from your audience, then create something deserving of that attention.
- EMOTION: Distinguish the range and types of emotion expected (and avoided) by readers within your genre.
- SIGNIFICANCE: Know what matters and make decisions that support the meaningful details that make your story worth telling.
- ESCALATION: Keep raising the stakes and increasing the risk so that each moment tops and transforms the last.
- RIDE: Devise an emotional rollercoaster for your reader so you meet and exceed their expectations, then bring them back safely.

- ALIGNMENT: Center all your efforts, specifics, and choices on the energy that drives your character.
- PATTERN: Use closure, causality, and tension to pull your reader inexorably through your story.
- CONTRAST: Seek the extremes of differentiation that attract attention and amplify stakes on the page via obstacles and opponents.
- EVENTS: Place your characters in meaningful, intentional collisions that require high-stakes choices and unleash energy.
- VOID: Anchor your character in the need, lack, or injury that creates predicaments for them in every context.
- ACTION: Cast each character with a single, dynamic, transitive verb that summarizes all their efforts in every moment of the story.
- OBJECTIVE: Identify the story goal that pulls each character through the story against overwhelming odds.
- RELATIONSHIPS: Force your characters to have intense, unexpected impact on each other as often as possible so they connect meaningfully.
- TACTICS: Express your character's action via a series of strategic re-actions specific to each scene based on their experience and decisions.
- OBJECTS: Focus your characters on tangible, challenging targets in each scene so that their tactics remain specific, external, and dynamic.
- ARC: Organize those tactics and objects in a rising crest, transforming characters by varying direction to beat the odds and reach an emotionally satisfying resolution.

I hope that you find these methods and exercises useful in your process. Thank you for taking the craft seriously and aiming for art when you can. Thank you for being a brave magpie who refuses to settle for scraps.

The secret of life is paying attention.

Whenever I teach a class, I feel so grateful that I got to spend that time with my colleagues. I learn more from fellow genre fictioneers than they'll ever learn from me. The questions they ask, the comments they make, the unexpected insights and sidebars and gauntlets they throw down make me a stronger writer and a better person.

Writing about my process has been such a freaky, funny, fascinating experience...verbalizing my ideas taught me so much about what I thought I knew and what I needed to know better, so thank you for that too.

Go write! Write *hard*. Write great books, because the rest of us need them.

Damon Suede,
New York City, 2017

"There's magic in the world. There is. People will tell you there isn't—they just want you to get back to work and be quiet and not ask questions. These are people who don't know where to look or who were not blessed with eyes that could see magic. Magical eyes. If you have them, develop them."

Tennessee Williams[94]

About the Author

Thank you so much for reading *Verbalize*. I hope you've found it practical and useful to your writing process.

As a working author, you know how important reviews and word of mouth can be to a book's success. When you have a moment, please leave a good word for this book on Amazon mentioning whatever specifics you found helpful so writers who'd benefit from verbalizing their stories can find what you dug and why.

BIO:

Damon Suede grew up out-n-proud deep in the anus of right-wing America, and escaped as soon as it was legal. He has lived all over and along the way, he's earned his crust as a model, a messenger, a promoter, a programmer, a sculptor, a singer, a stripper, a bookkeeper, a bartender, a techie, a teacher, a director... but writing has ever been his bread and butter. He has been happily partnered for over a decade with the most loving, handsome, shrewd, hilarious, noble man to walk this planet.

Damon is a proud member of the Romance Writers of America and currently serves on its national Board of Directors. He has been a full-time writer for print, stage, and screen for over two decades, which is both more and less glamorous than you might imagine. He's won some awards, but counts his blessings more often: his amazing friends, his demented family, his beautiful husband, his loyal fans, and his silly, stern, seductive Muse who keeps whispering in his ear, year after year.

Damon also loves teaching workshops and seminars. If you'd like him to present to your group or conference hit him up at:

- **DamonSuede.com**
- **Twitter (@DamonSuede)**
- **Facebook (http://damonsuede.com/fb)**
- **Newsletter (http://damonsuede.com/news)**

Appendix: Genre Examples

The following are titles used as examples throughout the course of the book. All of these books are stand-outs, and if you don't know them already, well worth a read, whatever your preferred literary stomping grounds.

- **Douglas Adams:** *The Hitchhiker's Guide to the Galaxy*
  - **Zaphod Beeblebrox** (*Flout*), **Arthur Dent** (*Plan*), **Marvin** (*Condemn*), **Ford Prefect** (*Wing*), **Trillian** (*Plot*)
- **Isabel Allende:** *The House of the Spirits*
  - **Alba de Satigny** (*Redeem*), **Esteban Trueba** (*Force*), **Clara del Valle** (*Divine*)
- **Jane Austen:** *Emma, Mansfield Park, Northanger Abbey, Persuasion, Pride and Prejudice, Sense and Sensibility* **(see expanded Austen discussion below)**
  - **George Knightley** (*Scold*), **Emma Woodhouse** (*Claim*)
  - **Edmund Bertram** (*Comfort*), **Fanny Price** (*Endure*)
  - **Catherine Moreland** (*Amplify*), **Henry Tilney** (*Simplify*)

- Anne Elliott (*Yield*), Captain Frederick Wentworth (*Command*)
- Elizabeth Bennet (*Provoke*), Fitzwilliam Darcy (*Preserve*)
- Colonel Brandon (*Grant*), Elinor Dashwood (*Assess*), Edward Ferrars (*Honor*), Marianne Dashwood (*Indulge*)
- **Peter Beagle:** *The Last Unicorn*
  - Amalthea (*Cherish*), Mommy Fortuna (*Mislead*), Molly Grue, (*Dare*), King Haggard (*Steal*), Prince Lir (*Save*), Schmendrick the Magician (*Bungle*), Unicorn (*Seek*)
- **Jim Butcher:** *Storm Front* (Dresden Files #1)
  - Harry Dresden (*Suspect*)
- **Lewis Carroll:** *Alice in Wonderland*
  - Alice (*Wonder*), Cheshire Cat (*Perplex*), the Hatter (*Spurn*), Queen of Hearts (*Threaten*)
- **Raymond Chandler:** *The Big Sleep*, *Farewell My Lovely*, et al.
  - Philip Marlowe (*Question*)
- **Lee Child:** *Killing Floor*
  - Jack Reacher (*Grasp*)
- **Arthur C. Clarke:** *2001*
  - Dr. David Bowman (*Explore*), HAL (*Regulate*)
- **Suzanne Collins:** The Hunger Games trilogy
  - Katniss Everdeen (*Hunt*), Gale Hawthorne (*Consume*), Peeta Mellark (*Feed*)
- **Agatha Christie:** *Murder at the Vicarage*, *Death on the Nile*, et al.
  - Jane Marple (*Probe*)

- ○ Hercule Poirot (*Outwit*)
- ▪ **Roald Dahl:** *Charlie and the Chocolate Factory*
  - ○ **Charlie Bucket** (*Respect*), **Grandpa Joe** (*Encourage*), **Willy Wonka** (*Astonish*)
- ▪ **Patrick Dennis:** *Auntie Mame*
  - ○ **Mame Dennis** (*Embrace*)
- ▪ **Charles Dickens:** *Bleak House, A Christmas Carol*
  - ○ **Lady Dedlock** (*Treasure*), **John Jarndyce** (*Help*), **Krook** (*Collect*), **Harold Skimpole** (*Cadge*), **Esther Summerson** (*Manage*), **Josiah Tulkinghorn** (*Corrupt*)
  - ○ **Bob Cratchit** (*Endure*), **Jacob Marley** (*Warn*), **Ebenezer Scrooge** (*Deny*)
- ▪ **Alexandre Dumas:** *The Count of Monte Cristo*
  - ○ **Edmond Dantès** (*Avenge*), **Benedetto** (*Covet*), **Giovanni Bertuccio** (*Arrange*), **Baron Danglars** (*Cheat*), **Abbe Faria** (*Bestow*), **Fernand Mondego** (*Betray*), **Gérard de Villefort:** (*Condemn*)
- ▪ **Umberto Eco:** *The Name of the Rose*
  - ○ **Abo,** (*Protect*), **Adso of Melk** (*Observe*), **Bernardo Gui** (*Condemn*), **William of Baskerville** (*Read*)
- ▪ **James Ellroy:** *L.A. Confidential*
  - ○ **Lynn Bracken** (*Lure*), **Ed Exley** (*Expose*), **Sid Hudgens** (*Exploit*), **Jack Vincennes** (*Grease*), **Bud White** (*Muscle*)
- ▪ **Laura Esquivel:** *Like Water for Chocolate*
  - ○ **Elena de la Garza** (*Starve*), **Tita de la Garza** (*Cook*), **Pedro Muzquiz** (*Consume*)
- ▪ **Fannie Flagg:** *Fried Green Tomatoes at the Whistle Stop Café*

- ○ **Ruth Jamison** (*Soothe*), **Idgie Threadgood** (*Defy*)
- ■ **Erle Stanley Gardner:** *The Case of the Velvet Claws* (Perry Mason #1)
  - ○ **Perry Mason** (*Prosecute*)
- ■ **William Goldman:** *The Princess Bride*
  - ○ **Buttercup** (*Spurn*), **Inigo Montoya** (*Avenge*), **Westley** (*Rescue*)
- ■ **Robert Graves:** *I, Claudius*
  - ○ **Caligula** (*Pervert*), **Claudius** (*Fool*), **Empress Livia** (*Poison*)
- ■ **H. Rider Haggard:** *King Solomon's Mines, She*
  - ○ **Allan Quatermain** (*Explore*)
- ■ **Alex Haley:** *Roots*
  - ○ **Kunta Kinte** (*Uproot*), **Kizzy Waller Lea** (*Stay*)
- ■ **Dashiell Hammett:** *The Maltese Falcon, The Thin Man*
  - ○ **Brigid O'Shaughnessy** (*Double-cross*), **Sam Spade** (*Honor*)
  - ○ **Nick Charles** (*Shake*), **Nora Charles** (*Stir*)
- ■ **Thomas Harris:** *The Silence of the Lambs*
  - ○ **Jame Gumb** (*Covet*), **Hannibal Lecter** (*Savor*), **Clarice Starling** (*Save*)
- ■ **Frank Herbert:** *Dune*
  - ○ **Paul "Muad'Dib" Atreides** (*Wake*), **Chani** (*Subdue*)
- ■ **Patricia Highsmith:** *The Talented Mr. Ripley*
  - ○ **Dickie Greenleaf** (*Overwhelm*), **Freddie Miles** (*Disdain*), **Tom Ripley** (*Manipulate*), **Marge Sherwood** (*Doubt*)

- **Homer:** *The Iliad, The Odyssey*
  - **Achilles** (*Vanquish*), **Agamemnon** (*Forfeit*), **Odysseus** (*Trick*)
- **Stephen King:** *Misery, The Shining*
  - **Paul Sheldon** (*Plot*), **Annie Wilkes** (*Pen*)
  - **Dick Halloran** (*Answer*), **Danny Torrance** (*Shine*), **Jack Torrance** (*Abuse*), **Wendy Torrance** (*Shield*)
- **Choderlos de Laclos:** *Les Liaisons dangereuses*
  - **Azolan** (*Serve*), **Chevalier Danceny** (*Court*), **Marquise de Merteuil** (*Dominate*), **Madame de Tourvel** (*Worship*), **Vicomte de Valmont** (*Ruin*), **Cécile Volanges** (*Indulge*), **Madame de Rosemonde** (*Excuse*), **Madame de Volanges** (*Deny*)
- **Madeleine L'Engle:** *A Wrinkle in Time,* **etc.**
  - **IT** (*Control*), **Charles Wallace Murry** (*Connect*), **Meg Murry** (*Disrupt*), **Calvin O'Keefe** (*Protect*), **Mrs. Whatsit** (*Guide*)
- **Stieg Larsson:** *The Girl with the Dragon Tattoo*
  - **Mikael Blomkvist** (*Bait*), **Lisbeth Salander** (*Hack*)
- **Harper Lee:** *To Kill a Mockingbird*
  - **Atticus Finch** (*Defend*), **Scout Finch** (*Trust*)
- **Ursula K. LeGuin:** *The Tombs of Atuan*
  - **Arha/Tenar** (*Master*), **Kossil** (*Tyrannize*), **Manan** (*Serve*), **Penthe** (*Accept*), **Sparrowhawk** (*Seek*), **Thar** (*Teach*)
- **Anita Loos:** *Gentlemen Prefer Blondes*
  - **Lorelei Lee** (*Lure*), **Dorothy Shaw** (*Prod*)
- **George R. R. Martin:** *A Game of Thrones*

- Robert Baratheon (*Spend*), **Khal Drogo** (*Conquer*), **Cersei Lannister** (*Coerce*), **Jamie Lannister** (*Betray*), **Tyrian Lannister** (*Negotiate*), **Jon Snow** (*Earn*), **Arya Stark** (*Exact*), **Catelyn Stark** (*Charge*), **Ned Stark** (*Guard*), **Sansa Stark** (*Face*), **Daenerys Targaryen** (*Rule*), **Viserys Targaryen** (*Demand*)
- **W. Somerset Maugham:** *The Letter*
  - **Leslie Crosbie** (*Plead*), **Robert Crosbie** (*Defend*), **Howard Joyce** (*Suspect*)
- **Daphne du Maurier:** *Rebecca*
  - **the second Mrs. de Winter** (*Expose*), **Maxim de Winter** (*Bury*), **Mrs. Danvers** (*Enshrine*), **and even offpage, Rebecca** (*Torment*)
- **Judith McNaught:** *Whitney, My Love*
  - **Whitney Stone** (*Agitate*), **Clayton Westland** (*Seize*)
- **Stephanie Meyer:** *Twilight*
  - **Jacob Black** (*Pursue*), **Edward Cullen** (*Protect*), **Bella Swan** (*Protest*)
- **Margaret Mitchell:** *Gone with the Wind*
  - **Rhett Butler** (*Challenge*), **Scarlett O'Hara** (*Claim*), **Ashley Wilkes** (*Refuse*), **Melanie Hamilton Wilkes** (*Accept*)
- **Toni Morrison:** *Beloved*
  - **Beloved** (*Devour*), **Sethe** (*Sacrifice*)
- **Walter Mosley:** *Devil in a Blue Dress* (**Easy Rawlins series**)
  - **Easy Rawlins** (*Handle*)
- **Charles Portis:** *True Grit*

- ◦ **Rooster Cogburn** (*Recover*), **Mattie Ross** (*Punish*)
- ▪ **Annie Proulx:** *Brokeback Mountain*
  - ◦ **Ennis Del Mar** (*Hold*), **Jack Twist** (*Share*)
- ▪ **Marcel Proust:** *In Search of Lost Time*
  - ◦ **The Narrator** (*Recall*)
- ▪ **Philip Pullman:** *The Golden Compass/Northern Lights, The Amber Spyglass, The Subtle Knife* (**His Dark Materials series**)
  - ◦ **Lyra Belacqua** (*Outsmart*), **Iorek Byrnison** (*Fight*), **Mrs. Coulter** (*Compel*), **Will Parry** (*Champion*)
- ▪ **Anne Rice:** *Interview with the Vampire , The Vampire Lestat* (**The Vampire Chronicles**)
  - ◦ **Lestat de Lioncourt** (*Ravish*), **Louis de Pointe du Lac** (*Crave*)
- ▪ **J.K. Rowling:** *Harry Potter and the Philosopher's/Sorcerer's Stone, ...and the Chamber of Secrets, ...and the Goblet of Fire, ...and the Order of the Phoenix, ...and the Half-Blood Prince, ...and the Deathly Hallows*
  - ◦ **Dumbledore** (*Keep*), **Hermione Granger** (*Prove*), **Hagrid** (*Nurture*), **Draco Malfoy** (*Spite*), **Harry Potter** (*Gather*), **Severus Snape** (*Vex*), **Voldemort** (*Shatter*), **Ron Weasley** (*Defend*)
- ▪ **Carl Sagan:** *Contact*
  - ◦ **Ellie Arroway** (*Search*), **Palmer Joss** (*Find*) **but in the film** (*Convince*)
- ▪ **William Shakespeare:** *Antony and Cleopatra, Hamlet, Macbeth, Twelfth Night*
  - ◦ **Antony** (*Battle*), **Cleopatra** (*Seduce*)

- Claudius (*Betray*), Gertrude (*Neglect*), Hamlet (*Test*)
- Lady Macbeth (*Scheme*), Macbeth (*Dream*)
- Olivia (*Adore*), Orsino (*Relish*), Viola (*Play*)
- John Steinbeck: *The Pearl*
  - Juana (*Mind*), Kino (*Plan*), the Doctor (*Trap*)
- Neal Stephenson: *Snow Crash*
  - Juanita Marquez (*Code*), Hiro Protagonist (*Hack*), Dmitri "Raven" Ravinoff (*Kill*), Y.T. (*Navigate*)
- Bram Stoker: *Dracula*
  - Dracula (*Drain*), Renfield (*Worship*), Van Helsing (*Stake*)
- Patrick Suskind: *Perfume*
  - Giuseppe Baldini (*Imitate*), Dominique Druot (*Sustain*), Jean-Baptiste Grenouille (*Scent*), Laure Richis (*Attract*)
- J.R.R. Tolkien: *The Hobbit, The Lord of the Rings* (see expanded Tolkien discussion below)
  - Bilbo Baggins (*Brave*), Elrond (*Direct*), Gandalf (*Unite*), Gollum (*Covet*), Smaug (*Desolate*), Thorin (*Withhold*)
  - Frodo Baggins (*Bear*), Samwise Gamgee (*Support*), Aragorn (*Protect*), Saruman (*Betray*), Sauron (*Bind*)... with recurring *Hobbit* characters maintaining their actions, natch.
- Robert Van Gulik: *The Chinese Nail Murders*, et al.
  - Judge Dee (*Judge*), Sergeant Hoong (*Keep*), Ma Joong (*Muscle*), Chiao Tai (*Mind*), Tao Gan (*Risk*)
- Alice Walker: *The Color Purple*

- - Shug Avery (*Celebrate*), Celie Harris (*Question*), Mister (*Crush*)
- Sarah Waters: *Fingersmith*
  - Maud Lilly (*Copy*), Sue Trinder (*Dupe*)
- Edith Wharton: *The Age of Innocence*
  - Newland Archer (*Challenge*), Countess Ellen Olenska (*Defy*), May Welland (*Bend*)
- T.H. White: *The Once and Future King*
  - Arthur/Wart (*Right*), Merlin (*Conjure*)
- Tennessee Williams: *A Streetcar Named Desire*
  - Blanche Dubois (*Conceal*), Stanley Kowalski (*Penetrate*)
- P.G. Wodehouse: *Jeeves and Wooster*
  - Reginald Jeeves (*Fix*), Bertie Wooster (*Mix*)

Pride and Prejudice Actions

While we're on the subject of examples, a few students have asked if I'd break out all of the actions for a single novel as a baseline example. Since I've used Jane Austen's *Pride and Prejudice* so often in explanations throughout, I thought it would provide a familiar and useful test case.

The film and television adaptations have a habit of shifting the tactics for several main characters (Lady Catherine and Mr. Bennet, notably) to compress the story and alter tone, so I'm going to the source. I came to this list of actions for the cast of *Pride and Prejudice* through rereading the novel so many times.

What remains timeless and compelling is the character actions. They appear right on the page, often articulated in Austen's own words. She provides all the character actions (and tactics) with sharp clarity, and I took many of the verbs right from her.

I started with Lizzy and Darcy, analyzing the tactics they use in their scenes to discern the common denominator—their actions—in those tactics. Her *provoke* and his *preserve* made themselves apparent very quickly in the big moments in the novel: the three proposals, the two dances, the intense verbal sparring. All of Lizzy's tactics *provoke*. All of Darcy's tactics *preserve*. They are perfectly, theatrically *mis*matched, as Austen intended.

Next I looked at the secondary characters to see who was *reflecting* and who *rejecting* the actions and tactics of the main couple, and how much *force* they apply at pivotal moments. Mrs. Bennet *pesters* from the first page of the book, and Mr. Bennet *teases*, ditto. In their awful marriage you can see the root of their daughter's wit and willfulness. Likewise the other four sisters:

- Jane *believes* everything and everyone for good and ill.
- Lydia *fancies* food, flattery, and dancing...to her mother's glee.
- Kitty *follows* "wherever Lydia leads."
- Mary *exhibits* relentlessly: music and homilies not worth the hearing.

In Meryton, Sir William Lucas just wants to *include* everyone in everything, while his wife *rumors* the petty news she's privy to as his Lady. Their spinster daughter

Charlotte has *settled*, just as she *settles* for an offer from Mr. Collins, who in his turn *flatters* himself and everyone else within earshot. Mr. Denny *amuses* the young ladies, which lays the groundwork in Meryton society for Wickham's arrival.

In Darcy's circle, Bingley's puppyish desire to *please* is charming and worrisome. Caroline's relentless *scorn* and Louisa's need *to fault* everyone she meets put the reader on guard. Thankfully Darcy has one bright spot back at home, his young sister Georgiana *respects* his desire *to preserve* Pemberley since he *preserved* her honor before she could elope.

Actions in the negative column are even starker. Loathsome Wickham *squanders* everything: his fortune, his friends, his future, not to mention the Bennets' reputation. Lady Catherine *demands* obeisance which her sad daughter Anne *abides* in hope of Darcy. These antagonists bring out the worst of our two main characters' actions, warping Lizzy's *provoke* into public insolence and Darcy's *preserve* into arrogant rigidity.

But luckily Mr. Gardiner lives to *assist* and clever Mrs. Gardiner *checks* both her hysterical in-laws and Lizzy's impressions against the reality of Pemberley. By the time the story ends, Lizzy *provokes* Darcy into preserving his own best principles and Darcy *preserves* Lizzy's family with inadvertent respectability.

- Elizabeth Bennet (*Provoke*)
- Fitzwilliam Darcy (*Preserve*)
- Mrs. Bennet (*Pester*)
- Mr. Bennet (*Tease*)

- Jane Bennet (*Believe*)
- Lydia Bennet (*Fancy*)
- Mary Bennet (*Exhibit*)
- Kitty Bennet (*Follow*)
- Charles Bingley (*Please*)
- Caroline Bingley (*Scorn*)
- Louisa Bingley (*Fault*)
- George Wickham (*Squander*)
- Mr. Collins: (*Flatter*)
- Charlotte (Lucas) Collins: (*Settle*)
- Lady Catherine de Bourgh: (*Demand*)
- Anne de Bourgh (*Abide*)
- Sir William Lucas (*Include*)
- Lady Lucas: (*Rumor*)
- Georgiana Darcy (*Respect*)
- Mr. Gardiner (*Assist*)
- Aunt Gardiner (*Check*)
- Mr. Denny (*Amuse*)

Just looking at that list of actions, you can discern the dim outline of the narrative, the juicy conflicts, the promised scenes. They suggest relationships and groupings, pairs and parties, as the synonyms slide together and the antonyms hint at sparks. You can feel the story wanting to be told, all the energy crackling in the verbs waiting for you to plug in.

Taking this point a little further, Austen's stylistic coherence offers a perfect ecosystem to examine verbalization in the wild. Her body of work features a very tight cast of character types, finding subtle variety and texture in generic roles over the course of her six published novels. For example, the stock role of "The Cad" recurs in all of Austen's books with notable shifts which personalize each individual cad. Consider:

- Frank Churchill (*Charm*) from *Emma*
- Henry Crawford (*Seduce*) from *Mansfield Park*
- Frederick Tilney (*Betray*) from *Northanger Abbey*
- William Eliot (*Exploit*) from *Persuasion*
- George Wickham (*Squander*) from *Pride and Prejudice*
- John Willoughby (*Spoil*) from *Sense and Sensibility*

All of these ne'er-do-wells are the same basic *type*; each presents as slick, sleek Mr. Wrong. Some are clever, some crude. Some are wealthy and titled, some penniless and predatory. Some prevail, some fail and turn tail. Their aims and ends vary drastically. Their sins range from amusing insult to ruinous treachery. Austen even judges them differently: Willoughby and Churchill get off lightly while Wickham and Crawford prove thorough villains.

As handsome, flashy gadabouts, all of them skate through trouble on guff and bluff...but their individual actions (and tactics) render them as very different cads in each case, precisely *mis*matched to bring out the worst of the heroine of that Austen novel. Ironically, all the actions of their fellow cads turn up as each other's *tactics* in the other books. And so their destructive impacts and fates suit their individual narratives anchored by those distinctive actions.

What they share is *inauthenticity*, a selfish, reckless disregard for honor and the people who trust them. In Austen's hands, each cad's actions and tactics bend that stock character from stereotype toward archetype.

Give it a go yourself! See if you arrive at different options that reflect how *you'd* tell the tale. If you're curious about this kind of analysis, coming up with a list of interconnected actions and tactics can be a fun and fascinating way to read a beloved classic. Remember: there's no "right" answer. Verbalize the story with the actions and tactics that would allow *you* to write it properly.

The Lord of the Rings Actions

Taking on an epic series reveals even greater power and flexibility in verbalization.

Beginning with *The Hobbit* and building through *The Lord of the Rings*, Tolkien's fantasy saga plays out in a majestic sequence of actions so clear, so dramatic that he often uses the action itself to explain or describe characters and scenes. Because so many of the characters participate in thousands of pages of text, Tolkien frontloads drama and tension via potent actions with loads of built-in friction and tactical flexibility.

- **Bilbo Baggins (*Brave*), but in the Jackson films (*Fight*)**
- **Gandalf (*Unite*)**

- Thorin Oakenshield (*Withhold*), but in the Jackson films (*Reclaim*)
- Elrond (*Direct*)
- Gollum/Sméagol (*Covet*)
- Beorn (*Daunt*), but in the Jackson films (*Guard*)
- Elvenking/Thranduil (*Control*)
- Master of Laketown (*Barter*)
- Bard (*Guard*), but in the Jackson films (*Conceal*)
- Smaug (*Desolate*)

Many of these characters reappear in the Lord of the Rings trilogy, continuing those actions in more complex and terrifying contexts. Because the later trilogy targeted adult readers, the tactics also shift in darker and more unsettling ways. In *The Hobbit*, Bilbo *braves* the rudeness of the dwarves, but by *The Fellowship of the Ring* he must *brave* retirement, the Ring's corrupting influence, and his accelerated decrepitude. In *The Hobbit*, Gandalf *unites* thirteen dwarves to hire a burglar, but in the trilogy he *unites* a great Fellowship to destroy the Ring, and by *The Return of the King*, he *unites* the armies of the West for the catastrophic Battle of the Pelennor Fields. Each character's action remains constant, but over the books the tactics unpack staggering gradations of emotion and evolution.

- Frodo Baggins (*Bear*)
- Samwise Gamgee (*Support*)
- Meriadoc "Merry" Brandybuck (*Dare*)
- Peregrine "Pippin" Took (*Risk*)

- Tom Bombadil (*Aid*)
- Saruman (*Betray*)
- Aragorn (*Protect*)
- Legolas (*Perceive*)
- Gimli (*Best*)
- Boromir (*Question*)
- Sauron (*Bind*)... viz: "and in the darkness **bind** them"
- Witch-king of Angmar (*Panic*)
- Galadriel (*Bestow*)
- Eomer (*Restore*)
- Treebeard (*Preserve*)
- Eowyn (*Prove*)
- Theoden (*Keep*), but in the Jackson films (*Resist*)
- Grima Wormtongue (*Poison*)
- Shelob (*Devour*)
- Denethor (*Scorn*), but in the Jackson films (*Spoil*)
- Faramir (*Earn*)
- Arwen Undómiel (*Pledge*), but in the Jackson films (*Sacrifice*)

Worth noting: Almost all the changes that fans groused about in the adaptations, Jackson's and others, arose from actions shifted for dramatic effect in an effort to compress the story and make the characters more filmable. That's why Thorin suddenly mutates from a pompous curmudgeon into a broody matinee idol, how Tom Bombadil vanishes from *The Fellowship of the Ring*, and why Arwen's role becomes so pivotal and melodramatic onscreen.

Again, as a practical exercise, try breaking down an adaptation you disliked and compare it to the actions from the source material and see if you can grok the story logic. Those decisions may be silly, but with millions of dollars on the line, they aren't made lightly. You'll also discover a lot about the endemic differences between telling stories in film versus fiction.

Notes

1. Specifically, I drew on "actioning," old-school dramaturgy, and the rehearsal process of London's Joint Stock Theatre Company and Cheek by Jowl forty years ago. Unlike a lot of iffy, self-indulgent performance theories that anchored acting choices in pop psychology or improv, these companies always started *from the text*. I first encountered actioning while rehearsing in London by way of Max Stafford Clark's *Letters to George*. It seemed a pragmatic and effective alternative to Stanislavsky's so-called Method, which (though neither Stanislavsky's nor a single method) is wildly hyped, misrepresented, and overused. The verbalization method I present in these pages isn't literally "actioning" in that sense, but it draws on the same theatrical traditions, criticism, and logic.

2. This is a paraphrase of a quote by Isaac Newton: "If I have seen a little further it is by standing on the shoulders of Giants." He was adapting a quote from 12th century John of Salisbury's *Metalogicon*: "We are like dwarfs sitting on the shoulders of giants." John had borrowed it himself from an earlier unknown author.

3. Richard Peck speaking at a PEN panel in NYC, Feb. 8, 2010.

4. *The Left Hand of Darkness* by Ursula K. LeGuin, "Introduction", p. xxvii.

5. Edward Abbey, *A Voice Crying in the Wilderness*, p. 13.

6. Earliest instance is in S. Harris "THEN A MIRACLE OCCURS" cartoon in the Nov/Dec 1977 issue of *American Scientist*.

7. In the Hindu parable, several blind men touch an elephant, each trapped by a limited perspective, saying an elephant is like a snake (trunk), a tree (leg), a spear, (tusk), a fan (ear), a wall (side), a rope (tail) because they each touch a different part and cannot form a coherent, shared picture. The original source is likely the *Rig Veda* and thence the *Chandogya Upanishad* and the *Udana*.

8. H.P. Lovecraft, *Selected Letters III*, p. 193.

9. from Thoreau's *Journals*, Volume 14 (August 1860-August 1861).

10. At 42 (in 1932), Hitler is confirmed as a German citizen and (through Goebbels) declares for presidency, making him a serious force in German politics for the first time. At 42 (in 1955), Parks refuses to move to the back of the bus and gets arrested, starting the Montgomery Bus Boycott and sparking the civil rights movement.

11. Kahlil Gibran, *The Prophet*, p. 28.

12. Elizabeth Bowen, "Notes on Writing a Novel" included in *Collected Impressions*, (1950).

13. Ezra Pound, *Selected Prose, 1909-1965*, p. 23.

14. quoted in *Ridiculous Theatre: Scourge of Human Folly: The Essays and Opinions of Charles Ludlam* by Charles Ludlam, p. 82.

15. cited in *Business Writing: What Works, What Won't* by Wilma Davidson, p. 1.
16. In addition to Knights, another essay with a similar thrust is "Diabolic Intellect and the Noble Hero: or the sentimentalist's Othello" by F.R. Leavis in his book *The Common Pursuit*.
17. Dwight Swain, *Techniques of the Selling Writer*, p. 133.
18. Dr. Keith Oatley, *Such Stuff as Dreams*, p. 125. This quote expands upon T.J. Scheff's ideas in *Catharsis in Healing, Drama & Ritual* about aesthetic distance presented viz Scheff's, p. 61: "At aesthetic distance the repressed emotion is restimulated but the result is not overwhelming."
19. see Dwight Swain, *Techniques of the Selling Writer*, Chapter 4, "Conflict and How to Build It."
20. William Shakespeare, *The Tempest* (IV.1)
21. Seneca the Younger, *De Providentia*.
22. "Picasso Speaks" in *The Arts*, edited by Marius de Zayas.
23. Carl Sagan, *Cosmos*, in Episode 9.
24. Ralph Waldo Emerson, "Character," *Essays: First and Second Series* (New York: Library of America, 1990), 36.
25. William J. J. Gordon, *Synectics: The Development of Creative Capacity*.
26. William Strunk Jr., *The Elements of Style*, p. 73.
27. Jasper Fforde, *One of Our Thursdays is Missing*, p. 21.
28. Max Morenberg, *Doing Grammar*, p. vi.

29. Emily Dickinson, "Poem 675".

30. See *Dialogues of Alfred North Whitehead* by Lucien Price (1954), specifically Ch. 29, June 10, 1943.

31. For a more in-depth discussion of the topic, see Raph Koster, *A Theory of Fun for Game Design*, p. 96.

32. Plato, *Theaetetus*, 155c-d.

33. Synapse: from the Greek *synapsis* (συνάψις), meaning "conjunction," (συν "together" + ἅπτειν "to fasten").

34. Nicole K. Speer, Jeremy R, Reynolds, Khena M. Swallow, and Jeffrey M. Zacks, "Reading Stories Activates Neural Representations of Visual and Motor Experiences", (*Psychological Science*, Vol. 20, No. 8 (August 2009), pp. 989-999; Nicole K. Speer, Jeffrey M. Zacks and Jeremy R. Reynolds, "Human Brain Activity Time-Locked to Narrative Event Boundaries" (*Psychological Science*, Vol. 18, No. 5 (May, 2007), pp. 449-455; Vittorio Caggiano, Leonardo Fogassi, Giacomo Rizzolatti, Antonino Casile, Martin A. Giese and Peter Thier, "Mirror neurons encode the subjective value of an observed action", (*Proceedings of the National Academy of Sciences of the United States of America*, Vol. 109, No. 29 (July 17, 2012), pp. 11848-11853.

35. Nihar Patel, "Billy Wilder's Rules of Good Filmmaking." This quote summarizes a longer anecdote Wilder shares in Cameron Crowe's *Conversations with Wilder*, p. 19.

36. Jorge Luis Borges, from the "Preface" to *Dr. Brodie's Report*, p. 11.

37. Barry Arons, MIT Media Lab, "A Review of the Cocktail Party Effect" (*Journal of the American Voice* I/O Society, Fall 2008).

38. Leo Tolstoy, "Three Methods Of Reform", on p. 29 in *Pamphlets: Translated from the Russian* (1900) translated by Aylmer Maude.

39. Brian Boyd, *On the Origin of Stories*, p. 361. This truncated sentence comes from Boyd's discussion of Dr. Seuss, but the idea applies more generally.

40. See also Harry Levin's wonderful book *Playboys and Killjoys* on this same archetypal duo about the characters we laugh *with* (playboys/wavy lines) and the characters we laugh *at* (killjoys/straight lines). Steve Kaplan's *Hidden Tools of Comedy* also does a great analysis of this technique. Showbiz types have used Straight/Wavy for years but Kaplan really breaks the binary down cogently.

41. Lisa Cron, *Wired for Story*, p. 90.

42. cited in *Little Book of Random Quotations II* by Kurt Vogler, p. 105.

43. Henry James, "The Art of Fiction", *Longman's Magazine* 4 (September 1884).

44. Cited in *Savage Art: A Biography of Jim Thompson* by Robert Polito, p. 7.

45. Maurice Merleau-Ponty, *Sense and Non-sense* in "The War Has Taken Place," his discussion of the SS and anti-Semitism.

46. Paul Éluard, French surrealist poet, quoted in Stephen Dunn, "Poets, Poetry, and the Spiritual", *The Georgia Review*. Vol. 52, No. 2 (Summer 1998), p. 270.

47. Roy Peter Clark, *The Glamour of Grammar*, p. 14.

48. Virginia Tufte, *Grammar as Style*, p. 125. See also linguist Dwight Bolinger, *Aspects of Language*, p. 120. ("Many languages...put the known first and the unknown or unexpected last.")

49. Will H. Hays, former postmaster general of the United States, later the head of cinematic censorship, in "Things Do Not Happen" in the *Washington Times*, (December 17, 1922), p. 55.

50. John Webster, *The Duchess of Malfi*, (V.5.70-72).

51. Joseph Gordon Pearce, *The Biology of Transcendence: A Blueprint of the Human Spirit*.

52. One of the most quoted verses in the *Bhagavad Gita*, from Chapter 2, line 47. There's a great collection of the various translations of this passage here, which reveals its subtlety.

53. Attempts to define narrative action range from the clinical to the poetic:

- Aristotelian scholar Samuel Butcher characterizes Aristotle's definition of action as "an inward process, a psychical energy moving outward" in *Aristotle's Theory of Poetry and Fine Art*, p. 123.

- Dante described action as "spiritual motion" or "movement of spirit" (*moto spiritale*). cf. *Dante* by Francis Fergusson, p. 50..."For Dante, *amor* = the movement of the spirit toward what it perceives as pleasant or good = "action (in Aristotle's terms)"

- Francis Fergusson (commenting on Butcher, Aristotle *and* Dante) calls action "**the focus or movement of the psyche towards what seems good to it at the moment.**"
- The Atlantic Theatre Company and David Mamet used to define action as "**the physical pursuance of a specific goal.**" *Practical Handbook for the Actor*, p. 13.
- Director Richard Boleslavsky described action as an organism, "Look at that tree. It is the protagonist of all arts. It is an ideal structure of action. **Upward movement and sideways resistance, balance and growth.** *Acting: The First Six Lessons*, p. 43.
- Gustav Freytag says in *Technique of the Drama*, p. 26: "**By action is meant an event or occurrence, arranged according to a controlling idea, and having its meaning made apparent by the characters.**"
- In *Games for Actors and Nonactors*, p. 42, director Augusto Boal calls action "**the abstract idea...transformed into a concrete will.**"
- Acting teacher Morris Carnovsky described action as "**an expression of the *energy* between the Self and Object**, an 'oscillating' character—back and forth, back and forth." *Actors Talk about Acting*, edited by Lewis Funke and John Booth)
- Oakley Hall boils it down further in *How Fiction Works*, p. 113: "**Character in action is what fiction is.**"

- William Packard claims "**Action is someone's wanting something.**" *The Art of the Playwright*, p. 14.
- Sam Smiley says in *Playwriting*, p. 43: "**Action in drama is change, as both process and deed.**"
- In *Acting Under the Circumstances*, p. 39, Richard Brestoff says, "**Action is the movement from the soul to the body... From the thing an actor *feels* to its physical form.**"

54. Incidentally, for any Group-Theatre groupies or other showbiz types paying attention: all of this theory predates the "Method" by several centuries. Action, intention, and objective are ideas Stanislavsky borrowed from his theatrical forebears and articulated in the nascent language of psychology. Mrs. Siddons (1755-1831) discusses the importance of articulating a specific action and intention to play Lady Macbeth.

55. William Shakespeare, *Hamlet*, (III.2).

56. F. Scott Fitzgerald, *F. Scott Fitzgerald on Writing*, p. 53.

57. William Ball, *A Sense of Direction*, p. 91.

58. Ulysses S. Grant, in an 1885 letter written in Mount McGregor, NY, to his physician, Dr. John Hancock Douglas. (cf. *The Captain Departs: Ulysses S. Grant's Last Campaign* by Thomas Pitkin).

59. Dwight Swain, *Creating Characters: How to Build Story People*, p. 45.

60. Elmore Leonard, *Elmore Leonard's 10 Rules of Writing*, p. 61.

61. Constance Hale, *Vex, Hex, Smash, Smooch*, p. 64.

62. cited in *Strategy, Leadership and the Soul: Resilience, Responsiveness and Reflection* by Jennifer Sertl and Koby Huberman, p. 87.

63. Ray Bradbury remarks quoted back to him in "An Interview with Master Storyteller Ray Bradbury" by Jason J. Marchi, in the *Hollywood Scriptwriter* (January 1999).

64. ...although superfans grouse at the notion the One Ring is inanimate, a complaint we'll address in the section which follows.

65. William Flesch, "Love, MacGuffins, and Death". As Flesch says, "We want the happy ending, but not too soon—we want (as George Ainslie says in his great essay on "Money as MacGuffin") to **build up an appetite for it not ruined by being satisfied too soon.**"

66. Alfred Hitchcock, Lecture at Columbia University, 30 March 1939 (Typescript, N.Y. Museum of Modern Art: Department of Film & Video).

67. Havelock Ellis, *The Dance of Life*, p. 236.

68. Sophocles, *Women of Trachis*, lines 592-593. The full quote is "Knowledge must come through action; you can have no test which is not fanciful, save by trial."

69. Richard Boleslavsky, *Acting: The First Six Lessons*, p. 43.

70. Hannah Arendt, "Isak Dinesen: 1885–1963", in *Men in Dark Times*, p. 105.

71. Brian Boyd, *On the Origin of Stories*, p. 222.

72. Antonio Machado, from "Proverbs & Songs XXIX" in *Castilian Fields*, 1912.

73. Stephen Nachmanovitch, *Free Play: Improvisation in Life and Art*, **p. 52.**

74. **Max Euwe,** *Strategy and Tactics in Chess* **(1937).**

75. **John Gardner,** *The Art of Fiction*, **p. 35.**

76. **William Wayte,** *The Chess Player's Chronicle* **(January 1878), vol. 2, no. 13, p. 31.**

77. **Yoshida Kenko,** *Essays in Idleness.*

78. **Martha Graham, "An Athlete of God", NPR broadcast and transcript circa 1953.**

79. **T.S. Eliot, Preface to** *Transit of Venus: Poems by Harry Crosby* **(1931).**

80. **Damon Suede, "Desire Paths",** *RWR Magazine* **(December 2017).**

81. **E.L. Doctorow, quoted in Charles Ruas,** *Conversations with American Writers*, **p. 211.**

82. **A lot of my approach to objects (aka scene goals) comes directly from the work of Cheek by Jowl and my experience with British actors, writers, and directors who'd spent significant time with the company. I've used it for so long it's woven into me, but for a deeper look at the theory, please read** *The Actor and the Target* **by Declan Donnellan, who founded Cheek by Jowl with Nick Ormerod, and whose ideas on "the Target" changed the way I looked at dramatic intention both as a performer and a writer.**

83. **In** *The Actor and the Target*, **Donnellan advises actors, "Instead of always wondering 'what am I doing?', it is more helpful to ask 'what is the target making me do?' Or: 'what is my partner doing to me?'"**

84. Dr. Keith Oatley, *Such Stuff as Dreams*. p. 201.

85. Arthur Schopenhauer, *The World as Representation: Second Aspect*, Volume I, chapter 3, paragraph 31 (1844).

86. Seneca the Younger, Letter 71: "On the Supreme Good", line 3.

87. Flannery O'Connor, *The Habit of Being: Letters of Flannery O'Connor*, p. 199.

88. Formulated by Empedocles, this system of divisions is also the root of the four classical elements, the doctrine of humors, and thence three thousand years of Western metaphysics. See *Ancient Philosophy, Mystery and Magic: Empedocles and Pythagorean Tradition* by Peter Kingsley.

89. Elizabeth Bowen, "Notes on Writing a Novel" included in *Collected Impressions*, (1950).

90. Aristotle, *The Poetics*, chapter 25.

91. George Eliot, *Middlemarch*, (Oxford World Classics, 1998) p. 140.

92. Peter Brooks, *Reading for Plot*, p. xiii.

93. Anton Chekhov, "Letter to Maxim Gorky" (3 January 1899).

94. From an interview with James Grissom, during the preparation of *Follies of God: Tennessee Williams and the Women of the Fog*.

Bibliography

As an inveterate recommender of books, I've done my best to contain the books listed here to those I used explicitly as references and research for this title. Additional titles related to verbalization, character, and storytelling in all media are listed on my website here.

Character

Characters & Viewpoint by Orson Scott Card

The Art of Character: Creating Memorable Characters for Fiction, Film, and TV by David Corbett

Creating Convincing Characters by Nicholas Corder

Developing Characters for Script Writing by Rib Davis

Characters Make Your Story by Maren Elwood

Writing the Character-Centered Screenplay by Andrew Horton

Standout Characters: How to Write Characters Who Make Readers Laugh, Cry, and Turn the Next Page by Mary L. Mercer

Writing Characters Who'll Keep Readers Captivated: Nail Your Novel by Roz Morris

Character Development and Storytelling for Games **by Lee Sheldon**

Creating Characters: How to Build Story People **by Dwight Swain**

Creating Character Arcs: The Masterful Author's Guide to Uniting Story Structure, Plot, and Character Development **by K.M. Weiland**

Creating Characters: The Complete Guide to Populating Your Fiction **by the Writer's Digest Editors**

Genre craft

Elizabeth Bowen, "Notes on Writing a Novel" included in *Collected Impressions,* **(1950).**

Reading for Plot **by Peter Brooks**

Mastering Suspense, Structure, and Plot **by Jane Cleland**

Wired for Story: The Writer's Guide to Using Brain Science to Hook Readers from the Very First Sentence **by Lisa Cron**

GMC: Goal, Motivation, and Conflict for Writers **by Debra Dixon**

The Art of Dramatic Writing: Its Basis in the Creative Interpretation of Human Motives **by Lajos Egri**

How Plays Are Made: The Fundamental Elements of Play Construction **by Stuart Griffiths**

The Hidden Tools of Comedy: The Serious Business of Being Funny by **Steve Kaplan**

Manuscript Makeover: Revision Techniques No Fiction Writer Can Afford To Ignore by **Elizabeth Lyon**

On Writing Romance: How to Craft a Novel that Sells by **Leigh Michaels**

The Art of the Playwright: Creating the Magic of Theatre by **William Packard**

Make Your Words Work by **Gary Provost**

Fire Up Your Fiction: An Editor's Guide to Writing Compelling Fiction by **Jodie Renner**

Writing a Killer Thriller by **Jodie Renner**

Playwriting: The Structure of Action by **Sam Smiley**

The Playwright's Guidebook: An Insightful Primer on the Art of Dramatic Writing by **Stuart Spencer**

Writing with Emotion, Tension, and Conflict: Techniques for Crafting an Expressive and Compelling Novel by **Cheryl St. John**

Techniques of the Selling Writer by **Dwight V. Swain**

Grammar & Language

Oxford American Writer's Thesaurus by **David Auburn and Rae Armantrout**

Spellbinding Sentences: A Writer's Guide to Achieving Excellence and Captivating Readers by **Barbara Baig**

It Was the Best of Sentences, It Was the Worst of Sentences: a Writer's Guide to Crafting Killer Sentences **by June Casagrande**

Chamber's Thesaurus, 12th Edition **(2012)**

Line by Line: How to Edit Your Own Writing **by Claire Kehrwald Cook**

Sister Bernadette's Barking Dog: The Quirky History and Lost Art of Diagramming Sentences **by Kitty Burns Florey**

The Deluxe Transitive Vampire: The Ultimate Handbook of Grammar for the Innocent, the Eager, and the Doomed **by Karen Elizabeth Gordon**

The New Well Tempered Sentence: A Punctuation Handbook for the Innocent, the Eager, and the Doomed **by Karen Elizabeth Gordon**

Out of the Loud Hound of Darkness: A Dictionarrative **by Karen Elizabeth Gordon**

Torn Wings and Faux Pas: A Flashbook of Style, a Beastly Guide through the Writer's Labyrinth **by Karen Elizabeth Gordon**

Vex, Hex, Smash, Smooch: Let Verbs Power Your Writing **by Constance Hale**

Sin and Syntax: How to Craft Wicked Good Prose **by Constance Hale**

Grammar for Fiction Writers **by Marcy Kennedy & Chris Saylor**

Say What?: The Fiction Writer's Handy Guide to Grammar, Punctuation, and Word Usage **by C.S. Lakin**

Doing Grammar **by Max Morenberg**

Woe is I: The Grammarphobe's Guide to Better English in Plain English, **3rd ed. by Patricia T. O'Conner**

Roget's Thesaurus of Words for Writers: over 2,300 Emotive, Evocative, Descriptive Synonyms, Antonyms, and Related Terms Every Writer Should Know **by David Olsen, Michelle Bevilacqua, Justin Cord Hayes, & Robert W. Bly**

The Elements of Expression: Putting Thoughts into Words, revised and expanded **by Arthur Plotnik**

Spunk and Bite: A Writer's Guide to Bold, Contemporary Style **by Arthur Plotnik**

The Synonym Finder by **JJ Rodale**

Roget's 21st Century Thesaurus, Third Edition **(2005)**

The Only Grammar & Style Workbook You'll Ever Need: A One-Stop Practice and Exercise Book for Perfect Writing **by Susan Thurman**

Eats, Shoots & Leaves: The Zero Tolerance Approach to Punctuation **by Lynne Truss**

Grammar as Style: Exercises in Creativity **by Virginia Tufte**

When You Catch an Adjective, Kill It: The Parts of Speech, for Better and/or Worse **by Ben Yagoda**

Criticism

George Ainslie, "Money as MacGuffin", in *Addiction and Self-control*, edited by Neil Levy. (2013)

On the Origin of Stories: Evolution, Cognition, and Fiction by Brian Boyd

Seymour Chatman, "What Novels Can Do That Films Can't (and Vice Versa)" in *Critical Inquiry*, Vol. 7, No. 1, *On Narrative* (Autumn, 1980), pp. 121-140

The Dark Voyage and the Golden Mean: A Philosophy of Comedy by Albert Cook

The Poetics (with the Tractatus Coislinianus, reconstruction of Poetics II, and the fragments of the On Poets) by Aristotle, translated by Richard Janko

Action and Character According to Aristotle: The Logic of the Moral Life by Kevin L. Flannery, SJ

Acting and Action in Shakespearean Tragedy by Michael Goldman

Shakespeare and the Energies of Drama by Michael Goldman

Story Proof: The Science behind the Startling Power of Story by Kendall Haven

How to Read a Play by Ronald Hayman

Aristotle on Comedy: Towards a Reconstruction of Poetics II by Richard Janko

Jane on the Brain: Exploring the Science of Social Intelligence with Jane Austen by Wendy Jones

How Not to Write a Play **by Walter Kerr**

Tragedy and Comedy **by Walter Kerr**

L.C. Knights, "*How Many Children Had Lady Macbeth? An Essay in the Theory and Practice of Shakespeare Criticism*" **in** *Explorations*.

F.R. Leavis, "**Diabolic Intellect and the Noble Hero: or the sentimentalist's Othello**" **in** *The Common Pursuit*.

Playboys and Killjoys: An Essay on the Theory and Practice of Comedy **by Harry Levin**

Such Stuff as Dreams: The Psychology of Fiction **by Keith Oatley**

The Passionate Muse: Exploring Emotion in Stories **by Keith Oatley**

Essays on Aristotle's Poetics **by Amélie Oksenberg Rorty**

The Lost Second Book of Aristotle's "Aristotle: The Poetics" **by Walter Watson**

Acting & Performance

A Sense of Direction: Some Observations on the Art of Directing **by William Ball**

Playing Shakespeare: An Actor's Guide **by John Barton (+the PBS series)**

Acting: The First Six Lessons **by Richard Boleslavsky**

A Practical Handbook for the Actor **by Melissa Bruder, Lee Michael Cohn, Madeleine Olnek, Nathaniel Pollack, Robert Previtio, and Scott Zigler**

Actions: The Actors' Thesaurus **by Marina Caldarone & Maggie Lloyd-Williams**

Conversations with Wilder **by Cameron Crowe**

The Actor and the Target **by Declan Donnellan**

Words into Action: Finding the Life of the Play **by William Gaskill**

Shakespeare's Game **by William Gibson**

In Various Directions: A View of Theatre **by Tyrone Guthrie**

Act One: An Autobiography **by Moss Hart**

The End of Acting: A Radical View **by Richard Hornby**

Play Directing: Analysis, Communication, and Style **by Francis Hodge and Michael McLain**

Directing the Action: Acting and Directing in the Contemporary Theatre **by Charles Marowitz**

Acting and Reacting: Tools for the Modern Actor **by Nick Moseley**

Letters to George: The Account of a Rehearsal **by Max Stafford-Clark**

Hitchcock/Truffaut (revised edition) **by Francois Truffaut**

Neurology, Psychology, and Philosophy

Barry Arons, MIT Media Lab, "A Review of the Cocktail Party Effect." (*Journal of the American Voice* I/O *Society,* Fall 2008)

The Reader's Brain: How Neuroscience Can Make You a Better Writer by Yellowlees Douglas

The Secret History of Emotion: From Aristotle's Rhetoric to Modern Brain Science by Daniel M. Gross

Donald Horton & Richard Wohl, "Mass Communication & Parasocial Interaction: Observations on Intimacy at a Distance", *Psychiatry* 19:215-29, 1956

The Actor and the Observer: Divergent Perceptions of the Causes of Behavior by Edward Jones & Richard Nisbett

Ancient Philosophy, Mystery and Magic: Empedocles and Pythagorean Tradition by Peter Kingsley

A Theory of Fun for Game Design by Raph Koster

Myth and Meaning: Cracking the Code of Culture by Claude Levi-Strauss

Understanding Comics: The Invisible Art by Scott McCloud

Keith Oatley, "A Feeling for Fiction" in *Greater Good* (1 September 2005)

The Archaeology of Mind: Neuroevolutionary Origins of Human Emotions by Jaak Panksepp PhD and Lucy Biven

Nicole K. Speer, Jeremy R, Reynolds, Khena M. Swallow and Jeffrey M. Zacks, "Reading Stories Activates Neural Representations of Visual and Motor Experiences" in *Psychological Science*, Vol. 20, No. 8 (August 2009), pp. 989-999...

Nicole K. Speer, Jeffrey M. Zacks and Jeremy R. Reynolds, "Human Brain Activity Time-Locked to Narrative Event Boundaries" in *Psychological Science*, Vol. 18, No. 5 (May, 2007), pp. 449-455

Vittorio Caggiano, Leonardo Fogassi, Giacomo Rizzolatti, Antonino Casile, Martin A. Giese and Peter Their, "Mirror Neurons Encode the Subjective Value of an Observed Action" *Proceedings of the National Academy of Sciences of the United States of America*, Vol. 109, No. 29 (July 17, 2012), pp. 11848-11853

Acknowledgments

Thank you to all the actors, directors, producers, and designers who raised me in showbiz, on- and offstage, and provided me with most of the raw material and methods that have allowed me to earn my crust spinning yarns for almost thirty years.

Thank you to all my students and colleagues who've attended my workshops and helped me discover and distill the techniques presented in these pages.

Thank you to Emily Jordan, who gets my weirdest jokes and calls me on every scintilla of my BS, making me a better writer, a better person thereby.

Thank you to Ruth Casie, for the savvy suggestions, impeccable insight, and constant encouragement.

Thank you to Lyla Bellatas, for sprinkling magic and mayhem over the manuscript, as she does.

Thank you to Mary Calmes, for her open heart, ruthless eye, and uncanny sense of the precise solution to most any problem.

Thank you to Lynn West, who helped at all hours of the day and night to make this book clearer than seemed possible and better than I'd imagined.

Thank you, thank you to Geoff Symon, my amazing husband who keeps me sane, safe, and sated no matter how weird the weather gets. I'll just keep trying to deserve you.

And thank you to *you*, dear reader, for spending time with me studying ways to verbalize your stories. I believe that books are the single greatest thing on the planet; they beat back darkness and doubt and pull us toward possibility. Anyone who loves books and makes books better helps us all stand in the light.

Any mistakes, delusions, or offenses are mine. My gratitude is oceanic.

Index

A

actions, xiii, xviii, xix, 7, 20,
27, 28, 30, 43–46, 49, 50–
51, 57, 62, 65, 71, 72, 75, 79,
80, 83–86, 87, 89, 92, 93,
94, 104, 105, 106, 108, 111,
113–18, 119–27, 127–34, 135–
42, 143–44, 171–73, 174–80,
180–84, 184–91, 195–201,
223, 224, 225, 226–32, 238,
239, 241, 245, 248, 251,
252–58, 258, 259–68, 268–
70, 272–75, 277, 280–81,
293–98, 298–301, 306, 308,
309, 310, 311
advancement, 79, 94, 129,
140, 198, 207, 233, 255,
259
agency, 85, 106, 114, 115, 148,
156, 158, 165, 235, 270
alignment, 82, 119, 132, 137,
166, 181, 252
breakdown, 196, 197, 201–7,
207–14, 217–22, 223, 236,
248
clarity, 63, 116, 117, 129–32,
136, 137, 144, 148, 152, 158,
180, 228, 294
conjugation, 46, 120, 136–
37, 142, 179, 191, 201
consistency, 32, 84, 85, 116,
124, 125, 135, 137, 141, 172,

178, 181, 182, 183, 195, 201,
204, 206, 229, 270
direction, 121, 259–68
energy, 50–51, 52, 71, 72–74,
76, 80, 81–86, 97, 98, 103,
106, 113–16, 113, 119–21, 127,
129, 131, 134, 135–36, 144,
149, 165, 167, 174, 176, 179,
181, 184, 185, 186, 196–98,
201–6, 213, 219, 259, 260–
62, 274, 280, 281, 296
friction, 62, 75, 106, 132, 135,
136, 141, 169, 191
genre, 135, 139, 183, 200,
215–24, 268
impact, 77, 85, 86, 116, 120,
135, 144, 181, 190, 252,
269, 270
intention, 20, 58, 93, 94,
103, 106, 114, 115, 117, 128,
129, 134, 135, 136, 137, 139,
140, 143, 144, 145, 146, 147,
148, 149, 153, 154, 155, 163,
167, 175, 176, 179, 197, 232,
233, 257, 260, 272, 275,
280
negativity, 102, 103, 140, 175,
176
recycled, 60, 85, 139, 175,
195, 217, 263
source, 20, 98–103, 113, 119,
127–33, 136, 137, 138, 141,
180
subtlety, 127, 129, 137, 150–
51, 207

emotional legibility, xii, xiv,
16, 17, 18, 19, 20, 29, 32,
36, 50, 55, 57–60, 63, 71–
74, 76, 78, 85, 88, 92, 96,
97, 101, 102, 113, 116–17,
120, 125, 128, 153, 158, 164,
176, 196, 198, 206, 225,
230, 238, 240, 248, 257,
265, 272, 275, 276
exposition, 129–30, 159, 208,
244, 245, 265
failure, 73, 119, 137, 163, 164,
176, 212, 225, 233, 252,
255, 257, 274
generality, 7, 12, 13, 18, 36,
46, 49, 50, 114, 163, 174,
176, 178, 179, 228, 232,
235, 240, 241
goals, xiv, 20, 76, 93, 94, 98,
99, 102, 104, 105–10, 114,
115, 117, 125, 127, 128, 134,
141, 142, 143–44, 144–54,
155–62, 163–69, 179, 190,
199, 204, 211, 225–26,
226–32, 232–39, 239–45,
281
impersonal ads, 7, 11–18, 24,
55, 109, 130, 199, 222
implementation, xv, xvi, 5–
11, 11–18, 18, 19, 20, 21, 29,
31, 42, 55, 76, 96, 108, 127,
223, 224, 238, 267, 272
inactivity, 176, 211, 212, 232
inertia, 93, 148, 150–51, 174,
211, 212, 241, 267
interviews, 7, 9, 10, 11–18, 21,
130
motivation, 105, 106, 107,
108, 110, 115, 125, 172
objectification, 241

paradox, 185, 201, 207, 210,
213, 214
predicaments, 89–96, 103,
142, 212, 227, 254, 271, 281
psychology, 7, 8, 9, 12, 20,
24–28, 98, 101, 177
reflection/rejection, 189,
190, 191, 267, 268, 294
relationships, 49, 73, 125,
132, 137, 168, 169, 184–91,
198, 206, 245, 256, 261,
280, 281, 296
specificity, 174
subtext, 103, 114, 206, 208
success, 65, 137, 163, 164,
200, 233, 239, 248, 252,
255, 257
traits, xviii, 3, 5–11, 11, 12, 13,
16, 17, 19, 21, 42, 71, 115,
119, 207
transformation, 31, 49, 50,
72, 73, 74, 94, 107, 155,
177, 178, 181, 198, 232, 249,
259, 260, 268–78, 280
trivia, 7–11, 11–18, 20, 21, 25,
26, 51, 113, 187
voids, 96–104, 109, 127–31,
136, 137, 141, 142, 165, 169,
172, 176, 183, 218, 219,
280, 281
weakness, 179
characters, 27, 32, 34, 269
antagonists, 102, 189, 191,
217, 295
cads, 187, 297, 298
classic, 23, 26, 42, 118, 173,
298
heroes, 49, 127, 129, 132, 137,
138, 187, 224, 234, 255,
257, 275, 297

Additionally, if you're interested in a fresh, fun approach to book promotion, check out...

Your A Game: winning promo for genre fiction by Damon Suede & Heidi Cullinan

Promoting genre fiction grows more competitive every day, yet no two authors or careers are alike.

Our solution: a chooseable adventure so you can pick the path toward the career you've always wanted. We offer a promo game plan tailored to your personal style, strategy, and measure of success.

Your A Game explains the tools and rules of kickass genre marketing to let you make your best next move. We break down the tricks and traps facing all novelists so you can:

- build your personal brand into a professional force.
- polish your public presence, online and in person.
- reach your ideal market and access your fans.
- raise each project to the next level.

Your career should be fun. Start playing *Your A Game* now.

CPSIA information can be obtained
at www.ICGtesting.com
Printed in the USA
LVHW03s0302150818
587029LV00007B/181/P